T0347400

Economic Citizenship in the European Union

High unemployment and rising social exclusion are the most tangible indicators that the European social model is in crisis. Traditional institutional mechanisms to incorporate people into the world of work, such as collective bargaining and employment regulation, are now being called into question.

Economic Citizenship in the European Union explores the macro-economic, productive and institutional pressures faced by Europe's social model, and assesses a number of economic and political programmes aimed at resolving the crisis. It also considers the role of the European Union in building a social dimension to the European economy.

The findings suggest that the future of traditional institutions of Social Europe is under threat. However, they also stress that we are not on the threshold of the 'Americanisation' of European life. This study finds that the influential political forces that reject the dismantling of Europe's social model should not become preoccupied with defending inherited institutions. Instead this book argues that they should encourage the construction of new forms of social solidarity compatible with the complexities of modern economic life.

Paul Teague is Professor of Industrial Relations at the University of Ulster. He has written extensively on the themes of European integration and labour markets, and EU social policy.

Routledge Research in European Public Policy
Edited by Jeremy Richardson,
Nuffield College, University of Oxford

Economic Citizenship in the European Union

Employment relations in the
new Europe

Paul Teague

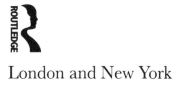

London and New York

First published 1999
by Routledge
11 New Fetter Lane, London EC4P 4EE

Simultaneously published in the USA and Canada
by Routledge
29 West 35th Street, New York, NY 10001

Typeset in Baskerville by Routledge

British Library Cataloguing in Publication Data
A catalogue record for this book is available from the British Library

Library of Congress Cataloging in Publication Data
Economic citizenship in the European Union: employment relations in the
new Europe / Paul Teague.
Includes bibliographical references and index.
1. Industrial relations – European Union countries. 2. European Union
countries – Social policy 3. Manpower policy – European Union countries.
4. Labour market – European Union countries. I. Teague, Paul.
HD5765.A6E265   1999
331'.094–dc21   98–39658

ISBN 0–415–17051–6

Contents

Illustrations

Figures

Tables

Series editor's preface

The European integration project must be judged in terms of its benefits to the citizens of the fifteen member states. Are their lives better as a result of the growth of supranational governance or not? In many ways the answer must be yes, whatever one's position in the current debate over the further expansion of the EU's competence. One need not be a Europhile to see the benefits to European citizens of transnational regulation of such diverse policy areas as environmental pollution, product safety, food standards, and pension rights, for example. The shift from national to supranational regulation has an obvious logic for those policy problems that are so clearly transnational in nature. Thus, we have seen a steady shift (inexorable some might say) away from national to supranational regulation, often supported by rather diverse and competing interests, such as polluters and environmentalists. The polluters seek lower transaction costs in having one set of Euro-level regulations with which to comply instead of fifteen sets of different national regulations. Environmentalists also believe that it is better to have Euro-regulation of a problem which by its very nature is transnational in scope. The EU seems to have matured into a regulatory state of some kind, with an 'engine' that seems capable of finding more and more problems to regulate. As we have seen more recently, however, increased Euro-regulation also brings problems if it is perceived to be part of a European-level 'nanny state'. An overbearing Brussels is part of the cause of the increase in Euro-scepticism across most of the member-states today.

Another reason for this scepticism is that the costs and benefits of European integration are seen as increasingly unevenly distributed. There are always winners and losers when public policy changes, whether the change is decided at the national or supranational level. Why else would there be so much Euro-lobbying? Increasingly, we hear the argument that the winners at the Euro-level, more often than not, are business interests. As we near the end of the century, the EU is seen by many as a business-driven project. Whether or not one accepts this rather simple-minded argument, it is fairly clear, nevertheless, that trade unions and their members (and the many other workers not in unions) have tended to lose out. As the Single Market project has been driven forward, and as greater emphasis is placed on the need to increase Europe's competitiveness against the rest of the world, traditional trade union and citizen claims get pushed aside. In practice, the almost hegemonic view that Europe's competitiveness must be increased has been a euphemism for reduced social protection, weaker unions, and greater acceptance of the vagaries of market forces. As Paul Teague points out in this volume, the traditional model of economic citizenship in Europe is now under severe strain, with high and persistent levels of unemployment, a decline in the economic functionality of the social institutions that have sustained economic citizenship in the member-states, and the fragmentation of social coherence.

This innovative study of Social Europe (the traditional European economic system which saw governments trying to reconcile social justice with market competition) therefore focuses on what is probably the key 'domestic' policy failure of European integration, most evident in the high unemployment across the Union. The political and economic risks of not reversing this policy failure are, as he argues, very high indeed. The result could be a thorough fragmentation of Europe, whereas success in addressing the adverse effects on workers and citizens of the move towards greater competitiveness might reclaim the tradition of successful delivery on the twin policy objectives of economic development and social integration.

A key element of economic citizenship is, of course, the system of employment relations in Europe. These form the central focus of the volume, as they have been subject to the most severe stress, as the result of economic forces and changes in productive systems. This study analyses the erosion of corporatist systems; the challenges to existing institutional arrangements across Europe, and the possible implications of various European-level policy innovations such as a Europe of the regions, monetary union and social policy.

The discussion of the policy co-ordination deficit within the EU is especially challenging, as Teague concludes that Social Europe cannot be protected by national action alone. Again, we see an argument familiar in other policy areas examined in this series on European public policy; namely, that solutions must be found at the supranational level. Simply because the problems of making, or re-creating, Social Europe are so intractable, there appears to be a 'logic' which drives policy problems upwards in the policy system. The concern for us all, is that European policy makers have been much more effective in achieving market integration than in building institutional structures which can support a Social Europe.

This volume, therefore, is an important contribution to our understanding of both the policy problems to be addressed and the nature of the processes by which the problems which have emerged might be solved. The costs of further policy failure are likely to be high for European citizens and for the integration project as a whole. Citizens will need to be convinced that what we might call the 'European journey', though difficult, brings with it a degree of protection from pure market forces, consistent with the model that most Europeans have known since the Second World War. Without that assurance, citizen support for the European integration project will be more problematic.

Jeremy Richardson
Oxford, October 1998

Acknowledgements

I have amassed many debts in the course of writing this book. I owe a special thanks to a long-time friend, John Grahl, who, over the years, has helped me form and clarify my views and arguments. The British Academy furnished me with a grant to help defray the costs of spending a sabbatical year at Cornell University and for that I am deeply grateful. I am also grateful to Harry Katz, Lowell Turner and Jonas Pontusson not only for making my stay at Cornell enjoyable and productive, but also for commenting on several draft chapters. Jeremy Richardson was very supportive and kind throughout this project and his advice certainly improved the quality of the text. Most of all, I would like to thank my wife Ann and our children, Ellen and Éoin, for ensuring that I remember that there is life beyond the university. Finally, I would like to thank the following journals for permission to use portions of published articles: 'Institutions and labour market performance in Europe', *Political Studies*, Vol. 46, No. 1, 1998; 'Europe of the regions and national systems of industrial relations', *Economic and Industrial Democracy*, Vol. 16, No. 2, 1995; 'Lean production and the German model', *German Politics*, Vol. 5, No. 2, 1997; 'Monetary Union and Social Europe', *Journal of European Social Policy*, Vol. 4, No. 2, 1998. In addition, I want to acknowledge the following for permission to use tables and figures: CEDOFOP for Table 3.2; *International Labour Review* for Table 3.1.

Part 1

Economic citizenship in transition

1 Convergence, citizenship and European employment relations

Introduction

Capitalism in Europe is widely seen as standing apart from the economic systems of other developed countries, particularly the USA and Japan. A range of factors makes the European economy distinctive, but the most important have been attempts by governments in the region to mesh social justice with market competition. Over the years, various labels have been used to capture these efforts, with welfare capitalism being the most frequently used term. Nowadays, the fashionable mantle is Social Europe. No exact definition has been developed for Social Europe, but discussions of the theme invariably cover two key institutions: the welfare state and collective bargaining, coupled with thick regulations governing employment relations. That these two institutions have played a central role in European economic life during the past half century should be beyond contention. To sketch the situation in schematic terms: the economic status of those in employment was determined by collective bargaining, more or less reinforced by legislation, while the rights and obligations of those not in jobs, such as the retired and the unemployed, depended primarily on the welfare state. Thus, Social Europe represents a form of economic citizenship embedded in an extensive array of public and collective institutions. No other industrialised country found it appropriate to organise economic and social relations in a similar way.

The argument developed in this book is that the traditional European model of economic citizenship is under severe strain and needs reforming in several important respects. Perhaps the most visible and troublesome sign that all is not well with existing citizenship arrangements is the high levels of unemployment that have stubbornly remained in some countries for nearly two decades. Overall, the European unemployment rate stands at about 10 per cent, which suggests that the seamless boundary between markets and social institutions that characterised the Europe of the 1950s and 1960s is coming apart. No one factor, such as the oil price shocks of the 1970s or an excessively deflationary macro-economic environment in the 1980s, is responsible for this situation. Rather, economic citizenship in Europe is encountering multiple pressures that range from the outmoded orientation of some labour market regulations to the constraining effects of deeper market integration inside the European Union (EU). In combination, these pressures have weakened the *economic functionality* of the social institutions that have sustained economic citizenship in the member-states. Increasingly, European countries are finding it difficult to organise their economic and social systems in ways that combine efficiency and equity. The pressures have also caused a fragmentation of social coherence since a widening gap is emerging between labour market governance and new emerging patterns of employment and work.

Highlighting the stresses in 'organised' employment systems in Europe should not be taken as yet another clarion call for their abolition, or another doom-laden account of their imminent collapse. On the one hand, this book is a challenge to those who continue to promote Social Europe in an uncritical way, as if it were some vibrant, well-functioning, economic and political arrangement. On the other hand, it seeks to emphasise that renewing economic citizenship in Europe most go beyond a blind defence of inherited institutions. In many European capitals, there appears to be a deep reluctance to adopt, in any full-blown form, the heavily market-oriented economic system of the USA. The idea of finding a European way that combines efficiency and equity, albeit in different institutional forms from the 'actual existing' social model, is still alive. As far-reaching and multi-dimensional reform will be required, it remains an open question whether the project of renewing economic citizenship will succeed. If it fails, the likelihood is a more thoroughgoing fragmentation of Social Europe, with some countries trying to maintain existing welfare and employment systems in a disordered and distorted form, while others move more decisively to the American model. If it succeeds, then Europe can reclaim its tradition of being the place where economic development and social integration go hand in hand.

It would be foolhardy to attempt a book that charts the difficulties of both welfare states and employment systems in Europe. Thus, my focus is largely on the employment relations components of economic citizenship. Even so not all the pressures and problems that can be found in European industrial relations are investigated fully. The discussion is divided into three parts. Part 1 examines some of the emerging tensions between industrial relations institutions and labour market performance as well as new forms of production that affront many of the well-established principles of work organisation in the region. In particular, Chapter 2 assesses the changing role of institutions in European labour markets. It examines the functioning of wage-bargaining regimes and finds that while the much-predicted move to pay decentralisation has not happened, it is no longer appropriate to describe multi-tier bargaining in Europe as corporatist. Perhaps a better label would be 'credibility' bargaining as most pay determination systems have become institutionally locked into the drive by most member-states to gain a reputation as a responsible candidate for European monetary union. The chapter also argues that the conventional juxtaposition in employment relations between coordination and flexibility is no longer appropriate since most member-states are moving, pragmatically, to a form of 'regulated flexibility'. Thus, although there is still widespread aversion to full-blooded neo-liberalism, virtually every European capital has now accepted that the postwar social democratic model of economic citizenship is exhausted.

Chapter 3 argues that productive changes to European economies may be undermining the long-standing 'cognitive' structures associated with European industrial relations. A powerful 'convention' in European employment relations is the necessity for labour market collective goods to simultaneously promote enterprise efficacy and social equity. Germany is seen as the most successful example of this type of industrial relations system. At the same time, labour market actors in other countries have used this convention as an 'imagined employment relations framework', even though they may not have been able to build smooth-functioning collective labour goods in practice. This chapter suggests that the idea of 'high road' industrial relations systems may be coming under pressure from the widespread diffusion of lean production principles in Europe. The renowned German system of labour market organisation is used as a test case to show just how menacing lean production can be to employment institutions that seek to mesh efficiency and equity. The main point that emerges from the analysis is that changes to productive systems may be obliging us to rethink the most appropriate institutions to 'mediate' between economy and society in Europe.

Part 2 casts a critical eye on two alternative visions of a reconstituted economic citizenship in the EU. Chapter 4 examines the viability of the 'Europe of the Regions' programme as a new institutional order for European industrial relations. In recent years, the combination of renewed economic integration, political decentralisation within member-states and the emergence of successful industrial districts has encouraged the argument that economic citizenship in the future will be tied to regionally defined productive and administrative complexes. This argument is closely examined and found to be unpersuasive. On the one hand, it underestimates the continued importance of national institutions in European industrial relations and overestimates the degree to which economic life has been 'regionalised'. On the other hand, it paints too benign a picture of the potential of regional economic systems in an era of deeper European integration. For sure, some regions may be successful in this scenario, but others will be less so and it is far from certain that the necessary mechanism would be in place to help them cope with difficult economic times. In essence, advocates of a 'Europe of the Regions' are asking labour market actors to take a leap into the dark on the basis of little more than speculative thinking. This is not going to happen.

Chapter 5 assesses the significance of the active labour market regimes that the member-states have been building over the past decade or so. The importance of active labour market policies is traced back to the emergence of a 'New Keynesian' school of thought in economics. Although it has a wide theoretical canvas, the essential New Keynesian insight with regard to the labour market is that the design of institutions can have a decisive influence on employment and unemployment outcomes. Thus, for example, if welfare systems are organised in a way that guarantees the jobless unlimited duration of benefits, the unintended consequence may be the accentuation of long-term unemployment. To help address the high unemployment problem in Europe, New Keynesianism has promoted an employment policy agenda around the theme of active labour market measures. This employment policy programme has important implications for the institutional shape of economic citizen regimes, since it redefines the boundary between individual entitlements and responsibilities in European employment systems. Overall, this chapter adopts a positive view of New Keynesianism and its associated labour market programme. However, it is argued that that the political support for this approach may be strengthened if greater efforts were made to integrate active labour market policies with the wider battle against social exclusion in Europe.

Part 3 is concerned with the relationship between European integration and economic citizenship. Chapter 6 charts the evolution of EU social policy and attempts to assess whether a meaningful plinth of employment rights supports the single market between the member-states. The analysis departs from the standard analytical framework for the assessment of EU social policy. Frequently, EU labour market measures are assessed against two benchmarks: (1) the extent to which the EU has been able to enact on a Europe-wide basis the corporatist structures long associated with national employment systems; and (2) the progress that has been made towards building an EU social constitution which would effectively create a European system of economic citizenship. These two benchmarks are criticised for misinterpreting the 'integration logic' behind EU social policies. For the most part, the EU is seen as attempting to build a 'symbiotic' social policy regime in which the national and European levels positively interact with one another. The purpose is not to enact employment relations policies that seek excessive centralisation or harmonisation, but a common social policy agenda in the context of institutional diversity. At the same time, Chapter 6 argues that the realisation of a symbiotic social policy has been held back by a number of institutional fault-lines between the member-states and the European centre.

Chapter 7 explores the connections between monetary union and social Europe. Creating a single currency is the most ambitious programme entered into by the member-states and is likely to have far-reaching effects on national economic and social systems. The monetary union project is widely seen as having a negative impact on Social Europe. Governments cutting back on welfare expenditure and downgrading social objectives to meet the Maastricht criteria for membership of a single currency club are the pieces of evidence usually offered in support of this view. This chapter develops a more nuanced argument. While fiscal retrenchment to prepare for a single currency is accepted as being bad news for national social systems, it is argued that rebuilding economic citizenship in Europe would be strengthened by a monetary union that departs somewhat from the Maastricht plan. In particular, the mismatch between deep market integration and relatively weak EU regulatory structures has created a macro-economic coordination deficit. One of the consequences of this deficit has been to intensify the pressures on the already hard to manage national welfare systems. A monetary union that allows for greater national fiscal freedom and which holds social dumping pressures in check may create a warmer macro-economic climate for the reform of economic citizenship. However, Chapter 7 cautions against overly radical plans for the recasting of the institutional architecture of the new Euro-zone. Instead, a well thought out programme of incremental reform is likely to be more credible and successful.

Overall, this book seeks to highlight three developments that are considered common to virtually all national employment relations systems in Europe. One is that almost every member-state is experiencing a lack of fit between the postwar model of economic citizenship and unfolding social and productive structures. Another is that national governments are reforming labour market institutions in the absence of a clear vision of a renewed Social Europe. For the most part, tentative pragmatic reforms have been the norm. This suggests that a key characteristic of employment relations systems of the future will be an ongoing effort to ensure some degree of balance between competitiveness and social justice. The old stable industrial relations institutions that exhibited a high degree of inertia may be withering a way. Finally, although the institutional shape of a new economic citizenship remains opaque, it appears less and less convincing to talk about reforming national industrial relations systems without stressing the importance of European integration. While a federal Europe is not in sight, complex interdependencies have arisen between the EU and the member-states. As a result, a democratic agenda for European institutions appears central to the broader task of revitalising national systems of economic citizenship.

The diversity approach to European employment relations

To some extent, the main arguments of this book cut across the consensus view about the current state of European employment relations. At the moment, it is fashionable to argue that few, if any, discernible patterns can be found in European industrial relations: that in regard to employment and labour market processes, Europe is living in an era of ambiguity (Hyman 1994; Crouch 1995). This view has its intellectual roots in the diversity approach to the comparative analysis of employment systems. In simplified form, this approach emphasises that each national system of industrial relations is distinctive because it is embedded in the social, historical and economic traditions of the respective country. Moreover, because labour market actors – usually taken to be trade unions, employers and government – have considerable, if not complete, autonomy in choosing employment strategies, then the likely outcome is industrial relations systems not conforming to any common patterns. Thus, national traditions, on the one hand, and strategic choice, on the other, dissolve any convergence tendencies across national employment systems.

The diversity approach has a number of strengths. It correctly takes to task crude convergence theories. Comparative industrial relations have their origins in the industrialisation thesis developed by Kerr and others nearly forty years ago. According to Kerr (1960), the combination of market competition, the diffusion of similar technological systems and the process of industrialisation itself would result in the gradual convergence of industrial relations systems across nations. Plainly, this thesis, developed in the Fordist era, underestimated the extent to which countries organise their human resources and labour market institutions differently to diffuse technological change and to face competitive pressures. In addition, it virtually assigned bodies such as trade unions and employers walk-on parts in the functioning of industrial relations systems. But if the history of industrial relations teaches us anything, it is that labour market actors have a decisive role in shaping the direction of employment systems. External, immutable laws that override human action do not govern industrial relations systems. A positive feature of the diversity approach is that it has highlighted the many weaknesses of the early convergence thinking with regard to comparative labour relations processes.

But the popularity of the diversity thesis is due more to the fact that it accords with everyday experience. Labour market governance structures do vary across Europe: to argue, for example, that the institutional architectures of the British and German industrial relations systems are the same would be to court open ridicule. Some countries practise centralised wage bargaining while others engage in decentralised forms of pay determination. Whereas trade union membership rates hardly get into high double figures in France and Spain, the density rate for Sweden is an impressive 84 per cent. Thus, when divergence appears so commonplace, the diversity approach seems the most coherent perspective for the study of European industrial relations. Such a position would be unassailable if it were not for a lingering doubt that it does not capture the full story.

In particular, once we scrape away the veneer of diversity it is possible to detect a range of similar themes, even common patterns, across European industrial relations. Almost everywhere, employment systems are grappling with issues around the theme of labour market flexibility. The consequences of European monetary union are dominating the agenda of trade unions, employers and governments in virtually all the member-states of the EU. If Europe is living in seventeen shades of ambiguity, as Hyman (1994) would have us believe, then why is there not one successful example of a national trade union recruiting and organising atypical workers on a widespread basis – the most rapidly growing part of the European labour force? Or why more generally is the forward march of labour not advancing in any tangible form in any country? Thus beyond the initial intuitive appeal of the divergence thesis, similarities, even convergence of sorts, can be found in European industrial relations. But it is not good enough to cast doubt on the diversity approach by simply setting out rhetorical questions; we need to flesh out some of the reservations in more detail. Consider the concrete examples of European rules on dismissals, labour market outcomes and the hot issue of monetary union.

Beneath the veneer of diversity

Widespread differences exist in the operation of employment dismissal regimes in Europe. In some countries, the dismissal and (discharge) laws are rooted in civil codes, in others they are part of the common law. The judiciary enjoys latitude in some regimes when enacting this legislation, whereas in others the role of judges is tightly constrained. In some instances the dismissal laws are integrated with the systems of collective bargaining and worker representation, whilst in others they are relatively independent. Big differences also exist in the roles of administrative and public authorities in the dismissal process. Even the definition of what constitutes a dismissal is virtually country-specific. Thus, it is beyond dispute, to use a pun, that wide variations exist in European dismissals regimes. But, as Hepple (1997) points out, despite these important differences, a common trend towards loosening the regulatory grip of the law has emerged across the various systems. Hepple points to the weakening of the role of administrative authorities in countries such as France, Spain and Portugal; to the widespread dilution of the rules governing the use of part-time and temporary workers; and to the strengthening of employer authority in the dismissal process in countries such as the UK, Belgium, Italy and Sweden. These examples beg the straightforward yet penetrating question: if the diversity story is fully valid what accounts for national dismissals regimes moving in the same direction?

A second example relates to wage systems and employment outcomes. In labour economics it is commonplace to contrast the sharply differing performances of US and European employment systems. On the one hand, the USA is regarded as having an impressive employment generation machine that creates large numbers of new jobs. Less benignly, many of these new jobs are of poor quality, and overall the American labour market produces high levels of wage inequality. On the other hand, employment growth in Europe is seen to be poor, resulting in high levels of joblessness. At the same time, poverty and wage inequality have been contained due largely to the presence of welfare states and labour market regulations. Thus, the stark alternatives appear to be either more jobs and less equality, or fewer jobs and more equality. Irrespective of the validity of this observation, the only way such a contrast can be made is if labour market outcomes in Europe are sufficiently similar. But such a broad equivalence of outcomes fits uneasily with the divergence thesis: if national industrial relations systems in the region are distinctive, then levels of employment and unemployment as well as wage distribution should vary too.

The robustness of the diversity thesis is also challenged by the monetary union project. It is now certain that the EU will form some type of single currency club before the year 2000. For the past five years, the member-states have been scrambling to meet the Maastricht criteria for membership of an Euro-zone. As shown in Chapter 7, this economic policy agenda has important repercussions for the management of labour markets and welfare systems. Nearly every member-state has squeezed social budgets, if not enacted cutbacks. Wage bargaining has been tightly constrained, causing a gap to open up between productivity performance and real compensation. In other words, the member-states are searching for real devaluation in currencies so that they are in a better position to face the rigours of a single currency club. Thus, an economic agenda formed outside the thicket of rules governing national labour markets is rebounding and influencing important spheres of industrial relations activity in almost every member-state. Another way of putting this is that the direction of European economic integration is creating some degree of convergence in the labour market agenda inside (and outside) the EU.

Thus, on closer examination, the picture of European industrial relations is more complex than that presented by a straightforward diversity argument. A strict or narrow diversity approach is hard-pressed to explain convincingly why the pattern of change in national dismissal laws is so similar. It is at odds with national labour market outcomes being so much in line with each other. And it looks shallow in view of the employment relations agenda in Europe being dominated by the impetus towards a single currency. In the face of such criticisms, the only convincing response of supporters of the diversity thesis can be to challenge the extent or depth of these common trends. Thus, Greece could be held up as an example of a country that has not slavishly followed the Maastricht convergence criteria for monetary union. Norway could be singled out as a European country that has maintained low unemployment and high wage equality. And Ireland and Denmark could be pointed to as countries where dismissal rules have not been changed.

So when evidence surfaces of similarities in European labour markets, the danger is that the search for exceptions simply intensifies. Such an approach offers a convenient escape for those reluctant to concede that many of the common trends in employment systems that can be detected suggest a weakening of Social Europe. But this position is unconvincing as it portrays an excessively binary thinking to the question of work and employment: if industrial relations systems are not uniform then they must be diverse. Yet in the circumstances in which economic and social structures in Europe still remain nationally engrained, industrial relations similarities will always be broad or approximate, they will never be complete, and they will certainly not be iron laws of convergence – they will be patterns. Exceptions will always be found to common trends, but that does not invalidate a loose convergence story. The problem with the diversity thesis is that it simply leaves insufficient theoretical room to explain trends that transcend national frontiers.

Despite its superficial appeal, then, the diversity approach is actually partial and incomplete. Regarding employment institutions and processes in Europe as a labyrinth, crudely delineated by national borders, is an oversimplification. European industrial relations are more accurately portrayed as consisting of diverse forms, but also sharing some commonalties in terms of underlying traditions, objectives and orientations – experiencing similar influences and pressures, and exhibiting broadly the same labour market outcomes. To be sure, divergent and convergent trends do not sit neatly and tidily beside each other. Moreover, there is no widely agreed framework to understand the interactions between the two influences. Thus, the debate about divergence and convergence is set against a murky theoretical background that tends to produce analytical incompleteness, or at least arguments with loose ends. For example, in the absence of robust theoretical foundations, a common practice is to use a 'checklist' approach that simply contrasts the way national systems are similar or distinct. Although useful, narratives of this kind tend to be too mechanical, not giving a full insight into the texture of the convergent and divergent influences at play.

Employment relations and economic citizenship

A different approach is developed in this introductory chapter to explain centripetal and centrifugal forces in European employment systems. This approach may not solve all the methodological problems associated with an academic inquiry on this topic, but it does permit a sharper insight into the pressures facing economic citizenship in Europe. The starting point is to suggest that industrial relations activity is an important dimension to economic citizenship – the rules and obligations set down for the incorporation of people into economic life. A defining characteristic of economic citizenship is its close association, even inherent link, to the nation-state. Nationality and citizenship are complementary in the sense that the establishment and delineation of rights and privileges are normally based on national identity. With the boundary between citizenship and nation-states being contiguous, so industrial relations systems are also tied to country-specific traditions and institutions. This observation takes on board many of the positive features of the diversity thesis and is consistent with the claim that most employment relations processes are nationally embedded.

But the argument does not end here. Although nationally specific, the employment relations institutions that contribute to the formation and maintenance of economic citizenship display similarities across countries. In particular, it is suggested that national industrial relations systems consist of three main spheres, regulation, voice and cognition, and that the interaction of these three spheres heavily influences the specific configuration of economic citizenship in a given country. Viewing employment relations in this way allows us to see convergence and divergence trends as co-existing in the European labour market rather than as opposites or as somehow in collision. The argument developed in the rest of the chapter is that the difficulties experienced by virtually all systems of economic citizenship in Europe can be traced, in part, to a number of common Europe-wide pressures and developments operating on the three spheres of regulation, voice and cognition. Of course, in addition to these destabilising convergence influences, national systems of economic citizenship are grappling with country-specific shocks. Though they are very important, dealing with these national peculiarities would bog down the analysis too much. By showing how the ebb and flow of European employment relations is influenced by similar tensions and processes, the intention is to highlight why economic citizenship in Europe is on the defensive and requires reforming in one way or another. However, before the analysis can begin properly some preliminary remarks are needed about the meaning of the spheres of regulation, voice and cognition.

The sphere of regulation

The regulation of employment, in essence the balance between power and trust in worker–employer exchange, is a central concern of industrial relations. A battery of legal, institutional, economic and social processes is usually seen as influencing this relationship, but a narrower approach is adopted here. For the most part, the sphere of regulation is taken to mean the legal framework governing employment relations institutions and processes. The better known term of 'juridification' could easily be used. Indeed, Voigt's definition of juridification, that it 'is concerned with the conditions for, and limits of, the effectiveness of the law as a steering mechanism' (cited in Clarke 1984: 38), nicely captures the thinking behind the sphere of regulation. The concern is with the legal codification of permissible and non-permissible labour market activity and the extent to which this boundary is delineated and upheld.

Mueckenberger (1984) suggests that the legal regulation of employment relations processes should be divided into three categories: (1) laws that afford individuals protection in the working environment; (2) the legal codes (and machinery) that underpin collective bargaining and industrial conflict situations; (3) the statutes that relate to the deployment of labour inside the organisation. Together these categories give rise to established distinctions in labour law regimes. One is the difference between substantive and procedural law. Substantive law is concerned with the fixing of standards, for example health and safety conditions or the character and extent of parental leave provision. On the other hand, procedural law is about laying down frameworks to guide employment relations activity, for instance the machinery for the hiring and firing of workers and mechanisms for employee involvement. Another difference, to some extent tied to the above distinction, is between collective and individual labour law. Collective labour law refers to the regulation of organised interests in the employment system – normally taken to be trade unions, employers and governments – and the legal codification of collective procedures. Individual labour law, on the other hand, relates to the rights and responsibilities conferred on individual employees and employers over and above those established by collective arrangements.

A longstanding controversy in industrial relations is the role and importance of labour law. There are many different strands to this debate. One economic view is that labour law is required to create public goods in the labour market. Establishing universal legal rights, entitlements and obligations in the labour market contributes to the elimination of negative externalities from the employment relationship (Edwards 1993). Another, more political, perspective is that labour law is necessary to redress the structural imbalance in power relations between employers and employees. A further outlook emphasises the connections between labour law and wider social processes. According to this view, employment legislation is more or less the formal articulation of informal ground-level norms and routines that govern social expectations about work. A fourth, cynical approach is that beyond the extreme cases of industrial conflict or crude violation of individual rights, labour law is unimportant. This account sees employers or employees paying little regard to the prevailing regime of labour market regulation. As we can see, the role of the law in employment systems is very much a contested matter.

At the same time, the individual spheres of regulation in national labour markets in Europe are well developed and complex, yet there are important differences between systems. In southern Europe, for example, although labour legislation is extensive, it is only weakly enforced. In France, legal (and other state) regulations have a pervasive role in the industrial relations systems due to the underdeveloped character of collective bargaining and the relatively weak role of trade unions inside companies. In Sweden, a peculiar characteristic of labour law is its integration with a well-developed system of active labour market policies. Germany, or at least the old West Germany, has one of the few systems where strong complementaries have emerged between the labour law framework and collective bargaining processes. Labour law has gained a new prominence in Britain, which has traditionally been cool towards juridification. Ironically, the greater use of employment law is the result of successive Conservative governments attempting to re-regulate the labour market along neo-liberal lines. Thus, although it is diverse, the sphere of regulation is an important dimension to national industrial relations systems almost everywhere.

Over the years, the sphere of regulation has been important for Social Europe in a number of ways. First, it represented the most formalised and legitimate source of sanctions against labour market behaviour deemed inappropriate or unacceptable: the sphere of regulation established the democratic perimeter to employment systems. Second, it codified and made transparent the norms and routines that hold together employment systems. For example, for most of the postwar period, most labour lawyers writing legislation were heavily influenced by the industrial world of production – male full-time workers, seeking collective rights at the workplace. Codifying these norms in legal statutes had the effect in many instances of advancing worker protection. Third, because it is normally connected with other parts of labour market governance, the sphere of regulation has been a good indicator of the relative strengths of capital and labour inside the employment system, the extent to which the law is upholding economic citizenship, and the character and texture of employment relations processes in general.

The sphere of voice

Economy and society are not independent arenas of human action. At the same time, economic and social structures are not automatically contiguous. To a large extent, the connections between the two are heavily influenced by what Piore (1994) calls mediating mechanisms – social and political institutions in business and civil life. These bodies attempt to make coherent and compatible the demands of commercial organisations with regard to the structuring of work, and the expectations of employees for rewarding and stable careers. Mediating mechanisms are successful if they provide a close fit between social demands and the capacity of the economy to deliver these on a sustainable basis. Another way of putting this is that social demands are not pursued in a manner that is disconnected from the economic system.

Thus, a key aspect of mediating mechanisms is to provide labour market actors with 'voice' arrangements – bodies that help formulate and articulate demands and procedures, and seek to resolve competing claims on economic and social resources. For most of the postwar period, trade unions and collective bargaining processes were the key mediating mechanisms that ensured that workers had a voice in the economic system. Corporatism is perhaps the most celebrated form of interest intermediation. A key feature of strong corporatist structures is the ability of encompassing trade union and employer associations to formulate strategies, negotiate agreements and bind members to deals. Under such a system, workers are integrated into economic life through collective provisions. Economic citizenship is worked from a collective contract towards the status of individuals. Germany and the Nordic countries developed the most mature and embedded corporatist structures in Europe. Streeck and Schmitter (1985) argued that these structures gave rise to unique political systems that they called associative orders. For the most part, associative orders represent a shift of economic governance away from parliamentary and elected institutions to trade unions and employers, which were given special public status that marked them off from other interests groups. Acquiring public status meant that the two sides of industry were expected to resolve disagreements in a manner that bene-fited wider society as much as sectionalist interests. Thus, organised labour and business became the epicentre of economic and political coordination.

Other countries created different forms of corporatism, but few devel-oped into associative political orders. In some cases, experiments in corporatism as mediating mechanisms were spectacular failures, the most well known being the British social contract of the 1970s. Thus, although trade unions and collective bargaining were influential everywhere, the extent to which they were successful as social mediators varied consider-ably. It is a testimony to the embeddedness of the industrial world of production that discussions about the interlocking of economic and social structures in postwar Europe have been dominated by the role of trade unions and employer organisations. Yet other social institutions have played an important role in coordinating economic activity and promoting social inclusion. In southern Europe, the institutions associated with indus-trial capitalism were much less prevalent and mature. Family and informal community networks were more important as a way of connecting economic and social activity. Decentralised, more amorphous forms of mediation were also central to the success of the regional economic agglomerations in Italy made famous by Piore and Sabel's *Second Industrial Divide* (1984). A chief characteristic of these arrangements was the creation of bonds of trust and the suspension of self-interested calculation in the absence of formal rules or institutions for the realisation of social compro-mises.

Thus, widespread variation can be found in an important part of indus-trial relations activity in Europe. Although they do not follow any one pattern or category, voice mechanisms in most countries nevertheless have shared similar properties. Above everything else, they have ensured that collective institutions have played an important role in holding together systems of economic citizenship. Frequently, trade unions have had a deci-sive role to play in the type of training received by individual workers. Information and consultation systems inside the enterprise were usually predicated on the presence of collective representative bodies for the aggregation of individual employee views. In other cases, voice mechanisms added to economic functionality by helping to organise commercial networks and the wider labour market. In some instances, they contributed to the overall legitimacy of the political system (Pizzorno 1978). All this is a far cry from other employment relations systems, particularly in the USA, where often 'exit' was the only viable option for workers (to some extent this explains why turnover rates are much higher in the USA than in Europe). Thus, the building of collective voice mechanisms in Europe has ensured a reconciliation of economic and social claims in a manner that has favoured individual workers.

The sphere of cognition

A third important aspect of employment systems is the sphere of cognition. Different influences make up this sphere, but at its centre are education and training systems. In the 1980s, an important theoretical innovation in European industrial relations research was the notion of societal effect. In comparing the competitive performance of enterprises in Germany and France, Maurice *et al.* (1986) argued that the contrasting national educational systems had a decisive impact not only on work organisation but also on the patterns of behaviour between managers and workers. To borrow from more recent French writing on conventions, they argued that each education and training system created contrasting conventions of identity and participation (Salais and Storper 1997). Conventions of identity, with regard to productive activity, relate to the competencies and characteristics people automatically associate with certain occupational categories. Conventions of participation concern the working environment and conditions that are seen as congruent with different employment groups. In a nutshell, Maurice and his colleagues were arguing that a by-product of the education and training system is the creation of reference points that not only influence the way individuals perceive their roles in the labour market, but also guide the manner in which employers shape their internal employment systems even before they recruit specific employees.

Thus the sphere of cognition refers to the frameworks of understanding and interpretation beyond formalised industrial relations institutions, although invariably embodied within them, that facilitate, guide and shape human action in relation to work and employment. Education and training systems play an important role in creating society-wide rules and norms with regard to learning. But conventions also arise from coordinating business activity on the ground. To help overcome the problems of uncertainty and limited information that could paralyse economic life, economic actors invariably develop informal codes to govern economic and social interactions. For example, it is now widely accepted that informal social codes played a pivotal role in the creation of a delicate balance between cooperation and competition among vertically disintegrated small firms in the 'third' Italy. Other examples of how 'micro' conventions contributed to the ordering of economic transactions can be found in a fascinating volume edited by Sabel and Zeitlin (1997).

Conventions play yet another role in that they give rise to long-term, deeply embedded, economic and social norms. In particular, long-term conventions invent economic and social categories that help order and give meaning to everyday life. One example, which is frequently used to show the gender bias of many economic systems, is the categorisation of household work as a non-commercial transaction. Yet when domestic servants are employed to do such activity, it immediately falls into the realm of legitimate business activity. Another example would be the convention of unemployment. From feudal days and before, economic idleness has long been a feature of societies. Before industrialisation, however, it was not categorised or labelled as unemployment. Thus when farm labourers were without full-time work in winter months, it was simply expected that they would use earnings accrued during the summer and autumn months to see them through to the spring. They were not considered unemployed.

But the emergence of the large factory changed all that. For the first time, unskilled workers were incorporated into productive activity on a mass scale. Invariably, these Fordist workers were without the family and other social networks that cushioned the fall out of work for those in the countryside or associated with a particular craft guild. Accordingly, when the great depression brought widespread destitution and poverty there was no developed social procedure to deal with widespread unemployment. Thus, before the problem could be effectively addressed the convention of unemployment had to be invented. If the term 'unemployment' had not gained legitimacy as an economic category, it is hard to see how modern social benefits systems would have emerged in any fully-fledged form.

Though we recognise that conventions play an influential role in social and economic life, these conventions should not be regarded as all-powerful social constructs. If it is a flaw of mainstream economics to regard human action everywhere as rational, then it is a shortcoming of sociology sometimes to regard individual behaviour as the outcome of institutional rules. People are not slaves to markets or institutions. The conventions approach attempts to avoid such 'totalising' assumptions by suggesting that individuals are not tied to particular routines or codes of behaviour. Rather, it suggests that people use conventions as frameworks of action, which can be revised and adapted to particular circumstances.

Thus, conventions are not immutable laws, external to society, but part and parcel of human behaviour itself.

Many of the conventions that have helped organise European economic life have been closely associated with the Fordist world of production. To some extent, these cognitive structures encourage an organised and ordered view of employment relations processes. Firms either pursued high value-added/high-skill commercial strategies or adopted low-wage, cost-based, competitive tactics. Training was organised either to give prominence to external labour market processes – the situation where qualifications are embedded in a recognised economy-wide certification process – or to promote internal labour markets where employers have more control over the skill formation process. Clearly delineated occupational structures allowed for a hierarchical structuring of work organisation as well as of the labour market more generally. In other words, many of the labour market conventions underpinning Social Europe are heavily associated with the notion of organised capitalism. Yet all around there are signs that these conventions are fraying. Talk of the boundary-less career, the rise of job insecurity, the emphasis on life-long learning, and the blurring of the high and low road to competitive success is an indication that conventions are undergoing a process of radical change. The framework of actions tied to the traditional model of Social Europe may no longer be in line with ground-level economic activity.

Spheres of activity, employment relations systems and economic citizenship

The spheres of regulation, voice and cognition are the main sub-parts of employment relations systems. They are all interconnected in ways that impact decisively on labour market structures and outcomes. For example, they strongly influence the relationship between external and internal labour markets – the extent to which an economy relies on transferable skills and the degree to which enterprises formalise on-the-job training. In addition, they help shape labour market access and mobility – the degree to which education and training structure pathways into occupations; whether organised interests enact labour market closure; and whether employees devise career plans inside the enterprise. Furthermore, they impact on labour market status and equality by promoting occupational hierarchies and identities. Finally, they play a big role in labour market equity: the co-mingling of the three spheres shapes the wage distribution of an economy, and the presence or otherwise of labour market insiders and outsiders.

The three spheres do not necessarily interlock in mutually reinforcing ways: connections between spheres can be disjointed and the spheres may even on occasion come into collision. A longstanding observation about French industrial relations is that the extensive use of labour law has impeded the development of trade union activity, particularly inside enterprises. In other words, the sphere of regulation crowds out the sphere of voice. At the same time, it is possible for the three spheres to be complementary. Consider Germany where positive interactions between regulation, voice and cognition lie behind the successful postwar system of industrial relations. The well-known framework of enterprise-level works councils is instructive of how the whole system operates. It is widely accepted that these bodies promote social compromises and trust relations between managers and workers in a manner that improves competitive performance.

Although the law mandates that companies establish works councils, it is not legal regulation that accounts for their success. Other countries have legislation mandating employment involvement, but this invariably does not achieve the same results as the German works councils. The sphere of cognition makes an important contribution to the German model of employee involvement. More specifically, strong craft-based trade unions, acting in a paternalistic way to protect their skill ethos, bring a unique blend of independence and a spirit of cooperation to work council discussions. It is such qualities that allow the councils to have highly charged discussions on issues on which management and worker representatives have divergent views, without losing sight of the need for accommodation and agreement.

By helping to shape and guide industrial relations activity, the spheres of regulation, voice and cognition make two important contributions to economic citizenship. One is supporting a vertical relationship between individuals and the governance structures of the state. Many of the functional aspects of economic citizenship grow out of this relationship. It sets out, for example, the legal entitlements and responsibilities of people in the world of work. The other contribution is the formation of horizontal relationships between citizens themselves, something that gives rise to bonds of trust and loyalty, as well as to codes of labour market behaviour. An important by-product of the 'horizontal' dimension to economic citizenship is the legitimation of a hierarchy of status that involves the distribution of rights and privileges between different groups of workers. Together, the vertical and horizontal relationships underpin contract and status in the labour market. They also form the foundations of solidarity and mobilisation processes in an industrial relations system by creating normative sentiments about fairness and probity.

Common trends in European employment relations

So far the argument is that the spheres of regulation, voice and cognition, which make up employment relations systems, give rise to distinctive forms of national economic citizenship. Thus, due weight has been given to the diversity thesis that labour market structures are nationally specific. But this section departs from the diversity approach by arguing that a range of common trends can be identified in European industrial relations. First of all, it is plausible to point out that employment systems in the region share similar political traditions. Largely arising from the activities of trade unions, churches and political movements, a social dimension was 'invented' for the process of industrialisation in Europe. After all, the region is the birthplace of socialism and social democracy, which shaped the character of wage labour in virtually every European country. Thus, the search for balance between equity and efficiency, and between markets and institutions is an engrained part of European development. In many respects, it remains the centre of economic and political debate in the region.

Moreover, the experience of two world wars this century has left an enduring legacy on the social and economic contours of Europe. As Hobsbawn (1994) points out in his monumental study of the twentieth century, the horrible experiences of the Second World War legitimised widespread public intervention in the economy, the creation of a wage relationship that was institutionally connected with the wider macro-economic and political regime, and a move towards deeper European integration, if not unity. Thus although postwar reconstruction took different institutional forms across Europe – Keynesianism and the welfare state in Britain, the social market economy in Germany, state planning in France – all shared the same umbilical cord. Ironically, it is precisely in the areas of public intervention, the wage relationship and European integration, where some of the sharpest exchanges are now taking place about the current state and future direction of Social Europe. Thus, many of the contemporary controversies about the European labour market have a common origin; the past, by helping to frame the employment relations processes of today, is influencing the future. To focus on European diversity is therefore to play down the shared experiences of and connections between separate countries. These bonds may not add up to an 'imagined community', but they do create a sense of economic and social mutuality that tie different countries together. It is this sense of mutuality that sustains the notion of Social Europe as a political programme. Without the widespread belief that Europe is travelling along a similar trajectory of economic and social development, such a programme would be ephemeral.

In addition to sharing common traditions, European industrial relations are presently encountering similar pressures, mostly economic in character. One of the economic influences facing Europe, and other advanced countries for that matter, is economic maturity. In a persuasive account, Rowthorn and Ramaswamy (1997) show that the processes of economic maturity are leading to deindustrialisation across the Organization for Economic Cooperation and Development (OECD). They claim that economic development follows a similar pattern across industrialised countries. The process begins in the initial phase of industrialisation. At this point, there is a shift of labour away from agriculture, mostly.to industry but also to services. Then, as economic progress proceeds, the relative share of employment in manufacturing more or less plateaus, but the agricultural sector continues to lose workers to services. The next phase begins when agricultural employment stabilises at a low level, but industry starts to lose labour to service-related activities. At this point, the logic of deindustrialisation has taken hold.

Rowthorn and Ramaswamy stress that that the shift in employment away from industry to services is not a cast-iron law of path dependency. Rather, they argue that countries can deindustrialise negatively or positively. Negative deindustrialisation is a sign of relative economic weakness or failure. For example, a country may, because of a poor performing manufacturing sector or general economic weakness, experience a slow-growing service sector, resulting in industrial jobs lost not being absorbed elsewhere in the economy. Of course in this situation unemployment and economic inactivity rise. Alternatively, an economy can deindustrialise positively – the situation where the service sector expands at a rate fast enough to compensate for the relative decline in manufacturing jobs. Perhaps the contrast between negative and positive deindustrialisation is too stark: countries can simultaneously experience both trends. The USA, for example, has experienced a massive expansion of the service sector to offset the decline in the relative share of manufacturing jobs in total employment, but stagnant earnings and rising income disparities have accompanied this process. Nevertheless, the overall argument is convincing. Certainly it is consistent with the data for western Europe, although the shift to service-related activities is occurring at different speeds and with individual countries experiencing contrasting degrees of positive and negative deindustrialisation.

A second common trend among EU member-states, is economic openness. In part, economic openness refers to the greater intensity of international economic activity. Financial markets are now borderless, with the capacity to endorse or penalise the economic policies of particular governments. Foreign direct investment has increased relentlessly in the past decade. One consequence has been the slicing up of the value-added chain so that production takes place in many different geographical sites. Trade flows too have massively grown. Some of this reflects the increasing importance of intra-industry trade, in which countries exchange goods in similar product segments (as frequently happens within countries). But it also relates to the full entry of low-wage developing countries into the export and import game. An unresolved debate is whether these developments, normally lumped together under the term 'economic globalisation', are leading to the fragmentation of national economic governance structures.

This debate is sidestepped here, but a proposition that is put forward is that economic globalisation, alongside deeper economic integration inside the EU, is putting pressure on the social systems of virtually all the member-states. Over the past decade, the EU has pursued concerted action to deepen negative integration in Europe. One successful tactic deployed to increase commercial interconnections has been the mutual recognition principle that obliges each member-state to accept the regulations and standards for economic activity established by other member countries. This simple stipulation has effectively swept away problems associated with the harmonisation of institutional conditions for trade, and has dramatically increased the possibilities of entry and exit into different national markets. National markets long seen as fragmented in Europe are now 'contestable'. In this situation, individual national governments are reluctant to go it alone and enact radical social or economic programmes in case they trigger capital flight. The threat of capital flight may be imagined, but it is instructive that no government has been prepared to put it to the test.

Compounding this problem is a third common trend of poor macro-economic performance. Few European countries have been able to establish a monetary/fiscal policy mix to secure a low unemployment, low inflation and high growth environment. Part of the problem is that financing social and welfare systems has effectively closed off the possibility of using fiscal policies to get people back into work. Maintaining a social safety net is undoubtedly desirable but it has not been cheap. Even if the necessary space existed, it would still be an open question whether or not such a fiscal expansion strategy would be successful. Any one country using increased public expenditure to tackle unemployment in the context of deeper economic integration in Europe would very quickly find itself in trouble. Domestic demand would certainly be stimulated, but in all likelihood imports would flood in from other parts of Europe. Not only would any positive labour market impact be undermined, but the economy would also run into a balance of payments crisis. To avoid such problems an alternative strategy may be to enact a Europe-wide reflationary programme, but the member-states have repeatedly shied away from this option.

The story with regard to monetary policy is hardly brighter. Tight monetary policy has been the norm across Europe for some time now. In the 1970s, the reduction and control of inflation motivated this policy stance. Subsequently, the desire to establish currency credibility became central, as governments aspired to European monetary union membership. Obtaining a good rating from the financial markets was seen as a key part of the admission fee into a single-currency club. At the same time, creating a stable framework for European monetary integration has proved difficult. In the 1980s, currency relationships between EU member-states were managed by the European exchange rate mechanism (ERM). Although it established parities between different national currencies, the ERM also allowed for the national management of interest rates. In the 1990s, financial markets saw this dual structure of Europe-wide currency coordination alongside continued national monetary policy-making as incompatible. This perceived mismatch triggered a massive bout of speculation that caused the virtual collapse of the ERM. Ironically, the political fallout from this episode has been a renewed commitment on the part of the member-states to full monetary union. Halfway-house systems for monetary cooperation, such as the ERM, are regarded as vulnerable to speculative attacks and thus not sustainable in the long term. The dominant view is that a single currency is the only viable alternative. National efforts to create the macro-economic conditions for monetary union have been redoubled. Almost everywhere, the result has been economic austerity.

A tight monetary and fiscal policy regime has important consequences for employment relations processes, particularly collective bargaining. Keeping public expenditure in check constrains pay bargaining in the non-market sector. Pressures have also intensified for new organisational forms of public services which invariably impact on established working conditions and practices. Marsden (1997) has neatly documented the public services pay reforms taking place in several European countries. Although he emphasises that there is no trend towards a common public sector collective bargaining model in Europe, he nevertheless shows that different countries are addressing similar matters. Denmark, Italy and France, for example, have abolished wage indexing mechanisms, which in one way or another linked pay and prices. Privatisation and deregulation have obliged previously state-owned companies to introduce far-reaching changes to pay-setting and personnel management procedures. This trend has been most pronounced in Britain, but it has also happened in the telecommunications sector in France, and in the postal and rail services in Germany. A further development has been the introduction of new administrative and organising procedures for the determination of pay and working conditions. Britain, Ireland, Italy and Sweden have all made extensive changes to public sector collective bargaining to promote incentive and 'market'-based procedures.

Restrictive monetary policy normally produces high exchange rates which oblige companies to reduce costs to maintain competitiveness. Thus, the tradable sector becomes involved in a relentless search for productivity improvements with sharp implications for established employment relations practices. Overall, an austere macro-economic environment creates a cold climate for trade unions and other forms of labour market protection. Consequently, it is unsurprising to find that these institutions are on the defensive across Europe. As we shall see in Chapter 2, the new intense corporate environment in Europe has obliged almost every government to keep a tight lid on private sector pay increases and to introduce measures designed to make labour markets more flexible.

Economic pressures are not the only common trends operating on European industrial relations systems. A range of social changes is also at play. There is a complex, yet unresolved, debate about the extent and scale of any social transformations occurring in Europe and the exact implications for economic life. No attempt is made to address this post-Fordist debate – stirring up that hornet's nest would not be particularly worthwhile for the argument here. But one social development that does need highlighting is the large and growing number of women in the European workforce. Since the 1960s there has been a continuous increase in the percentage of women in total employment, although the rate of growth has slowed in the 1990s.

From about 1975, the entire growth of the European labour force can be accounted for by the increased participation of women. About 75 per cent of women in employment work in the service sector and, with this area of the economy being the main source of new jobs, the overall proportion of women in the workforce is likely to grow. Despite these positive trends, gender biases in the labour market are still apparent. Roughly, 35 per cent of all women in employment work part-time, a much higher percentage than men. Moreover, women continue to be less likely to hold jobs in managerial and technical occupational categories. They also still earn less than men. Overall, the picture is one of the growing labour market participation of women alongside pronounced gender-based labour market segmentation.

A number of unresolved questions arise from this picture. It is uncertain whether the relatively high concentration of women in precarious work is explained by the their greater willingness to accept such employment, or whether it is due to post-industrial economies creating a disproportionately high number of poor jobs. Working out this puzzle is central to under-standing trends towards stagnant earnings and wage inequality. Beyond answering such complex questions, there can be little dispute that the growth of women in the labour market is triggering big changes in employment relations processes. It signals that the nature and type of work now being done is radically different from that done in the heyday of the Fordist era. It suggests that social codes of behaviour, even the social struc-ture of organisations, require change. It indicates that new social demands, such will be made on employment relations processes.

Convergence and economic citizenship in Europe

Although it is not an exhaustive account, the above discussion highlights some of the similar developments in separate industrial relations systems in Europe. The main message is that a cold climate exists for employment relations processes and institutions. Many of the identified common pres-sures are causing deep-seated upheavals in the three spheres of regulation, voice and cognition. The result is nothing less than a destabilisation of the established form and character of economic citizenship in Europe. Consider the impact of economic maturity on social corporatism or soli-daristic wage bargaining. One of the main objectives of such pay determination systems is to keep wage differentials within a relatively narrow band. Such a strategy was easier when jobs were broadly similar across the manufacturing sector. But deindustrialisation disrupts organised occupational structures. Greater variation exists between jobs in the service sector, ranging from relatively menial unskilled labour to sophisticated state-of-the-art technical labour. With a wider range of skills and produc-tivity being associated with different types of job, wage differentials invariably increase. Solidaristic bargaining becomes difficult in these circumstances. It would be heroic to say that pressure for a wider spread of the wage structure played no part in the breakdown of celebrated exam-ples of solidaristic wage bargaining.

At the same time, economic factors do not fully explain the demise of solidaristic collective bargaining. Baccaro and Locke (1998) show how the pursuit of egalitarian pay bargaining gradually wracked Swedish and Italian trade unions with internal divisions and tensions. In Italy, for instance, solidaristic bargaining first triggered the creation of the *sindacati autonomi* (autonomous unions) in the 1970s which sought to pursue section-alist pay strategies. In the 1980s, further fragmentation occurred with the appearance of *Comitati di Buso* (COBAS) (grassroots committees) which argued for an even more hard-line economistic bargaining than the autonomous unions. With regard to Sweden, dissatisfaction had been brewing against the centralised corporatist wage structure from the early 1970s with the emergence of breakaway unions in the public sector (e.g. the creation of the PTK in 1973). In the early 1980s, a wide range of tensions erupted between different groups of workers – semi-skilled v. skilled, manual v. clerical, public v. private. A number of attempts were made to patch up these rivalries, but in the end the weight of divisions proved too much and the regime of solidaristic bargaining collapsed. This story shows that in addition to economic events, the institutional environment may have turned against this type of pay behaviour by trade unions. It lends support to the argument made by Mueckenberger *et al.* (1995: 18) that a trade union strategy based on the 'illusion that workers in the same class situation have the same interests that can only be accomplished collectively' may be outmoded.

The shift to service sector activity is also causing uncertainty about how to organise training and skill formation systems. Traditionally, the apprenticeship model has been widely regarded as the best method of equipping young people with skills and qualifications for working life. The aim was to give the young person a deep knowledge of both the conception and execution of tasks related to a particular craft. On completing training, the person was given a certificate that was transferable on an external occupational labour market. But this model of skill formation is coming under pressure with the demise of many craft-related occupational categories and the rise of new office jobs. Surveys show that in the new service economy employers are seeking to recruit labour with computer and communications skills (Soskice 1994). These new forms of labour demand are putting pressure on the organised and formalised apprenticeship model of training. Of course, it would be wrong to infer that the end of the apprenticeship model in Europe is nigh. Actually, a number of countries, such as Belgium, Ireland, Italy and Finland, have expanded this form of training.

At the same time, this aggregate trend should not be seen as evidence of well-functioning skill formation systems. Many apprenticeship programmes in Europe, if not undergoing large-scale reform, are experiencing considerable operational difficulties. Consider the Austrian case. In this country, employers have complained that the specification of some skills in the apprenticeship system is too narrow in light of the changes taking place in the economy. In response, the public authorities introduced a series of revisions designed to broaden the definition of skills and revamp the qualification structure to meet employer concerns. However, introducing these changes almost immediately gave rise to another set of problems. It quickly became apparent that small and medium-sized companies were finding it difficult to provide the wider range of work experience demanded by the new more broadly based apprenticeship scheme. This situation gave rise to two problems. On the one hand, a decline occurred in the number of apprenticeship places offered by small firms (which account for 60 per cent of all placements in manufacturing). On the other hand, the reliability of the new qualification structure for occupational labour markets was brought into question. Overall, it highlighted the problems of organising an economy-wide apprenticeship scheme at a time when the employment structure is fragmenting.

Traditional methods of company-level training are also being undermined by the shift away from manufacturing jobs. In many situations, on-the-job training was connected to well-developed internal labour markets. Employees with the most experience of the production process and widely seen as the most competent were normally given the task of training new recruits. These skilled workers usually enjoyed enhanced status within the organisation – consider the position of the *Meister* in Germany companies. In other words, organisational learning was bound up in formalised rules and patterns of recognition. But in the new service company, on-the-job training is looser and more informal. Internal labour markets are less pronounced, thus weakening organisational structures that support skill formation. Moreover, as Orr (1996) shows, technical white-collar workers relate to each other differently than manufacturing workers, particularly in the use of informal communication to exchange information and knowledge. As a result, on-the-job training becomes less a matter of building organised internal labour markets and more one of promoting a conversation between employees about their work experiences. In short, the growth of sevice sector related activities has undermined established conventions about the meaning of skill and the organisation of training provision.

In an elegant essay, Hyman (1997a) shows how the new service economy is placing stress on traditional voice mechanisms in European industrial relations. In particular, he argues that features of the new diversified workforce are making it difficult for trade unions to aggregate the interests of their members. This difficulty has a number of dimensions. First, on which employment constituency should trade unions focus recruitment and mobilisation activity – the new elite technical workers or those in the more precarious and unskilled segments of the service economy? The second dilemma relates to what interests are articulated – whether trade unions should focus on the wages struggle or move to a broader social agenda, and whether the focus should be on the enterprise or the wider community and political environment. The third question relates to the best organisational form for the trade unions to adopt to represent members – should they be occupational, sector- or company-based? All these tensions are emerging because structural change is impairing the role of trade unions as the institutional expression of collective action. In other words, organised labour is experiencing a crisis of interest representation.

Similar problems arise when we look at the impact of large numbers of women workers on industrial relations systems. Consider the impact on the sphere of voice. For most of the postwar period, the typical worker was male, working full-time and providing for a family. An employment structure made up of this type of wage earner had an influential impact on trade union activity. In particular, organised labour focused largely on the 'wages struggle' and on improving employment and working conditions inside the enterprise. Wider social issues were a secondary concern. But with the growth of women in the labour force this situation radically changes. One manifestation of the new workforce is the shift away from single-earner to two-earner families. In this situation, conventional collective bargaining demands on the part of trade unions reflect the needs of a much smaller section of their members. The new wage earners are more concerned about wider social issues, such as child-care provision. This reflects a desire on the part of women workers to be incorporated into economic life on different social terms than their male counterparts. In other words, economic citizenship needs new social foundations and the role of trade unions as social mediators needs transforming.

The 'genderisation' of the labour market has equally profound consequences for the spheres of regulation and cognition. Prevailing labour market conventions have not kept pace with the increasing numbers of women in employment. As a result, many established work practices and routines, as well as day-to-day frameworks of action, if not openly gender biased, are incongruent with the new employment structure. Enterprises that rely heavily on over-time working can hardly be considered gender-friendly as many women attempt to combine work with family commitments. Or patterns of behaviour that reinforce subservience between men and women are out of line with growing societal expectations for sexual equality. Slowly, through policies such as gender auditing of employment practices, these conventions are being challenged, but they have by no means disappeared. In the sphere of regulation, for more than half a century the assumption behind much employment law was a workforce made up of male full-time employees. But these assumptions are ill-suited to today's labour market. With the growth in the number of women workers a new agenda for employment protection has been created, dealing with issues ranging from sexual harassment inside the enterprise to nursery provision in the community. Most European countries are only just beginning to address these questions and still have a long way to go. Mueckenberger (1996) argues that the new job market requires nothing less than an overhaul of the way labour law regulates the individual employment relationship.

The common pressures on European industrial relations are undermining other parts of labour market governance. Grimshaw and Rubery (1997), for example, highlight the incongruity between established systems of unemployment benefits and the growing heterogeneity of workforces across Europe. In particular, they show that the eligibility conditions for benefits in many situations presume full-time continuous labour market participation. Yet, more and more of the European workforce is working part-time and on a temporary basis. The upshot of this incongruity is that members of the new atypical workforce, particularly young people and women, are slipping through the social safety net. Other examples of this process of labour market marginalisation can be given, but the basic point is that the protectionist coverage supposedly offered by Social Europe is coming apart. In many respects, the growing debate in Europe about social exclusion has been motivated by such concerns.

Moves towards a fully integrated European single market have intensified competitive pressures on European industry. One consequence has been to accelerate the pace of workplace change. A number of interesting studies have emerged about the pace and direction of corporate-level employment innovations. Most confirm the argument made earlier in the chapter that European industrial relations currently consist of a complex balance of convergent and divergent influences. Consider the case of the banking sector. Several investigations of the industry show that banks in different countries are facing similar pressures to restructure their internal work systems (see Thornley *et al.* 1997 and Anderson 1997). In particular, the diffusion of new technologies, the intensification of competition and the need to develop 'new products' to maintain customer loyalty have created a cold climate for traditional employment practices. The pattern of change to this new corporate environment has been strikingly similar across countries. Job losses have been enacted almost everywhere and employment security is now a thing of the past in European banking. Moreover, in many instances, internal labour markets have been reorganised in a way that has led to new forms of occupational segmentation in the industry.

At the same time, country distinctions remain. Anderson (1997) shows that whereas British banks are increasingly using part-time workers, Danish banks are keeping with the full-time salaried model. In addition, he shows that there has been a more extensive fragmentation of traditional collective bargaining structures in Britain than in Denmark. Thornley *et al.* (1997) develop a more nuanced account of workplace restructuring in

British and French banks. They argue that the two countries have a great deal in common in the way that banks are reorganising their employment systems. Yet they highlight that important differences persist in the way workplace reform has been interpreted in each country. French trade unionists, for example, were more likely to view the move to ERM-related practices as part of a wider political project to 'Americanise' the European labour market than their British counterparts. Another way of making this point is that while common pressures are putting strains on established collective bargaining (voice) mechanisms in both France and Britain, important nationally based cognitive structures still persist with regard to the world of work.

Nevertheless there is evidence that the traditional 'national' frameworks of action of some trade unions have been affected by the greater economic openness in Europe. Consider the building industry. Largely as a result of the emergence of a single market, the corporate contours of the building industry in Europe have been radically reshaped. Initially, deeper economic openness caused a wave of national mergers, resulting in greater domestic concentration of building firms. Then a process of Europe-wide corporate realignment took place, which brought to an end the largely national orientation of most building-related firms. As Cremers (1997: 634) points out, 'for the top 40 construction companies and the 10–15 biggest cement and building materials manufacturers, it has gradually come to be the case that they organise their operations on a Europe-wide basis'. The Europeanisation of the industry has brought new challenges to the essentially national framework of trade union action. It has made centres of corporate decision-making more remote and it has made lines of authority and channels of information more difficult to track and monitor.

National trade unions are presently inadequately organised to respond effectively to the Europeanisation of the industry. Clearly some changes will have to be introduced if they want to have any influence over the corporate strategies of the bigger firms. At the minimum, greater coordination and information-sharing between separate national trade union centres appears essential. However, on their own these changes may not be enough. To respond effectively to the Europeanisation of firms, organised labour may be obliged to become 'European' too. Becoming less 'German' or 'British' will not be easy for trade unions as they are deeply enmeshed in cognitive structures that emphasise the primacy of national action. Thus, dealing with the European challenge will require them to 'unlearn' conventional modes of action and interact, interpret and internalise a whole range of European activities, so that they can deal more effectively with the new realities of their industry. Whether such a transformation is possible is a moot point, but there are signs that trade unions are attempting to change in this direction (Marginson and Sissons 1998). Overall, the key point is that deeper market integration in Europe is challenging the 'national' cognitive structures of economic citizenship.

This theme has preoccupied Wolfgang Streeck (1995) for some years now. He develops a story about the impact of increased economic openness on European employment relations, which is nearly all doom and gloom. In particular, he argues that the heavily market-led process of European integration has placed a wedge between systems of economic citizenship and nation-states, creating big stresses on 'organised' national labour markets. In the sphere of regulation, a trend is emerging towards a loosening of legislative controls on the labour market. One way or another, most European countries are attempting to make labour law regimes less restrictive, thereby paving the way for the widespread diffusion of employment flexibility measures. Nowhere in the sphere of voice is there a forward march of labour. Most trade unions are on the defensive, complying with, even endorsing in some instances, austere labour measures in an attempt to remain important institutions in European society. In the sphere of cognition, established conventions about labour market action are beginning to break up. Trade unions are less and less prepared to evoke strike action against employers and are more eager to build social partnership edifices.

For Streeck, these developments are a far cry from the 'imagined' model of labour market organisation associated with Social Europe. Under this model, the labour market consists of a number of collective goods that constrain the behaviour of employers in a way that reduces negative externalities and promotes the social integration of workers into the economic system. In other words, collective labour market goods create the institutional conditions that simultaneously promote equity and efficiency in the one economic system. Streeck's argument is that deeper economic openness is undermining the operation of these institutional arrangements, thus allowing neo-liberalism to triumph in Europe. While this account is perhaps too pessimistic, it is hard to deny that the national foundations to Social Europe are under considerable strain in an era of deeper economic integration inside the EU.

Conclusions

The central message of this introductory chapter is that the spheres of regulation, voice and cognition that uphold economic citizenship in Europe are under severe pressure. Whether these pressures amount to a crisis of European employment relations is the source of much debate.

One optimistic argument is that talk of crisis is much exaggerated. Those who hold this view invariably point to *institutional resilience* as evidence of continuity, even stability, in employment systems. For instance, Wallerstein and Golden (1997) highlight the continued importance of centralised bargaining in all Nordic countries apart from Sweden, which they regard as supporting a 'little has changed' hypothesis. But this interpretation is flawed in several important respects. First of all, other studies that survey the Nordic countries just as well as Wallerstein and Golden arrive at different conclusions. For instance, Gill *et al.* (1998) show that the 'collective' institutional system of the Danish labour market is being impaired as a result of decentralisation and other pressures. Norway, recently held up as an example of the continued plausibility of 'solidaristic' employment systems (Kahn 1998), seems to be imploding in on itself. Developments indicate that there is not as much seamless continuity in the Nordic countries as Wallerstein and Golden suggest.

A second flaw in their argument, highlighted more fully in Chapter 2, is that they fail to examine the types of bargain that are emerging from centralised bargaining arrangements in the Nordic countries or elsewhere in Europe. The entirely plausible scenario of widespread and far-reaching changes taking place *within* traditional collective bargaining institutions is simply not explored. Yet the evidence is all around that everything is not well inside European industrial relations. On the economic front, high and persistent unemployment is a strong indicator that conventional collective bargaining is losing its economic functionality. On the institutional front, the demise of traditional patterns of trade union organisation and the distortions in regimes of labour market regulation, highlighted in the next chapter, suggest the presence of representative and governance gaps. On the ideological front, the decline in norms of egalitarianism and solidarity suggests that the glue that held together the European social model is no longer particularly adhesive.

In this opening chapter these tensions have been interpreted as signs that the existing model of economic citizenship in Europe is experiencing multiple pressures caused by big economic and social transformations. Thus, we have pointed to the incongruity between the increasingly integrated European single market and the largely national orientation of economic citizenship; to the mismatch between traditional forms of labour market governance and new forms of productive and social organisation emerging in many countries; to the lack of policy room that governments experience in dealing with the sweeping labour market changes taking place. All in all, the analysis has tried to show that these pressures and some additional ones are destabilising the three key spheres of national economic citizenship in Europe – the spheres of regulation, voice and cognition.

The story told is far from upbeat or optimistic: one would be hard pressed to make a convincing case for the so-called social market economies of northern Europe from the analysis. Yet, it also stands apart from the pessimism of accounts served up by Streeck and others. This chapter, and this book for that matter, neither accepts nor endorses the view that European employment relations are sliding down the greasy pole that will end in the Americanisation of labour markets. Such an outlook underestimates the political and social forces that stand opposed to full-blown neo-liberalism in Europe. Rather the central message is that the search is on for a new model of economic citizenship in Europe. In the following chapters I attempt to show that persisting with the past is no longer credible; why it is important to choose a reform past that avoids being too utopian on the one hand and yet is not too timid on the other; and why the EU is central to the renewal of economic citizenship in Europe.

2 Institutions and labour market performance in Europe

Introduction

In the literature on the role of institutions in European labour markets we are encouraged to accept one of two models. Either institutions are seen as dysfunctional for labour markets since they cause them to be inflexible, or a dense ensemble of interlocking institutions is regarded as necessary to coordinate the labour market (as happens in Germany). Much of the academic debate is taken up with assessing the relative merits of these models – flexibility or coordination. But if the functioning of most European industrial relations systems, outside Britain and Germany, is examined, it becomes apparent almost immediately that none of them can be described as fully flexible or completely coordinated.

On the one hand, institutions and rules are still considered important to provide those in employment with some degree of protection or to bring order to collective bargaining systems. On the other hand, these institutions do not appear to operate in a way that secures labour market coordination. In many instances, institutions and policies are not fully successful in performing the tasks that they are put in place to perform. Thus, the story of labour market institutions in most European countries is that, although they are regarded as necessary, they fail to reduce tensions or distortions in employment systems. In other words, most European industrial relations systems do not correspond to either of the two main paradigms. There appears to be a mismatch between much of what we read about labour markets in Europe and actual ground-level developments.

This chapter argues that as a result of this mismatch we should be sceptical about the coordination and flexibility stories of the European labour market. Advocates of the coordination model simply exaggerate the ability of European countries at the present time to create for an employment system an institutional framework that is coherent, integrated and well-functioning. In the first part of the chapter, the matter of pay bargaining – a key aspect of the coordination model – is examined to show how organised labour market behaviour is becoming increasingly elusive. At the same time, the flexibility scenario is unlikely to become a viable alternative labour market programme, as many governments in Europe remain committed, although to varying degrees, to the idea of a European social model. The second part of the chapter argues that the flexibility approach is limited in several important respects, and shows that the dominant trend in Europe is to mesh flexibility and regulation. The third part of the chapter suggests that the pragmatic, tentative approach to labour market flexibility reflects a deep-seated uncertainty in many European capitals about how labour markets should be governed. While it is becoming widely accepted that the traditional rules and regulations that did bring order and coherence to labour market systems are fragmenting, no clear lines of reform are opening up. The notion of a *governance gap* is developed to highlight this concern about the lack of fit between labour market institutions and ground-level employment dynamics, and it is suggested that the emergence of this gap should be regarded as a dominant trend in European industrial relations.

The wage bargaining problem

A large body of economics and industrial relations literature argues that uncoordinated forms of wage bargaining distort labour market outcomes (Soskice 1990; Dore 1994). In uncoordinated bargaining, for example, trade unions will be less aware of the impact of wage claims on the price level and as a result less likely to pursue moderate wage goals. Similarly if employees do not coordinate their wage offers and pursue only their individual self-interest, each will continually seek to leapfrog over the other in an effort to recruit and retain efficient workers. Layard (1990) gives a concrete example of how uncoordinated pay deals may have a distorting impact. He argues that some industrial sectors have inherently greater productivity growth than others, mainly due to technological factors and not to the efforts of workers. Thus, he points out that between 1979 and 1986 productivity growth in British manufacturing varied hugely between industries – doubling in man-made fibres while remaining constant in brewing. If pay had been based on productivity, wages in man-made fibres would have doubled relative to those in brewing. But in fact the wage increase was identical in both industries (70 per cent). In other words, competition for labour always tends to produce a going rate, and where enterprises with high productivity growth grant large pay increases, other industries end up paying the same in order to retain labour.

The central idea is that a pay increase for one group of workers can produce negative externalities for the economy or society as a whole. Calmfors (1993) suggests that there are at least seven types of negative wage externalities, which can produce sub-optimal labour market outcomes in one way or another. Those most discussed are the insider/outsider split, which leads to bargains neglecting the interests of the unemployed, and the wage spiral, where bargains imitate recent settlements rather than being based on anticipated developments. A further argument of this literature is that these *externalities* can be *internalised* by cooperative or coordinated behaviour (Rowthorn 1992). The bargaining system can either produce conventions or contagions. A system-wide convention reduces negative externalities. In particular, it reduces the potentially harmful effects of pay agreements on levels of inflation and unemployment or on other parts of the macro-economic environment. Contagion, on the other hand, is when the going rate for wage settlements is persistently out of line with prevailing macro-economic conditions. Leapfrogging – the process of bidding up wages – is frequently cited as an example of contagion.

Establishing a convention for pay rises is seen as dependent on the existence of coordinated bargaining. However, it is not always clear in the economic literature what coordinated wage bargaining amounts to in institutional terms (Boyer 1993). The industrial relations literature is stronger on this point. Here there is wide agreement that for coordinated bargaining to work, either trade unions or employer organisations or both *outside the firm* should have the capacity to formulate collective strategies, negotiate collective obligations and implement collective policies (Crouch 1994). In other words, extra-firm institutional arrangements are required to tie enterprise pay determination to economy-wide goals and to ensure that wage drift does not occur at ground level caused either by employers paying efficiency wages or by the 'local pushiness' of trade unions. Thus coordinated bargaining creates an interface between the macro- and micro-dimensions of the labour market and this gives rise to positive externalities.

Wage formation in Europe

The centralised wage-setting procedures in the Nordic countries heavily influenced this argument (Crouch 1993). Highly centralised and encompassing trade union and employer organisations had the authority to conclude and police national pay deals. As a result, wage levels were highly sensitive to changes in employment or inflation. A consensus exists that these corporatist wage systems were a key factor in allowing the Nordic countries to sustain virtual full employment for most of the 1980s while other parts of Europe were experiencing unemployment rates of 10 per cent and above (Glyn and Rowthorn 1988). Figure 2.1 categorises each country by the degree of labour market coordination and plots this against their level of unemployment. It confirms the view that the corporatist countries were able to hold down unemployment more successfully than other European countries.

A few years back, it was widely assumed that these arrangements were on the defensive. The argument was that centralised pay arrangements such as the rate of technological change and highly fluctuating patterns of demand were too rigid to adapt to contemporary business life. In addition, in the new global corporate environment it was presumed too difficult to insulate a cohesive system of industrial relations from the effects of external trade flows and international capital mobility. Employers, so the argument went, would become less committed to national pay determination and seek greater decentralisation of wage formation. But this prediction has not materialised, at least in any coherent form. As shown in the list of wage bargaining regimes below, centralised or sector-level collective bargaining is now the norm in virtually every European country.

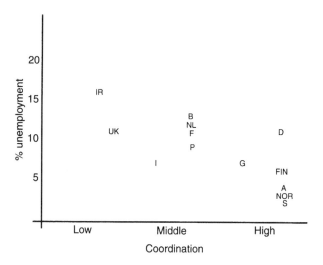

Figure 2.1 Average unemployment by level of coordination in wage bargaining, 1983–88

Notes:
A Austria; B Belgium; D Denmark; F France; FIN Finland; G Germany; I Italy; IR Ireland; NL The Netherlands; NOR Norway; P Portugal; S Sweden; UK United Kingdom

During the past few years the trend has been towards the recentralisation of wage fixing.

Wage bargaining regimes in the EU

Greece

'Informal' national wage bargaining prevails. Governments announce 'guidelines' for pay increases in the end-of-year budget. These guidelines are used as the basis for collective bargaining negotiations that take place between the social partners the following month. In addition, decentralised enterprise bargaining takes place within nationally agreed limits.

Ireland

National wage agreements have been in place since 1987. Most programmes have been based on general annual percentage increases in wages, subject to minimum absolute increases. Local bargaining clauses have allowed enterprise-level pay productivity negotiations subject to a centrally determined cap.

Sweden

The renowned system of centralised solidaristic bargaining has collapsed. Industry-wide and local pay determination are now the norm. Employer organisations appear resolute not to return to the past whilst trade unions are experimenting with new forms of pay coordination. Currently the trend is towards three-year pay agreements permitting only modest wage increases.

Portugal

The National Council for Social Concertation has played an increasingly important role in collective bargaining in the 1990s. Normally, pay determination takes place at the industry and local level, but the Council's recommendations on wage increases have been accepted more and more by the social partners. Meeting the Maastricht criteria for monetary union is widely seen as the motor behind this policy development.

Spain

In 1997, the government introduced a series of reforms to the 1980 Worker's Statute. An important feature of the reform package was the creation of a national structure for collective bargaining with only indirect government involvement. At the same time, an 'informal code' has been created between the social partners that wage determination should be consistent with government efforts to join EMU.

Finland

Non-binding framework agreements for wage increases are established by a centralised bargaining process. However these national pay guidelines are normally endorsed by individual unions which must give their consent before any collective agreement can be enacted. The latest two-year deal was concluded in January 1998, sanctioning only modest pay rises and allowing for some tax concessions.

Italy

Industrial relations reform in the early 1990s created a three-tier bargaining system. Old style incomes policies are established via centralised wage agreements. These deals normally tie wage increases to government inflation targets. Industry-wide bargaining is also permitted and local enterprise bargaining on such things as profit- and gain-sharing is encouraged.

The Netherlands

Central Agreements (*Centraal Akkoord*) are widely regarded as the key feature of the Dutch miracle. Since the early 1980s, national pay deals have for the most part maintained a regime of wage moderation, allowing for the restoration of employment growth and international competitiveness. Local-level bargaining is permitted provided it is non-inflationary.

Germany

A multi-layered bargaining system exists, involving national industry-wide and regional components. A dense network of employers and trade unions has ensured that the system operates in a coordinated way. Despite many industry-wide agreements providing opt-out clauses and growing pressure from employers for greater enterprise-based pay determination, the bargaining system is delivering pay and price stability.

Denmark

A system of 'centralised decentralisation' wage bargaining exists in the country. Central-level negotiations determine maximum permissible pay increases, whilst enterprises have sufficient freedom to create flexible pay structures. There is growing pressure for further decentralisation, but the centralised negotiations remain broadly intact and have complemented the government's fairly austere macroeconomic programme even though the country is not joining EMU.

Austria

The country has no economy-wide centralised pay negotiation system as is often assumed. Rather, a bargaining procedure between individual unions and relevant parts of the Federal Chamber of Commerce, the national employers' body, produces centralised pay deals for various sub-parts of the economy. Company-level pay bargaining is also permitted under the system. In recent years the trend, like almost everywhere else, has been towards pay moderation.

Belgium

After a drift towards pay decentralisation, centralised wage determination has recently been restored. In 1996, the government forced through an incomes policy that sets a maximum limit to wage increases based on a weighted average of projected labour cost increases among Belgium's major trading partners. To some extent this formula can be interpreted as establishing a European zone for national pay deals.

France

Collective bargaining takes place at the sector and local levels. Approximately 95 per cent of workers are covered by sector agreements. Average pay increases at both levels have been running at 2 per cent a year. High unemployment along with the desire to join EMU have promoted wage moderation. Currently the structure of collective bargaining is under review.

UK

During the 1980s industry-wide collective bargaining more or less crumbled in the UK. Enterprise bargaining is now the norm in the private sector, although it appears that decentralisation has not fragmented 'national' pay structures in many industries (going rates across industries are still evident). At the same time, centralised bargaining has largely persisted in the public sector, which governments have successfully controlled by setting tight cash limits for public expenditure.

To some, the persistence of centralised pay in certain countries and the renewal of this practice in others suggest that no deep-seated institutional fragmentation of longstanding features of European industrial relations is taking place. Or, to put the argument more positively, some level of institutional continuity is evident. For example, as Figure 2.2 shows, trade union density rates remain high or stable in many countries. Where organised labour is numerically weak, such as in France or Spain, this is to some extent compensated for by the coverage of collective bargaining agreements. Thus, while the trade union density rates barely get into double figures in the two countries, collective agreements cover about 85 per cent of the workforce. Such institutional characteristics of European industrial relations are far from trivial matters as they have an important impact on labour market outcomes. As Figure 2.3 shows, wage inequality, although not similar across Europe, is lower than the USA almost everywhere. Wide agreement exists that centralised bargaining by compressing wage structures is the key reason for this contrasting picture. With such important institutional features of European industrial relations still intact, it is not surprising that some conclude that talk about crisis or change in organised industrial relations in Europe is much overplayed (Traxler 1996; Wallerstein and Golden 1997).

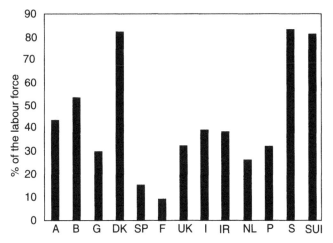

Figure 2.2 Trade union density in Europe, 1995

Notes:
A   Austria; B   Belgium; D   Denmark; F   France; G   Germany; I   Italy; IR   Ireland;
NL   The   Netherlands;   P   Portugal;   S   Sweden;   SP   Spain;   SUI   Switzerland;
UK   United Kingdom

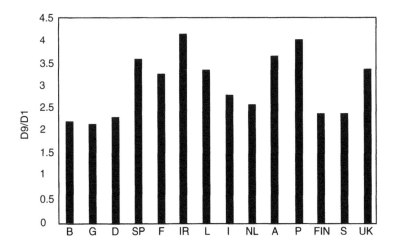

Figure 2.3 Wage dispersion in the EU, 1995

Notes:
A   Austria; B   Belgium; D   Denmark; F   France; FIN   Finland; G   Germany; I   Italy;
IR   Ireland;   L   Luxembourg;   NL   The   Netherlands;   P   Portugal;   S   Sweden;
SP   Spain; UK   United Kingdom

But a big shortcoming of assessments of this kind is that they conflate institutional continuity with industrial relations stability. In recent years important changes have been taking place as to what *collective bargaining structures do* in Europe, despite the persistence or renewal of centralised wage negotiating arrangements. The first signs that all was not well came in the 1980s when the functioning of traditional social corporatist arrangements started to run into trouble. To a large extent, the problem, apart from in Sweden, was not institutional, since many of the centralised bargaining systems operated as before, but one of economic functionality. Thus, most Nordic countries found it difficult to reach collective agreements that ensured continued low unemployment. In other words, the bargaining systems became lopsided: they could deliver on wage equality but not on employment. As a result, the widely acclaimed advantage of social corporatism, as a mediating mechanism that could connect national economic and social structures in the face of internal and external competitive pressures to keep unemployment low, began to look somewhat threadbare.

Moreover, the new centralised pay structures that have emerged in countries such as Spain, Finland, Italy, Portugal and Ireland do not appear to operate on the basis of old-style social corporatist logic. Instead, their *modus operandi* is tied to the imperatives of European integration. In particular, many of the centralised pay agreements appear little more than institutional appendages to national macro-economic regimes, more or less exclusively geared towards ensuring countries meet the criteria to join a single currency in Europe. The Maastricht Plan for European monetary union (EMU) sets down testing conditions for entry into a single currency. In addition, it lays out an elaborate institutional architecture for the proposed new Euro-zone. The democratic and institutional merits of this plan have been hotly debated. But in practice most of the member-states have been implementing policies designed to help them meet the entry fee for monetary union. In the area of fiscal policy for example, as the list of national fiscal strategies below shows, virtually all European countries, even those who have declared that they intend to stay out of the first phase of the new Euro-zone, have adopted rules more or less based on the Maastricht monetary union agenda.

National fiscal strategies in the EU, 1996–2000

Germany

Reduce general government deficit and debt-to-GDP ratio to 1.5 per cent and 60 per cent respectively; reduce public expenditure to 46 per cent (pre-unification spending level); lower tax burden and budget deficit; and lower social security contributions to below 40 per cent of gross wages.

France

General government deficit decline to 1.4 per cent of GDP; debt-to-GDP ratio at 59 per cent; phase in changes to direct taxation.

Italy

Reduce general government deficit and debt-to-GDP ratio to 2.8 per cent and 113 per cent respectively of GDP.

UK

Sound public finances over the business cycle and zero public sector borrowing requirement.

Austria

Reduce federal deficit to 2.1 per cent of GDP; freeze public expenditures on personnel, operating costs, social spending and subsidies to firms in real terms.

Belgium

Maintain general government primary surplus at around 6 per cent of GDP; reduce budget deficit to around 1 per cent of GDP; and reduce the debt-to-GDP ratio.

Denmark

General government balance in surplus over the business cycle.

Finland

Stabilise and then reduce central government debt-to-GDP ratio.

Greece

Reduce general government deficit and debt-to-GDP ratio to 0.9 per cent and 103 per cent respectively.

Ireland

Limit general government deficit to 1.5 per cent of GDP; only use contingency reserve to compensate for cyclical shortfall of revenue (0.7 per cent of GDP); meet all future EU targets.

Luxembourg

Central government expenditure to grow in line with medium-term GDP growth.

The Netherlands

Reduce tax and social security burden; and reduce public sector deficit to below 3 per cent of GDP.

Portugal

Reduce general government deficit and debt-to-GDP ratio to 1.5 per cent and 59 per cent respectively of GDP.

Spain

Reduce general government deficit and debt-to-GDP ratio to 1.6 per cent and 65 per cent respectively of GDP.

Aligning national economic governance structures to the single currency project has delivered *agenda* and *policy* shocks to organised wage-setting systems – both old and new – in Europe. These shocks have not undermined the institutional viability of centralised systems, but they have severely narrowed the room for bargains with a strong social content to be concluded. In short, the social corporatist equilibria of many centralised wage bargaining systems have been disrupted. The various labour market actors have different motivations in entering the agreements. Governments are using the central agreements to restrict pay increases so that the Maastricht hurdles are more easily jumped, and to widen the social and political legitimacy of the single currency project. Trade unions perceive the deals as a way of ensuring that organised labour has an institutional place in the new Euro-zone. This needs further explanation.

Almost all economists agree that the EU does not represent a particularly good common currency area to be governed by one money. Divergent living standards and economic structures, making it hard to enact credible macro-economic policies, are the main reasons why a single currency is not particularly suitable for the European economy. To some extent, these structural impediments to a smooth-running monetary union can be overcome if the participating countries ensure that their economic systems are highly flexible. But because of the longstanding commitment to Social Europe, most national economies, but particularly labour market regimes, are embedded in a complex array of institutional constraints. Thus, without the proper underlying structural conditions or the necessary compensating economic flexibility, the EU is not an especially good candidate for monetary union. Since structural convergence is not easily secured in the short run, a programme to free the European labour market of rigidities may become increasingly attractive to EU governments as the 2002 deadline gets closer. Thus, introducing a single currency could be the launching pad for the wholesale deregulation of the European labour market. Almost immediately, efforts to make the new single currency operate effectively could turn out to be the nadir for Social Europe. This point has not been lost on European trade unions and thus it should be no surprise that they are willing signatories to centralised agreements as part of a strategy to secure institutional lock-in in the new Euro-zone. For organised labour the 'new' centralised agreements represent a defensive strategy to prevent the Americanisation of the European labour market. But the trade-off for trade unions has been to accept an essentially employer-defined bargaining agenda. Controlling unit labour costs, improving competitiveness and managing fiscal retrenchment are the mainstays of the new agreements. Some old-type *quid pro quos*, in which social expenditure commitments are traded for pay moderation, can be found, but usually they do not add up to much. The new policy agenda gives some insight into why employers are going along with the recentralising of collective bargaining. Although a strong preference has emerged among employers for decentralised pay setting, this type of bargaining regime is not always beneficial to them. They can very quickly find themselves sucked into costly and distortional bargaining rounds, where they have to cede to wage demands in order to retain or recruit skilled workers. Thus it should not be assumed that employers somehow lose out through the presence of centralised agreements. Besides, as Streeck (1998) has pointed out, European employers have probably calculated that they would be unable to push through a wage flexibility programme. Political forces in favour of Social Europe may not be in the driving seat, but they are nevertheless still strong enough to mount an effective rearguard action against any attempt to introduce a thorough labour market deregulation programme. Thus, employers probably view the present central agreements as an acceptable second-best option in light of the prevailing political circumstances.

This account of the organisational logic behind the new collective agreements departs from standard discussions of developments in European employment relations. At present, the industrial relations academy appears divided into two camps: the optimists and the pessimists. For the optimists the new central agreements simply amount to the continuation of coordinated bargaining in different economic times. For the pessimists, pay recentralisation should be viewed as part of the wider rewriting of the traditional peace formula between European capital and labour, which secured a balance between labour market equity and efficiency. Although generating considerable contention, this optimistic/pessimistic divide is not a particularly fruitful line of debate since neither position is without flaws. On the one hand, the optimistic camp seems tied to a rather truncated view of social partnership, regarding it as a mode of decision-making rather than a way to organise the labour market. On the other hand, pessimists appear exceptionally rigid in their thinking. If the institutional framework for the labour market does not broadly conform to some notion of a coordinated employment system, then by definition it must resemble some variation of neo-liberalism. To be polemical, the pessimists see the USA and Germany as representing the only viable alternative paths to organising the labour market. Because of these various shortcomings, neither camp captures the full subtlety of current changes in European employment relations. The 'nothing has changed view' of the optimists hugely under-estimates the scale of the labour market changes taking place. At the same time, the pessimists are also off track: the current direction of centralised bargaining may be having a damaging impact on coordinated labour markets, but at the same time it is excessive to describe unfolding events as neo-liberalism in corporatist clothing.

Perhaps the best way to read the recentralisation of wage systems is that they reflect the emergence of a twin-track collective bargaining system in Europe. On the one hand, the industrial relations centre is exercising strict control over wages increases. On the other, greater variation and decen-tralisation are being permitted in virtually every other aspect of the employment relationship: centralisation and decentralisation are co-existing in Europe. In other words, in response to the pressures of European integration, the agreements have created a wedge between the macro- and micro-aspects of the labour market. While it is fairly apparent that the industrial relations centre in many member-states has become co-opted into macro-economic regimes dedicated to the realisation of a single currency in Europe, there is no such clarity with regard to ground-level developments.

Little reliable evidence exists on the scale, direction or depth of work-place change in Europe, but from the surveys that do exist three key themes emerge. First, employers are striving to increase the operational flexibility of enterprises through the use of annualised hours schemes, by increasing shift working and by introducing weekend work (European Commission 1993). Second, greater fragmentation is occurring in work organisation, although most countries are grappling with the themes of team-working, total quality management and new human resource management practices. Third, nowhere do trade unions appear to be on the offensive in enterprise-based collective bargaining systems. For the most part, trade unions are on the defensive, preoccupied with themes such as balancing job flexibility and employment security, if not openly engaging in concessionary bargaining. On occasions, trade unions have been successful in negotiating innovatory packages on such things as work sharing, but the trend has been for them to comply with employer-driven attempts at reorganising the workplace. Together these three trends are perhaps best captured in the term 'converging divergences' (Darbishire and Katz forthcoming). This term highlights the fact that distinct national systems of industrial relations are fragmenting at the same time as common patterns in workplace change are occurring across countries. Converging divergences alongside pay centralisation for monetary union are the foundations to twin-track industrial relations systems in Europe. These systems weaken the coordinating capacities of labour markets. On the one hand, the narrow focus of centralised agreements on pay and competitiveness reduces their ability to produce collective labour market goods. As Streeck (1992a) has argued, the key to the sustainability of organised labour markets in northern Europe was the ability of corporatist structures to integrate the distributional and productive sides of the economy. In addition to dividing up the economic pie, the central agreements created the institutional mechanisms to address the 'negative externalities' in the labour markets. But because of their constrained agenda, the vast majority of central agreements cannot operate in such a manner. On the other hand, the variegated enterprise-based employment systems that are emerging on the ground are causing the proliferation of specific agreements, each with different terms and conditions. The multiplicity of locally differentiated factors obscures general labour market conditions. In such a situation, the enterprise foundations to any type of social corporatist equilibrium between equity and efficiency become precarious. Thus twin-track industrial relations squeezes the coordinating capacities of labour markets by disrupting the institutional interfaces between the macro- and micro-aspects of the employment systems. To repeat, this is not to suggest that neo-liberalism is triumphing everywhere in Europe. But it does mean that we should be wary about the coordination story for the European labour market. Too many industrial relations developments are cutting against the grain of this argument to make it a convincing model.

The flexibility thesis

At the heart of the coordination argument is the notion that governing the labour market with rules and regulations can produce positive economic outcomes. A sharp contrast to this view is the flexibility thesis, according to which poor labour market performance in Europe is caused by too many rigidities in employment systems. On this perspective, excessive government intervention and over-powerful trade unions have reduced the flexibility of European labour markets. Trade unions and collective bargaining arrangements are regarded as the main obstacles preventing wages from adjusting to market conditions, resulting in workers being priced out of jobs. On the other hand, state intervention is held responsible for excessive legal and financial guarantees in the labour market that cause redundancies and discourage hiring. From this standpoint, if economic performance is to be improved, a number of flexibility measures need to be introduced.

Although several taxonomies of labour market flexibility exist, all tend to touch upon three interrelated themes. First, macro-economic flexibility which concerns the responsiveness of the general wage level in a country to increase in unemployment – this was one of the earliest aspects of labour market flexibility to be investigated as unemployment rates began to rise. If the problem is not one of aggregate demand, then a failure of the average wage level to respond to changes in economic circumstances can reduce unemployment. Second, mobility is broadly understood to include movements of workers between occupations, industrial sectors and geographical regions. The argument here is that mobility eases the problems of structural economic adjustment. Third and probably most important is enterprise flexibility. There are many dimensions to this level of flexibility – flexibility of wages; lack of hiring and firing rules; the variability of working time and its distribution over the week and year; the definition of work rules; and the mobility of employees between different work tasks in the company – in short every aspect of the firm's access to and use of labour.

Advocates of the labour market flexibility thesis are correct in suggesting that employment systems in Europe are heavily constrained by rules and regulations. The more important areas of labour market regulation include working time, working conditions, atypical work, employment protection, minimum wages and employee representation rights. Unsurprisingly the details of regulations vary, but certain patterns do emerge across countries. Apart from in Denmark and the UK, statutory provisions govern the length of the working week in Europe. The norm is for a 48-hour ceiling on the working week, but some countries, such as Spain and Greece, have more stringent regulations. On working conditions, all countries legally oblige employers to give employees health and safety protection at the workplace, as well as other benefits such as sickness and maternity/paternity leave. Both legislation and collective agreements are used to implement minimum wages, although the severity of these regulations differs significantly, with France probably having the toughest and Spain the weakest. A key aspect of employment protection is the regulation of the recruitment and dismissal of employees – hiring and firing rules. Germany, the Netherlands and Italy have the toughest hiring and firing rules, with Britain again the most lenient. With the exception of Denmark, Italy, Ireland and the UK, European countries have specific legislation regulating fixed-term contracts. The situation is different with regard to part-time work, as few legal texts or collective agreements explicitly regulate this form of atypical employment. Countries where no regulations apply include the UK, Denmark, the Netherlands and Portugal. Many European countries give employee representation rights at the workplace, with the exception of Ireland, the UK and Switzerland. Normally these rights are realised through the operation of works councils, although the status and authority of such institutions vary considerably.

A comprehensive account of the extent of labour market legislation in Europe is not possible here. Instead a synthetic index has been constructed to show the intensity of such regulations in each country. This involves grading the labour market rules, outlined above on a scale between 0 and 5 (0 being the lowest score, reflecting the relative absence of rules whilst a 5 means heavy employment protection), and then adding the values together to get a synthetic index score. Table 2.1 gives the result for most European countries, and it shows that labour market rules differ from one country to another. Fewer rules exist in the UK than elsewhere while there are four countries that share together the title of most regulated labour market. The big question is the impact of these different regulatory regimes on economic performance.

Table 2.1 Synthetic index (SI) of intensity of labour market regulations in Europe

Country	Working time	Working conditions	Atypical work	Employment protection	Minimum wages	Employees' represent-sation rights	SI
Belgium	1	2	3	2	1	1	10
Denmark	1	1	0	1	0	2	5
France	1	1	2	2	3	2	11
Germany	1	2	2	2	1	3	11
Greece	2	2	2	2	1	1	10
Ireland	1	1	2	2	0	0	6
Italy	1	1	2	2	2	1	9
The Netherlands	2	2	1	2	1	2	10
Portugal	1	1	1	2	1	1	7
Spain	2	1	1	3	2	1	10
UK	0	1	1	1	0	0	3
Austria	2	2	2	2	0	3	11
Finland	1	1	2	1	1	2	8
Norway	1	2	2	1	0	2	8
Sweden	2	2	2	1	1	3	11
Switzerland	1	1	1	1	0	0	4

Source: Author's own research

Figures 2.4a and 2.4b plot the synthetic index of the intensity of labour market regulations in European countries against their employment performance. Figure 2.4a shows the average percentage change in job creation between 1989 and 1995. Two points stand out from the table: (1) the UK employment growth rate is not particularly higher than in other countries even though its labour market is the least regulated; and (2) the overall job generation machine in Europe is pretty poor. The same story emerges with regard to unemployment (Figure 2.4b). Nearly two decades of flexibility measures have not enabled the UK to stand apart from the rest of Europe; the UK simply mirrors the general trend of fairly high unemployment. Figures 2.5a and 2.5b relate the synthetic index to wider measures of competitive performance – unit labour costs and investment rates. Again we see that there is no discernible difference between flexibility oriented and regulated economies. The general trend is for most European countries to keep unit labour costs under control on the one hand, but to experience unimpressive investment levels on the other.

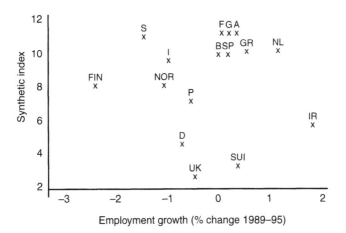

Figure 2.4a Intensity of labour market regulations and employment performance, 1989–95

Notes:
A Austria; B Belgium; D Denmark; F France; FIN Finland; G Germany; GR Greece; I Italy; IR Ireland; NL The Netherlands; NOR Norway; P Portugal; S Sweden; SP Spain; SUI Switzerland; UK United Kingdom

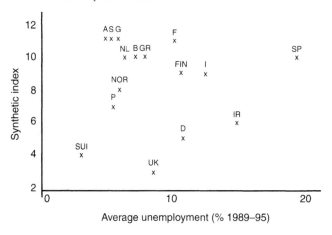

Figure 2.4b Intensity of labour market regulations and unemployment
performance, 1989–95

Notes:
A   Austria;   B   Belgium;   D   Denmark;   F   France;   FIN   Finland;   G   Germany;
GR   Greece; I   Italy; IR   Ireland; NL   The Netherlands; NOR   Norway; P   Portugal;
S   Sweden; SP   Spain; SUI   Switzerland; UK   United Kingdom

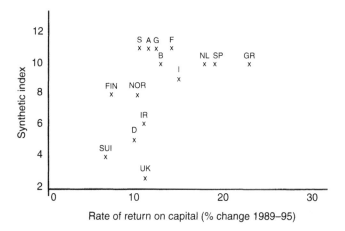

Figure 2.5a Intensity of labour market regulations and competitive performance,
1989–95: rate of return on capital business sector

Notes:
A   Austria;   B   Belgium;   D   Denmark;   F   France;   FIN   Finland;   G   Germany;
GR   Greece; I   Italy; IR   Ireland; NL   The Netherlands; NOR   Norway; S   Sweden;
SP   Spain; SUI   Switzerland; UK   United Kingdom

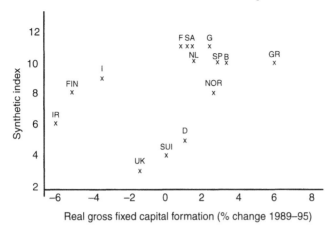

Figure 2.5b Intensity of labour market regulations and competitive performance, 1989–95: real gross fixed capital formation

Notes:

A Austria; B Belgium; D Denmark; F France; FIN Finland; G Germany; GR Greece; I Italy; IR Ireland; NL The Netherlands; NOR Norway; S Sweden; SP Spain; SUI Switzerland; UK United Kingdom

Thus the claim that flexibility and deregulation are the routes to better economic performance is not upheld by the evidence. This observation corresponds with the argument that the first-order effects of flexibility are to increase wage (and income) inequality (Machin 1996; Freeman 1994; Atkinson 1995; Solow 1990). Wage inequality, as shown in Figure 2.3, has increased more in countries, both in Europe and elsewhere, where the flexibility programme has been most actively pursued. Thus, for example, the UK has experienced the highest increase in wage inequality compared with other European or even OECD countries. One explanation why flexibility accentuates inequality is that it fails as a model of labour market competition. Where flexibility has been extensively introduced, the result has been the creation of insiders and outsiders in the employment system.

Enterprises given the opportunity to introduce thoroughgoing market principles into the employment relationship have actually done the reverse and insulated large numbers of workers from the pressure of labour market competition. A common reason for protecting core workers is the recognition that too much competition may disrupt the trust and social relations which codify and stabilise relationships between employers and employees. But creating groups of insider employees impairs the efficiency of key aspects of the labour market system, particularly wage-setting.

Thus, for example, even though unemployment may be rising in the economy, core workers may continue to receive pay rises above inflation. In other words, at the macro-level, wages are not responding sufficiently to changes in the level of unemployment, with the likelihood that a number of distortions may emerge.

But employers cannot extend privileged insider positions to all employees since the cost would be prohibitive. They therefore tend to use the scope given to them by labour market deregulation to expand the numbers of outsiders. As a result, in the wake of flexibility measures, the trend is for an increase in temporary and part-time contracts; hiring and firing; local or enterprise-based wage differentials; and the use of subcontracted labour. The result is more intensive competition, but largely among these groups of workers already exposed in varying degrees to economic and social exclusion, while core employees remain relatively immune from the dynamics of demand and supply (Bentolila and Dolado 1994).

Regulations and the loss of economic functionality

Widening the gap between insider and outsider employees is a key market failure of the flexibility model. It is this insight that has encouraged many to justify legal and government interventions in labour markets. To be sure, where employment systems have remained closely regulated in Europe, there has been no significant widening in wage inequality. At the same time, as shown earlier, the employment and economic records of these regulated labour markets are lacklustre. Thus the old institutionalist argument that equity and efficiency can go hand in hand, with one dependent on the other and each being mutually reinforcing, no longer appears to hold. A schism appears to have been created between the fairness dimension of labour market regulation in Europe and its positive contribution to economic performance. Employment rules have lost their economic functionality. This has not always been the case. In the past, labour market regulations were functional, particularly during the golden age of economic growth, in maintaining macro-economic stability and lowering micro-economic transactions costs (Boyer 1995).

Most European governments are in a quandary. On the one hand, they are deeply reluctant to adopt the flexibility model, given its socially divisive implications. But on the other hand, it is becoming increasingly apparent that the existing repertoire of employment regulations is now in some aspects dysfunctional. Almost everywhere the response has been to introduce greater flexibility without dismantling the overall regulatory framework. Consider the matter of part-time and temporary work.

In 1991 Belgium introduced new legal rules on atypical work which, despite facilitating the greater use of part-time and temporary workers, also codified and made more transparent the legal rights of such employees. In particular, a range of rules was introduced to regulate the amount of overtime that a part-time worker can perform; control the variation in hours by part-timers; and give such employees priority treatment with regard to full-time positions that become vacant in the company in which they work. The Balladur government in France in 1993 launched a similar initiative. As part of a wide-ranging package of labour market policies, a law was introduced with the objective of balancing new forms of employment with a measure of protection for the workers involved. Thus the law reduces employer social security contributions by 30 per cent in respect of part-time workers whose contracts meet certain requirements, including guaranteed minimum continuous duration of any period of working; the right to priority consideration when a full-time job becomes available; and the same working conditions as full-time workers (Teague 1994).

Reforms have also been introduced with regard to the organisation of working time. In the Netherlands, a 1995 Working Time Directive made it easier for firms to introduce more flexibility in working and operating time arrangements. Similar changes were made in Austria in 1994 when amendments to the Law of Working Time (*Arbeitszeitgesetz*) were made. Rules governing the recruitment and dismissal of workers – hiring and firing systems – have been relaxed in many countries, particularly Germany, Italy, Switzerland and Spain. Thus the search is on for a new balance between regulation and flexibility, but no finely tuned, coherent model has been found to mesh them together. Many countries are enacting reforms in a pragmatic, uneven way, resulting in the emergence of an awkward hybrid. Nevertheless, attempts at combining regulation and flexibility will continue to dominate European industrial relations for the next decade.

One reason why this is so is that enterprises on the ground are implementing flexibility innovations even in the context of strong regulatory arrangements. For example, a recent European Commission Report (1996) on labour market flexibility shows that enterprises have gone a long way towards decoupling weekly operating times and weekly working hours. Whereas the average contractually agreed working week (for full-time workers) in the EU is 38 hours, the average operating time of operating plants is 69 hours. This decoupling has been achieved largely by the greater use of flexible employment conditions, particularly with regard to shift work, night and weekend work. Virtually every member-state has experienced an increase in these forms of employment. As well as making operating times more flexible, an increasing number of enterprises are experimenting with systems of temporary and part-time contracts. These corporate moves towards flexibility are likely to add momentum to government-led attempts to weaken labour market regulatory regimes.

To some extent this observation is at odds with the conventional view of labour regulations and business strategies. Traditionally it is assumed that institutional rules heavily influence the choice of strategy adopted by enterprises. In some circumstances it is believed that a virtuous interaction can open up between the regulatory regime and commercial behaviour. Trade unionists often claim, for example, that employment rights which reduce the scope for cost-based competitive strategies lock enterprises into high value-added forms of activity, thereby creating the ground-level conditions for high labour standards. But at the moment the direction of influence seems to be going the other way: new employment practices at company level are creating extra pressure for the reform of labour market regulation regimes in Europe. Certainly, the smooth correspondence between rules and company-level behaviour that many accounts of labour market institutional arrangements assume no longer exists. Governments have less confidence in the ability of regulations to combine efficiency and equity in labour markets. Even the European Commission in its latest social action programme signalled that it would not be proposing any 'hard' new laws for the European employment system.

The governance gap

The two main arguments advanced thus far can be summarised as follows. On the one hand, institutions no longer organise the employment relationship in an orderly and coordinated way. On the other hand, there has been no large-scale shift towards labour market flexibility. Most European governments have engaged in a pragmatic loosening of regulatory rules for the labour market. This situation reflects a continuing political commitment across Europe to some vaguely defined social model, even though the organising capacity of current arrangements are fragmenting. Thus European industrial relations are caught somewhere between coordination and flexibility: a gap has opened up between the governance system of labour markets in many European countries and ground-level economic, social and commercial developments.

A governance system is frequently defined 'as the totality of institutional arrangements – including rules and rule-making agents – that regulate transactions inside and across the boundaries of an economic system' (Hollingsworth *et al.* 1994: 5). Here a slightly different view is taken, as labour market governance systems are primarily seen as mediating mechanisms that set out to connect economic and social structures – they are an attempt to incorporate people into economic life in a way that makes compatible the human resource needs of enterprises and worker demands for certain social guarantees. When these mediating mechanisms – trade unions, the system of labour law and so on – establish a symmetry between the economic and social spheres, then the labour market can be considered coordinated. In contrast, the flexibility agenda seeks to curb the role of industrial relations institutions as economic and social interlocutors so that the pursuit of efficiency can go on unencumbered by equity concerns. The contention of this chapter is that the mediation mechanisms governing the European labour market are fractured.

Thus the argument around coordination and flexibility does not fully encapsulate developments in European industrial relations. At the moment we are witnessing a growing disillusionment with the traditional social model in Europe and the start of the search for a replacement. So far the reforms enacted have been timid and piecemeal, doing little more than patching up existing labour market regimes. But arguments are emerging for bolder, more radical, innovations (Suriot 1995). For example, important assumptions underpinning much of labour law are considered ready for a rethink. A longstanding characteristic of the employment contract has been the notion of a relationship of subordination. But new systems of job assignments and work hierarchies that abridge the traditional distinctions between management and labour make such a notion look increasingly tenuous. Similarly, the blurring of boundaries between firms through the creation of corporate networks and the increasing use of contract and temporary work makes the object of the employment contract increasing difficult to define. Furthermore, the traditional model of full-time paid jobs which permeates much of labour law is now looking outmoded in light of the growth of atypical employment. Regulating this form of work by traditional labour law methods runs the risk of creating a mass of rules which become so confusing that they are rendered useless.

The character of collective goods produced by labour market governance structures is also coming under the spotlight. In an influential essay, Streeck (1992b) argues that a range of labour market institutions is required to establish an adequate pool of properly skilled workers for the economy. On this view, in the absence of institutions, firms will free-ride by allowing other enterprises to incur the costs of training and then poach skilled workers by offering attractive remuneration packages. Thus to lock a productive system into a high-skills/high value-added economy requires firms to be embedded in a dense ensemble of institutional arrangements. Regini (1995), who suggests that skills are being redefined in a root and branch way in most European economies, has convincingly challenged this standard view. Greater importance is being attached to problem-solving ability and the behavioural traits of employees rather than technical 'know-how'. The result is that firms are attaching less emphasis to the public provision of vocational training. Rather, they are creating teaching systems inside their own organisations through the use of team-working procedures and internal labour market systems. As a result, a gulf is opening between the qualifications' systems – normally apprenticeships – of national, publicly funded, training arrangements and the skill formation strategies of specific firms. Thus a reconceptualisation of the content, scope and purpose of collective public goods produced by governance structures is seen as timely.

A critical eye is being cast on some of the traditional mediating mechanisms themselves. In the past, for example, trade unions played an important role in promoting and maintaining fairness in European labour markets. By engaging in enterprise-level collective bargaining, they gave workers a degree of control over the social structure of the firm. But the role of organised labour as the guarantor of terms and conditions of work through collective representation is crumbling fast. Although patterns in European trade unions are diverse, almost everywhere trade unions are on the defensive. The extremely adversarial trade union systems of Britain and France have suffered the greatest damage, but even in countries with more consensual traditions, such as Germany, unions have been seriously weakened. A testimony to this halt to the forward march of labour has been the inability of trade unions in most European country to recruit atypical workers, the most rapidly growing part of the labour force, to any great extent.

These developments are profound because they represent not only an obvious loss of bargaining power, but also increasingly the impairment of the unions as representative agents. In this situation, question marks arise about their capacity to act as a mediating mechanism connecting economic and social life in Europe. At the very least, new forms of trade union activity appear necessary: for example, rather than trying to use traditional collective bargaining to give atypical workers a modicum of protection, trade unions may increasingly have to operate as institutional enforcers of individual rights for this part of the workforce. But even these changes may not be enough, thus raising the matter of more far-reaching adaptations involving new support structures other than trade unions to ensure that people are properly incorporated into economic life.

Closing the governance gap in the European labour market is seen as requiring changes beyond industrial relations arrangements. Important distortions have emerged in most welfare systems in Europe. Virtually every social benefits system in Europe distorts the labour market by creating disincentives to work. One common problem is the unemployment trap: the situation where a move from joblessness to employment may result in a relatively small increase in income or in some cases in an actual fall in living standards. But, as Chapter 5 highlights, to address the problem simply by reducing benefit levels may lock many people into low-paid, low-productive jobs with limited opportunities – the poverty trap. Thus, while the need for reform is evident, there appears no easy or straightforward adjustment route.

This is an important point: although a governance gap can be identified in the European labour market, and although areas where reform is required can be pinpointed, it is by no means certain that the appropriate actions to re-establish a complementarity between institutions and ground-level employment relations will be taken. Switching from one governance regime to another is often a hazardous business. Furthermore, any changes made may not necessarily create a new set of cohesive, interdependent institutions. Indeed, Boyer (1995) suggests that a deep institutional mismatch exists in the French labour market where there is a big public policy push to enhance education and training, but many enterprises remained tied to old style Fordist employment practices. Another possibility that cannot be discounted is that the pressures in favour of flexibility may become more intense, resulting in the deregulation policies pursued in the UK being imported to the rest of Europe. Thus much uncertainty exists about the future governance of the European labour market.

Conclusions

The essential message of this chapter could be expressed as scepticism about two contemporary metanarratives of labour markets – *coordination* and *flexibility*. It is suggested that labour market regulation and labour market institutions are ubiquitous in contemporary Europe, being both unavoidable and functionally necessary. On the other hand, institutional and regulatory frameworks are everywhere fragmented, incoherent and a source of friction: although they mitigate some of the most severe economic and social problems in employment relations, they nowhere establish anything approaching systemic organisation in the field of employment.

To refer first to the notion of coordination, it is clear that the Scandinavian social corporatist paradigm of centralised wage settlements is a thing of the past. Beyond that, retrospective analysis is in the process of dismantling the exaggerated claims that have been made for Scandinavian labour market structures, whose success was always contingent on a quite transitory political and economic equilibrium. Today German models are more fashionable but the same sorts of consideration apply. It is easy to accept the claims that German labour market institutions facilitated industrial adaptation in an increasingly turbulent international environment. But the converse also holds true – Germany's industrial success reduced the need for drastic labour shredding in the industrial sector, and helped to shield inherited institutions from the pressures which led, elsewhere, to dislocation or decay.

German models themselves are showing signs of dilapidation (see Streeck's 1993 account of German wage bargaining): the number of those excluded from prevailing standards of income, working conditions and security is increasing rapidly; a serious fiscal crisis makes some of the compromises of the 1980s, such as subsidies for declining sectors, difficult to continue and impossible to repeat; even the German training system requires modernisation in the light of new competitive pressures.

On the other hand, if institutions and regulation are everywhere incoherent, they are none the less ubiquitous and necessary even in this incoherence. The notion of thoroughgoing flexibility or, so to speak, an institutional vacuum is as remote from reality as that of national coordination. The protagonists of flexibility have correctly identified the presence of institutional disarray, intensified by extremely rapid change in technologies, markets and resource availability. But it is a wild idea to restore order by eliminating institutional structures as such. Where policy has been influenced by this second utopian aspiration – in Britain, above all, perhaps, in the construction industry – the result has only been the proliferation of crude economic and social malfunctions, which can be seen in all the domains we have considered: bargaining, skills and social legitimacy. Even in this extreme case an institutional vacuum is not produced; but the necessary process of institutional change and adaptation is distorted and delayed.

Finally, it is to institutional evolution, rather than to institutional design, that I wish to draw attention. The most effective role for public policy is to intervene in evolving practice and to contest the most obviously undesirable developments, rather than to pursue the illusory goal of coordination. We propose the defence of disadvantaged and insecure employees as the most important guiding principle of such intervention, on grounds both of efficiency and equity. No general scheme of labour market regulation follows from this principle. Protecting and strengthening the weakest members of the labour force may, in some cases, suggest more stringent or effective constraints on business practice. In other cases, relaxing constraints (for instance in the informal economy) or cutting taxes (especially on low-waged employees) may best advance the same goals. In both situations the only realistic aim is to influence labour market outcomes, not to rationalise labour market processes which will continue to display enormous diversity, fragmentation and incoherence.

3 Lean production and the German model

Introduction

Supporters of the European social model have traditionally argued that public interventions in the labour market promote both equity and efficiency. Old-style institutional arguments are normally used in support of this position. On the one hand, it is suggested that employment regulations close off the possibility of enterprises pursuing low-wage commercial strategies. Instead employers are encouraged to build up productive capacity. On the other hand, it is claimed that firms that comply with regulations and offer advantageous employment contracts and create good working conditions benefit by attracting the more capable in the labour market.

From this perspective, the European social model is an 'institutional supply-side' model of the economy that allows enterprises to be successful as workers simultaneously enjoy high social standards (Rodgers and Streeck 1994). The German high-skills/high value-added economy has long been the Mecca for those who hold this position. The doubting Thomases that expressed scepticism about equity and efficiency being amalgamated in one labour market are invariably presented with *Modell Deutschland*. Ailing economic systems such as Britain have been constantly encouraged to imitate key German labour market institutions, particularly its vocational training system. So long as the German economy was thriving, the notion of a European social model was a viable, plausible, political project.

This chapter argues that this traditional defence of the European social model may be losing credibility precisely because of the difficulties facing the German economy. At the moment, Germany is facing several formidable economic challenges; dealing with the aftershock of reunification and preparing for monetary union are among the most prominent (Streeck 1996). But this chapter concentrates on the pressures placed on

Germany by new emerging flexible patterns of production encapsulated in the term 'lean production'. This new production concept is seen as a threat to the German model because it strikes at some of its core assumptions. It tears up the idea that there is a high road and a low road to economic competitiveness. It offers a model of employment status that challenges the craft-based system in Germany. Whether the German model can withstand the pressures from lean production remains an open question: certainly some adaptation will be required. These developments cast a shadow over the alleged superiority of the German economic system and thus, indirectly, over the case for a European social model (Klodt *et al.* 1994).

This chapter is organised as follows. First, the German system of labour market coordination is set out. Then why this system is seen to combine economic efficiency and social equity is explained. Rather than discussing all aspects of the employment system in detail, attention will be focused on the training system, which is both a central part of the German model and representative of its general character. The following section outlines the main features of lean production and argues that it represents a new cognitive structure for corporate organisations and workstations. Next, the model of employment offered up by lean production is analysed. The following section assesses just how lean production is challenging the German model and the penultimate part of the chapter contrasts two alternative ways in which Germany can respond to the challenge – by muddling through or by learning through monitoring. The conclusions draw out the implications of the analysis for the wider debate about the European social model.

Institutional foundations of German success

Over the years a wide range of influences has been responsible for the impressive performance of the German economy. But one key factor has been a set of interlocking labour market institutions conducive to firms following high-quality, high value-added commercial strategies (Soskice 1994). Pride of place must go to the country's vocational training system that produces skilled workers of sufficient quantity and quality. The German apprenticeship system is built on two key foundations. One is a bank–industry relationship that allows corporate managers to include the interests of workers in business plans. Not only are managers able to make long-term investments, but they also have the opportunity to pursue in-depth training programmes. As a result, they create an organisational infrastructure that is suitable for employees to handle state-of-the-art machinery. The other is the willingness of young people to work hard at school to secure a place at the top end of the apprenticeship hierarchy and to accept low wages throughout the period of training. This ensures that on entering a company, a young person has a high level of general education and has in effect accepted to pay for part of their training. In brief, young people are prepared to make sacrifices for rewards in the future. This calculation reflects the close correspondence between a person's position in the occupational hierarchy and his or her position in German society as such.

A range of institutional arrangements ensures that these twin pillars of the training system are sustained over time. First, there is the system of pay determination. For the most part, wages are set at the sector and regional levels, leaving little room for enterprises to pursue their own pay policies. On the one hand, this makes it difficult for firms either to pursue cost-based commercial strategies centred on low wages or to engage in poaching by offering attractive remuneration packages to entice workers from competitors. On the other hand, it impedes workers from pursuing rent-seeking strategies – the danger of workers using firm-specific knowledge to pressurise for higher wages. In other words, wages are taken out of competition, allowing managers and workers within the enterprise to negotiate on other aspects of work and production organisation.

Second, several positive benefits arise as a result of employer associations playing an active administrative role in the training system. One is that they lower transaction costs associated with running an elaborate economy-wide training system. Companies require comprehensive up-to-date advice and guidance in organising apprenticeship schemes, and employer organisations deliver these services cheaply. In addition, they perform a monitoring role on behalf of government to ensure that national standards are being reached. As monitoring can only be effective if enterprises trust the external agency, employer organisations are likely to get better access to a firm than a public body. This ensures that the certification system is more credible and allows the private sector itself to put right any defects in training provision.

Employer organisations also operate as an external institutional sanction against free-riding behaviour. Not all companies will be prosperous all the time and when the rainy day comes the temptation is to cut back on training or to reduce the number of apprentices on the payroll. But employer organisations close off this option by exhorting the struggling company to maintain existing levels of training. Inside the enterprise, the system of work councils, which gives employees a voice in business decision-making, acts as a third institutional buttress for the apprenticeship system. Through this arrangement, employees receive guarantees that young people will not be used as replacements for older more skilled workers. They also secure input into the format and content of training provision. In return, management gains assurances that trade unions will not rent-seek after employees acquire skills, and a general commitment to cooperation in any production or organisational restructuring. All in all, the works council system, by promoting trust relations at the workplace, creates a favourable environment for the operation of high-skills training.

The German model: combining equity and efficiency

The symbiosis between the productive system of many German companies and the institutional structure of the labour market has locked the country into a high-skills, high-quality, economic trajectory. As a result, the country has been able to square the circle between economic efficiency and social equity. With regard to efficiency, not only does each part of the labour market governance structure carry out a worthwhile task, but every aspect dovetails with another. Overall, the system reduces many market failures associated with organising an employment system in a coherent way. It is this ability to reduce distortions such as free-riding behaviour that has earned the German model such wide acclaim. Consider the matter of skill formation. Since Gary Becker's seminal work in this area over thirty years ago (1964), it is well understood that creating well-functioning training systems is a complex, even hazardous task. A key problem is that for a number of reasons enterprises have a tendency to under-invest in skill formation (Buechtemann and Soloff 1994). For example, enterprises are frequently reluctant to invest in general skills – those skills recognised through an economy-wide certification procedure – either because the company will have to pay the employee the going rate for the job or because he or she may quit. But to pay the employee the market wage reduces the incentive to make the initial investment in training. A cheaper strategy may be either to hire a worker with the necessary skills from the external labour market or to poach such a worker from another firm.

An alternative route open to firms is to invest in company-specific training. Such a system certainly has its advantages since it can fine-tune worker skills to the particular needs of the company. In addition, it insulates the company from the threat of poaching, since the skills acquired by employees are not transferable. But company-focused training systems have a down side. On acquiring skills, employees become more indispensable to the company – in economic terms they become a quasi-fixed factor of production. In such a situation, a firm is exposed to rent-seeking by employees – an attempt may be made to pursue wage claims that exceed productivity performance. Additionally, an economy where firm-specific training predominates may be under-provided in general training. As a result, a mismatch may exist in the external labour market between the skills demanded by employers and those offered by potential recruits, causing tension in the movement of workers between firms. This analysis suggests that a high-skills/high value-added economy cannot be created by enterprises alone. Instead, institutional interventions are required to reduce free-riding behaviour and other distortions. The German system of labour market coordination is seen as a supreme example of how these distortions can be suppressed, thereby improving competitiveness.

In terms of equity, the German model creates a particular form of economic citizenship – the rights and obligations outside the sphere of individual contracts and market exchange that facilitate the incorporation of people into economic life (Grahl and Teague 1994). Again, the apprenticeship system plays a key role, for it confers upon individuals a level of status in the labour market. Specifically, the structure of skill formation promotes a professional model of employment status. Membership of a liberal profession is a status relationship, which runs in parallel with the contracts entered into by individuals. The specific natures of services and remuneration are governed by free contract, but are embedded in an invariant structure of obligations, which ensures the competence, responsibility and ethical probity of the practitioner. The client thus has a guarantee which makes it possible to transact with any recognised member of the profession. The counterpart of this for professional workers is precisely their mobility from one client to another. The objective of the German vocational training system is to extend this professional model of skill to as many workers as possible. Thus workers should receive high levels of training which are not tied to the specific needs of an individual enterprise but validated by objective qualifications recognised across the economy. As a result, the employment status of an individual does not arise from an advantageous contract with a particular employer, but from membership of a generally recognised association which encourages an ethos of skill and work discipline.

Thus the model of economic citizenship works from the provision of labour market collective goods towards the status of individuals. On the basis of interlocking institutions, the labour market is organised in a way that combines the social integration and involvement of workers with the reduction of market distortions, such as free-riding activity. This contrasts sharply with the human resource management (HRM) model of economic citizenship often found in (American) textbooks. For the most part, this model ties workers to individual enterprises. In its most benign form, it can be regarded as enterprise-level citizenship, as it is about creating a *Gemeinschaft* inside the firm to increase the attachment and loyalty of employees to their place of work. The vision is of enterprises operating as tiny communities in which the relationship between workers and managers is harmonious and consensual. Unquestionably, individuals and even groups of workers can benefit under such arrangements, but the danger is that enterprises may become disconnected from the operation of the wider labour market. Decentralising employee relations to the enterprise normally results in a proliferation of specific agreements, each with different terms and conditions. General labour market conditions become obscured by the multiplicity of locally differentiated factors. In such a situation, it is difficult to establish coordinating structures in the labour market. Thus, while an equilibrium of sorts can be established between equity and efficiency inside the enterprise with the implementation of HRM policies, it is doubtful whether a similar balance would exist in the wider employment system. Internal cohesion translates into external disorder.

The German model has important implications for the organisational design of enterprises as well as for society at large (Herrigel 1995). Because skilled workers see their honour and status being realised through completing integrated and sophisticated tasks in an autonomous manner, many German firms are structured in a hierarchical way. Pronounced demarcations exist between job roles and work jurisdictions so that the expertise of different skilled workers can be made transparent. Craft trade unions play a key role in the maintenance and reproduction of this structured system. Invariably, these unions dominate company-level works councils which give them important influence over the production, investment and employment plans of enterprises. Within the wider society, craft unions, being the backbone of organised labour, are given a special associative status. This status marks them off from other interest groups which mainly pursue their own sectionalist demands. Instead, trade unions are regarded as part of the web of institutions that promote order and cohesion in Germany.

Lean production and the emergence of a new 'industrial logic'

The merits of the German 'high road' to competitive success are considerable. Yet there are increasing signs that the model is coming under strain from the alternative system of flexible or lean production. The term 'lean production' was popularised by a team of researchers at MIT studying the performance of the automobile industry worldwide (Womack *et al.* 1990). One of their central conclusions was that Japanese car manufacturers are the most efficient. The ability to make quality cars cheaply was attributed to the production system in Japanese factories. This was named 'lean production' and the MIT report concluded that it could be used in a wide range of commercial settings other than automobile manufacturing. In the immodest language of the researchers, 'lean production is a better way of making things which the whole world should adopt ... as quickly as possible' (ibid.: 225)

Although lean production is not a precise menu of policies and arrangements, Sengenberger (1992) suggests it has a number of key elements: (1) the design and manufacture of products are integrated and synchronised rather than separated as under mass production techniques of the past; (2) just-in-time inventory systems are used so that production is closely in line with market demand – the aim is to reduce costs by avoiding shortages or stockpiles and wasted time, and to accelerate adjustment to changing consumer preferences; (3) total quality control systems are built into the production process so that virtually no defective products reach the market; (4) team-work is frequently used to allow for job rotation to reduce monotony and boredom; (5) cooperative industrial relations are pursued in the form of quality circles or other involvement schemes which encourage employees to make suggestions about how the production system could be improved. Thus, a distinguishing feature of lean production is that it focuses more on the nature of work organisation than on the narrow technical elements of manufacturing systems.

The boast that lean production will be the new universal production method of the twenty-first century is excessive. Companies are not uprooting existing organisational arrangements in deference to a new 'best way' (Oliver *et al.* 1996). Much uncertainty remains about the commercial and social implications of lean production techniques. Disputes exist about whether establishing tighter integration with sub-contractors amounts to the creation of a new partnership between buyers and sellers based on trust and cooperation, or whether it is simply a way to download inventory costs. A similar conflict exists about certain HRM policies associated with lean production. There is little consensus about whether team-working is a genuine attempt to broaden and deepen the skills of some workers, or whether it is a cynical exercise to intensify work by expanding the number of tasks a single worker performs. These arguments will rage for some time since evidence can be mustered to support a wide range of positions. As a result, claims that lean production represents a neatly defined and internally coherent model should be treated with scepticism (Berggren 1993).

At the same time, it would be wrong to underestimate the influence of the concept. In some respects lean production has been profoundly influential, as it has given rise to a new cognitive structure with regard to the organisation of the enterprise and the structure of work systems (Orlean

1994). Enterprise engineers and managers have been infused with new ways of thinking about the role of machinery, the organisation of work tasks, the concept of skills, relationships within and between firms, and so on. This new cognitive structure should not be regarded as establishing an 'iron law' for production systems – the one best way mentality. Rather it creates reference points or a series of conventions which individual managers interact with when addressing business strategies. Through a process of organisational learning or simply individual choice, they may choose to modify, reject or reinvent aspects of the lean production agenda (Dibella *et al.* 1996). Thus, lean production is important as an imagined organisational system that allows managers in different social and institutional settings to define the questions to explore and to cast others to one side. It is a new general cross-national production trajectory, although it does not tie organisations to particular employment and technological arrangements (Boyer and Freyssenet 1993).

The work organisation convention created by lean production departs from both the scientific management that governed job tasks in the mass production factory and craft-based work (Cappelli and Rogovsky 1994). To some extent, it represents a halfway house between these two extremes. Under scientific management most jobs were relatively unskilled and most workers performed single tasks repetitively. Little on-the-job training was required and virtually no learning took place. Work tasks were organised hierarchically, with close supervision of the individual employees. Craft-based work, as already pointed out, integrated conception and execution in work. Craft workers have a theoretical understanding of the tasks they are doing. Such highly skilled workers enjoy a high degree of autonomy at the workplace and normally do a range of tasks. Lean production promotes a work regime which departs from both these models. Thus, in order to remove repetition from the working environment job rotation is introduced. Tasks are made more meaningful, while close supervision is replaced by quality circles or some other type of involvement scheme. However, there is little job autonomy and the skill levels required are not particularly high so that few employees are engaged in a coherent, identifiable piece of work.

Table 3.1 codifies in a fairly schematic way the differences in job tasks among the three production regimes. Autonomy refers to the ability of workers to make decisions on their own. The Fordist worker is stripped of all capacity to act independently while craft workers enjoy a high degree of autonomy. Lean production is closer to the Fordist than to the craft situation, since there is heavy emphasis on group or team-based decisions. Variety is about the number of job tasks done by an individual worker. Virtually no variety exists in the workplace governed by scientific management principles, whereas the exact opposite is true for craft-based productive systems. On this score, lean production arrangements have more in common with craft workers than with Fordist workers. With regard to the significance of the tasks performed, there is little to separate lean and craft work systems: under each regime workers carry out important duties. Again, the Fordist factory is the laggard with individual work tasks amounting to very little. Task identity, which in essence measures whether the conception and execution of tasks are integrated, shows that craft workers have fairly enriched work settings. Lean production has more in common with scientific management on this issue. Overall, lean production amounts to a peculiar hybrid between Fordist and craft work.

Just as lean production challenges traditional conceptions of work and skill, it is also causing a radical rethink among policy-makers responsible for training provision almost everywhere in Europe. Significant innovations are being made to skill formation regimes so that organisations can diffuse work principles associated with lean production more easily. A generalised shift is occurring towards competence-based training systems. Table 3.2 shows that there are four main elements to the idea of competence. First, specialised competence relates to knowledge and technical aspects of training. The main objective is to develop skills among trainees that simultaneously meet the specific needs of enterprises and are transferable across firms. To establish this balance between general training and company-specific training, the specialised and in-depth knowledge and techniques associated with craft-based apprenticeship are being sacrificed. More emphasis is placed on practical know-how than on theoretical knowledge of the processes that lie behind the performance of a work task. Thus the transferable part of the skill acquired is much thinner than before.

Table 3.1 Differences in forms of work organisation

	Scientific management	*Craft-based work*	*Lean production*
Individual autonomy	None	High	Low
Variety	None	High	Moderate
Feedback from work itself	Moderate	High	Moderate to High
Significance of tasks	Low	High	High
Task identity (working on a coherent identifiable piece of work)	None	High	Low

Source: Adapted from Cappelli and Rogovsky (1994)

Table 3.2 What competence means

Specialised competence	Methodological competence	Social competence	Participatory competence
CONTINUITY	FLEXIBILITY	SOCIABILITY	PARTICIPATION
Knowledge, skills and abilities	Procedures	Modes of behaviour	Structuring methods
• Inter-disciplinary elements • Occupation-specific • Extended vertical and horizontal knowledge about the occupation • Enterprise-specific • Experience-specific	• Variable working methods • Situation solutions • Problem-solving solutions • Independent thinking and working, planning, execution and assessment of work • Adaptability	Individual: • Willingness to achieve • Flexibility, adaptability • Willingness to work Interpersonal: • Willingness to cooperate, honesty, fairness • Willingness to help, team spirit	• Coordination skills • Organisational skills • Combination skills • Persuasion skills • Decision-making skills • Ability to assume responsibility • Leadership skills
	Competence to act		

Source: Bunk 1994

The other three aspects of the competence-based approach are more to do with teaching trainees the behavioural skills that are conducive to lean production. Methodological competence is about giving young people the adaptability to perform in today's flexible work organisation. Social competence and participatory competence are more concerned with ensuring that trainees can function within team-work settings. Thus, the focus is on improving communication and interpersonal skills as well as on upgrading individual abilities in areas such as leadership and coordination within the enterprise. All in all, these features of competence-based training aim at getting the learner to internalise the behavioural patterns associated with working in a lean production organisation.

Variants on the theme of lean production

Lean production creates powerful new global conventions for the organisation of work which are adapted to fit specific national industrial relations traditions. The interplay between these transnational cognitive influences, on the one hand, and domestic employment systems, on the other, is highlighted in the way different car-makers have diffused lean production principles. Redher (1994), in an illuminating article, charts how different variations of the lean production theme have been introduced in car plants in Sweden and the USA. Volvo, the Swedish car-maker, has a long tradition of promoting humanistic and people-centred forms of work organisation. It set out to meet the competitive challenge of Japanese car producers by developing its own brand of autonomous team-working and flexible production systems. A new plant was established at Uddevalla, a small seaside town in north-west Sweden. Huge effort was made to establish a low-stress working environment as well as advanced, ergonomically designed, workstations. A system of team-working was created, with each group responsible for the full assembly of cars. The goal was to eliminate first-line management and to promote decentralised decision-making amongst teams. Careful planning went into team selection and each member was given extensive training. A battery of technological support systems and HRM innovations were put in place to hold the productive system together. Although productivity across teams varied, initial assessments of the experiment found rich communication and information flows between workers. In addition, the plant's industrial relations were problem-free, with a high level of cooperation between managers and workers. Unfortunately, because of low group profits alongside a general slump in the demand for cars, Volvo could not afford the high costs associated with running the plant. Uddevalla was certainly pioneering, but it was also expensive and it closed only three years after opening.

In the USA, General Motors (GM) responded to the Japanese challenge by opening the Saturn plant. Detailed planning and preparation, involving both management and unions, went into this venture. Saturn represented a big departure for GM in several important respects. The plant contained some state-of-the-art technological innovations in a green-field site that allowed the company simultaneously to reduce costs and improve quality. It also housed a highly integrated manufacturing and assembly system that was unlike any of the company's other factories. But most important of all, the system of team-working, alongside the new organisational values established to support this form of working, marked the beginning of a new corporate journey for the company. With regard to team-working, the emphasis was on balancing the needs of people and technology in the productive system. Comprehensive training was provided so that individual employees could work in a team setting. Realistic productivity targets were established for each team so that none was overburdened. A new system of management–union consultation was created to improve information sharing on all aspects of the production operation on an ongoing basis. The organisational goals of Saturn are to promote quality, mutual trust, continuous improvement, developing human potential, all of which are a far cry from the more adversarial industrial relations that characterise many other GM plants. Overall most of the innovations made by the company were heavily influenced by the lean production paradigm. Although the plant has some way to go to match the cost base of many Japanese producers, the Saturn project has nevertheless allowed the company to improve the standard and quality of the finished car. As a result, lean production ideas are central to the company's strategic thinking.

Uddevalla and Saturn were lean production experiments in new greenfield sites. Yet similar organisational principles have been used to transform work systems in more established car plants. Consider Rover, formerly British Leyland, the *bête noire* of UK manufacturing in the 1970s, when industrial unrest appeared ever-present. In the 1980s the company experienced almost continuous downsizing: output fell by about 50 per cent between 1979 and 1989 and in five traumatic years, 1978–83, the workforce was reduced from 147,000 to 80,000. Since the late 1980s, management has been attempting to recast the organisational framework and values of the company. In 1987, a programme of total quality was introduced. At the same time, a form of 'cell' working was created, consisting of teams of forty to a hundred employees. In addition, crossfunctional development teams were set up, which had the responsibility of developing, producing and marketing new models. Further changes came in the early 1990s when the company launched a new employment policy called the 'New Deal'. This package of reforms included single employee status; continuous improvement as a requirement for everyone; greater task flexibility; and the creation of a single pay structure. Not all of these changes were supported by the trade unions, but they were enacted nevertheless. Over the past decade, work organisation and human resource management inside the company has been radically transformed. Although they are not full-blown lean production, many of the changes have their origin in this approach to work.

Similar changes have been instilled into Fiat, another car producer with a turbulent industrial relations history. The decisive moment came in the late 1980s when management gained widespread concessions from the trade unions with regard to redundancies, the end of restrictive practices and greater employment flexibility. These reforms paved the way for a programme of HRM innovations in the 1990s under the theme of 'The Integrated Factory'. This programme is making far-reaching changes to the company's organisational structure, including a move towards process-rather than function-based departments; the integration of operations and production engineering; flatter managerial layers; the creation of relatively autonomous manufacturing cells; and greater employee involvement. Not all of these innovations have fully matured, which means that remnants of the past remain (Camuffo and Volpato 1995). Nevertheless, it is clear that Fiat management is steering the company down a lean production route.

Thus we see how lean production is being used in different national settings as a broad framework to reorganise work systems in the car industry. But in no country is this paradigm uncritically introduced or diffused. On the contrary, far-reaching efforts have been made to modify and adjust the underlying principles according to domestic circumstances. Nevertheless, similar issues are being addressed in each setting: quality; teamworking; cost reduction; involvement; continuous improvement. Thus we are experiencing a curious blend of uniformity and diversity. It is important to point out that lean production principles are applicable to economic sectors other than manufacturing. Consider the example of nurses in the UK public sector. In many Trust hospitals there is a big move to upgrade the work tasks of auxiliary nurses so as to weaken the reliance on highly trained nurses; in other words to increase the proportion of semi-skilled to skilled workers. Lean production ideas are also being used to blur the boundaries between separate professions. Consider another example for the UK health sector. Previously, occupational therapists and physiotherapists jealously protected their professional autonomy from each other. Now there are moves to integrate the two professions. The only conceivable way this can be done is to reduce the theoretical part of current training provision for each group and focus more on task-orientated matters. Lean production par excellence.

Lean production and the German model

This redefinition of skill and public provision of training for the world of work due to the spread of lean production ideas challenges key facets of the German model. First, the craft system of work organisation is called into question (Herrigel and Sabel 1994). Under lean production, the individual autonomy, the depth and significance of job tasks, and the high level of task identity enjoyed by craft workers are eroded. These developments in turn call into question the hierarchical structure of many German enterprises, which legitimises and sustains the craft-model of employment. Problem-solving, rather than being the main responsibility of individual skill workers, becomes a team exercise. As a result, the boundaries between different groups of workers become blurred. Greater emphasis is placed on the horizontal coordination of separate work teams than on maintaining a paternalistic structure of craft activity. More widely, these developments are a potential threat to the professional 'model' of labour market status enjoyed by many German workers.

Lean production promotes a model of economic citizenship that is closer to the American HRM system than to the idea of embedding the rights and obligations of people at work in a series of extra-firm labour market institutions. On paper at least, it is possible for lean production to drive a wedge between institutions and enterprises in an employment system. Certainly it poses questions about the way such relationships function in Germany. Under lean production, the skills and career path of workers are more intimately tied to the enterprise. This could diminish the professional model of skill in which social status is derived from being a member of a particular craft community. This in turn may dent the idea of craft workers enjoying pre-contractual employment rights – the notion that association with a particular skill ensures that a worker enjoys a relatively autonomous working environment and high social standards irrespective of the employer for whom he or she works. Further uncertainties then arise about the role of other parts of the institutional environment for the labour market. For example, should the German vocational training system be so geared towards occupational labour markets when lean production encourages skill formation inside internal labour markets?

To put the argument in a slightly different way: it is hard to see how the competence-based training associated with lean production is compatible with the German apprenticeship system. One difficulty with the competence approach concerns the issue of whether a reliable standardised certification system can be established when so much of the training occurs on the job and is geared towards the specific needs of companies. In Britain, where this training regime has been embraced more than anywhere else, the evidence is that a credible certification system in which both trainees and enterprises have confidence has yet to emerge (Steedman 1994). Some research suggests that enterprises are simply interested in giving trainees on-the-job training and little else (Marsden 1994). Other questions can be raised about the social implications of competence training. For example, can a collection of competencies, which are primarily geared towards modifying the behaviour of workers, be considered an efficient skill formation system? Who is the more skilled – the craftsperson who is the master of his or her craft or the person who is highly motivated, highly flexible and has good communication skills (Steedman 1994)?

As well as these equity considerations, lean production could disrupt the efficiency dimension of the German model. A coordinated labour market normally results in the macro- and micro-spheres of the employment system being positively interlocked. In particular, in a coordinated labour market firm-level pay arrangements are not in collision with the search for equilibrium between unemployment and inflation at the aggregate level, for example (Rowthorn 1992). Under lean production this positive interaction between ground-level labour market behaviour and national employment performance is far from assured. The danger is that by attenuating the links between enterprises and the wider environment, this productive regime may cause coordination failures in the labour market. Greater decentralisation, for instance, may produce a distorted wage setting system. Much research in labour economics suggests that pay decentralisation results in wages not responding adequately to the level of unemployment. Thus, unconstrained decentralisation leads to macro-level labour market distortions. Moreover when well-established labour market institutions are eroded, the danger is that trust relationships between employers and employees may be disrupted. Such a situation is likely to have harmful efficiency consequences: for example, transaction costs associated with maintaining employment contracts could increase, thereby making the chances of opportunistic behaviour by both employers and employees more likely.

The key point is that lean production may damage the role industrial relations institutions play as mediating mechanisms that bring together Germany's economy and society. Whether lean production actually emerges as a threat depends largely on whether the German model can prove itself as a superior competitiveness regime. Streeck (1993) argues that the big strength of the German system has been the blocking of the cost route to competitiveness, thereby obliging enterprises to travel the high value-added business road. Conquering niche markets has been the cornerstone of the German economic success story. But the significance of lean production is to promote a new competition that dissolves the boundaries between low-cost and niche markets. Lean production puts a premium on making high-quality products cheaply. It does so by designing organisational structures which ensure that employees can adjust to change and cope with problems (Sako 1993). In other words, with the arrival of the new production and organisational innovations, the juxtaposition between a high road and a low road of economic success looks suspect. Thus the business logic that allowed the German model to operate in an orderly and stable manner is rapidly deteriorating. The lean production threat has to be taken seriously.

Adapting to lean production: the costs of muddling through

Assessment of the impact of lean production on the German model is mixed. Some studies suggest that managers and workers inside firms are adopting 'modernisation pacts' aimed at reducing the specialisation and rigidities associated with craft work and diffusing principles of team-working (Lane 1995). Other research is less upbeat, suggesting that trade unions, through works councils, are resisting any diffusion of lean production techniques. As a result, many workplaces are the sites of jurisdictional disputes about occupational identities and employment practices. Herrigel (1996) refers to this opposition to change as self-blockage. Outside the firm, the picture is also unclear about how labour market institutions are responding to the lean production challenge. Muller-Jentsch *et al.* (1992) argue that national trade unions are responding positively by setting out an agenda which attempts to reconcile traditional craft skills with new work practices such as team-working. Lane (1995) points out that significant changes have been made to the German training system in order to make apprentices more polyvalent and flexible.

On the other hand, Jacobi and Hassel (1996) infer that employer organisations are strongly opposed to the introduction of workplace changes through extra-firm collective agreements which suggests a rethink on their part of the German model. Jurgens (1994) points out that when setting up a factory abroad, German employers invariably install lean production techniques rather that the domestic craft-based system. He takes this as another indication of employer unease with present work arrangements.

The uncertainty which characterises German employment relations at present can be seen in the Standort debate (for example, Klodt *et al.* 1994); the concern here is that, a world of increasingly mobile capital, high German labour costs and tax rates may deter productive investment and, in the long run, undermine competitiveness. As a result, quite disturbing questions are posed about both the welfare state and the system of employment relations. There is little doubt that some of this discussion is exaggerated; Germany remains, after all, the world's most successful industrial exporter. But the debate does indicate further pressures. Another straw in the wind may be the increasingly explicit objections of employers to constraints by *Tarif Autonomie* – that is, the system of industry-wide bargaining.

Thus a shadow is being cast over the vibrancy of the German model. It would be a mistake to suggest that lean production is causing the labour market coordination system to crumble. Deeply embedded work arrangements need something akin to an institutional revolution before they are uprooted. Lean production does not constitute such a frontal assault and thus it is misleading to say that the German model is about to collapse. At the same time, all the old certainties about the superiority of the German method of production are fragmenting. Important new pressures are operating on the country's employment system and some adjustments appear unavoidable. The key issue is the quality of this adjustment process.

One scenario is that no ordered or coherent response will emerge to lean production and as a result change will be a muddling-through affair. Such an approach could very well blunt the equity and efficiency advantages of the German model. Existing institutions would still be in place and connected to one another, but their economic and social functionality would be impaired. As a result, the country would move nearer to other parts of Europe where labour market institutions fail to produce big positive benefits.

Consider the area of training, where many labour market governance systems in Europe have been unable to face down market failures. This is particularly striking in the area of skill formation. For instance, the UK has gained the reputation of comprehensively failing the training challenge. In a damning assessment, Finegold and Soskice (1988) argue that Britain has become trapped in a low skills equilibrium. Market failures appear endemic within the economy: poaching and free-riding is widespread among enterprises; wage determination is fragmented to the extent that it encourages sectionalist and rent-seeking behaviour among trade unions; the financial system is too insistent on industry making profits in the short term which makes it difficult for firms to pursue meaningful training programmes. All in all, an incentive structure has emerged in Britain that actually nudges enterprises towards low value-added, low-cost commercial strategies. The consensus is that training policy in Britain is in the doldrums (Mayhew and Kweep 1994).

But everything is far from rosy in other parts of the European garden. Other countries are experiencing market (and government) failures in organising skill formation systems, although not on the same scale as Britain. Consider the case of France. Legislation requires every employer with ten or more employees to spend about 3.4 per cent of the total wage bill on enterprise-level education and training, or to pay a tax equal to the difference between its obligated and actual training expenditure. On paper, this legally based training regime appears a powerful way to lock firms into training activity. In practice, however, several shortcomings have surfaced. One is that firms have used creative accounting so that they neither spend the obligated amount on training nor incur a higher tax bill. Another problem is that there is little control over the quality of the training provided, causing the system to produce uneven outcomes (Bishop 1993).

Blemishes are also becoming apparent in the training systems of Nordic countries. In this group of countries, school-based vocational training is pursued to equip school-leavers with a high level of general education. The government picks up the tab for a large part of the training that is done, which explains, in part, why public expenditure on training is higher in these countries than any other part of Europe. But while the level of government sponsorship may be high, firms tend not to take an active interest in skill formation. As a result, there is a mismatch between the training provided by the state and the skills demanded by the private sector (Lynch 1994).

By disorganising the system of labour market coordination, lean production may push the German employment system nearer to the experience in the rest of Europe. Instead of strong institutions balancing equity and efficiency, Germany may get more involved in a process of almost continual reform and adaptation in an attempt to keep an ordered labour market. Were such a scenario to materialise, German pre-eminence as an economic power might not be blunted too much. But the drive to maintain competitiveness may result in growing labour market distortions: social inequalities may widen; disorganised pay-setting may set in; skill gaps may appear; and so on. The basic message is that in a muddling-through situation the German model loses some of its economic and social functionality.

The learning by monitoring option

A possible alternative to muddling through is what Sabel (1995) calls learning by monitoring. According to Sabel, fresh thinking needs to occur about how to organise the world of work. In particular, he argues that lean production and associated changes have triggered a huge wave of economic innovation and experimentation. The scale and direction of these changes have made well-understood models of the labour market, such as the high and low roads to corporate success, redundant. In the new complex economy, systems of governance lose their capacity to order and stabilise productive relations. As a result, economic or even corporate adjustment is more open-ended with neither managers nor workers able to specify, let alone control, the probable outcome of any reorganisation or restructuring project. In such circumstances all that labour market actors can do is to learn from each other. Thus, rather than attempting to build big institutional edifices or tie adjustment to particular outcomes, economic change is about building discursive relations between labour market actors so that the process of reorganisation and adaptation is grounded on several cooperative principles and codes of behaviour.

In the new commercial game neither side seeks to triumph and all parties fully commit themselves to a procedure of learning by monitoring. This procedure involves the parties 'continuously evaluating their possibilities: they do this by elaborating ways of assessing present as against past and potential performance or by comparing one class of solutions to a problem with others' (Sabel 1994: 127). In other words, nothing is either ruled in or out, and a range of alternatives is considered which allows actors to develop a shared view of what is jointly possible. The result is the formation of mutual commitment strategies with which every interest can identify. But learning by monitoring is not simply about recasting organisational systems and relationships inside the enterprise in a cooperative way. It also involves a wider process in which learning ripples outward and transforms the role of wider institutions – trade unions, training system and public authorities.

Thus, learning by monitoring is not about legitimising and making effective a particular model of the labour market. Instead it is more reflexive and enabling in character. On the one hand, it codifies and interprets the nature of changes that are occurring, and this, on the other hand, makes it easier for labour market actors to innovate (Dubious 1996). To carry out these two roles, extra-firm institutional arrangements must promote comparable work settings by generalising certain facets of work conditions, rules and remuneration. Without some level of comparability, it is more difficult to promote linkages and cooperation across firms. The other role of the institutional environment is to limit social exclusion. A large gap between the have and have-nots sends a signal that an economy encouraging permanent innovation can descend into a game of winners and losers. As a result, the willingness of employers to enter an open-ended restructuring process will be reduced. Overall, the emphasis is to establish fluid and loose institutional supports for strongly decentralised forms of corporate decision-making.

Certainly key aspects of Sabel's formulation are underdeveloped. Missing is any adequate discussion about the role of labour market institutions as constraints on the behaviour of labour market actors such as trade unions and employer organisations. This matter cannot be side-stepped given the scepticism that enterprises will voluntarily pursue corporate strategies designed to create a new symbiosis between individual commercial action and the collective labour market system (Streeck 1993). The premise of learning by monitoring appears to be that it is no longer viable to regulate an economy heavily. But more has to be said about how the trust relations that are required to underscore mutual obligations inside companies are to be created and sustained over time. At the same time, Sabel's argument corresponds with the extensive changes that are taking place in corporate organisation and management practice. Economic decentralisation and commercial innovations are happening almost everywhere and it is becoming clear that these are irreversible trends.

Overall, learning by monitoring has relevance to the debate about how German institutions should respond to lean production. For it encourages people to think of lean production as but one manifestation of a deep qualitative shift in the economy and society. If this view is widely adopted, then it is less likely that a strategy that seeks pragmatically to absorb lean production principles into existing labour market institutions – the muddling-through scenario – will be regarded as satisfactory. Instead, large-scale change will be regarded as necessary to keep pace with the ground-level upheavals taking place in the world of work. In a nutshell, existing governance systems of the labour market would be seen as outmoded – too rigid, too rule-bound, and too dense to connect easily with the new complex economy.

Learning by monitoring also suggests the type of reform path that should be followed in the recasting of institutions. It warns against any master plan for institutional change. Such an approach rests on the assumption that the new economy and society can be codified and matched together by an overarching governance structure. Thus, in the future, labour market institutions should not be tied to big visions of the economy, as new productive and work systems can no longer be mapped out in advance. If they are to have any *modus operandi* it is to be sufficiently adaptable to manage or guide a virtually continuous process of economic experimentation and innovation. This puts a premium on institutions which can be reformed from within. As for the functions of institutions, more emphasis is put on codifying information and drawing out the significance of the changes that are occurring than on regulatory activity. As Piore (1996) emphasises, institutions should be primarily seen as an attempt to construct a narrative that allows a fuller understanding of the learning and creative processes in the economy.

Some unfolding developments in Germany can be classified as learning by monitoring. For instance, the organisational changes that trade unions have made in Baden-Württemberg to exchange information and discuss forms of enterprise-level restructuring can be considered a type of this practice. But this kind of behaviour is by no means widespread, and it remains an open question whether learning by monitoring will emerge in any systemic way. Conjunctural factors are not working in favour of this option. The present climate of fiscal retrenchment is locking trade unions into a defensive mode on the one hand, and employers in an aggressive mode on the other. These conditions are hardly conducive to the creation of mutual commitment strategies. Thus, the future of the German model remains uncertain.

Conclusions

This chapter argues that lean production is posing serious challenges to the renowned system of labour market coordination in Germany. It suggests that it may be necessary to make important qualitative changes to almost every part of the system – the strategies of employers and trade unions, the functioning of the apprenticeship system, and so on. The underlying proposition is that because of the far-reaching changes taking place in the organisation of work and production, we have to rethink the institutional mechanisms used to connect the economy and society. In other words, the institutional foundations to economic citizenship in Germany need to be reviewed. If this is the case for Germany, it is doubly true for other parts of Europe.

In many European countries the mediating mechanisms that bound together economic and social structures have frayed: institutions are no longer as economically and socially functional as they once were. But now that the widely acclaimed superiority of the German model is also under threat we have nothing less than a crisis of the European social model, and its associated national systems of economic citizenship have been put thoroughly on the defensive. In this situation it is unconvincing to extol the virtues of the conventional methods used in the region to regulate the labour market. Eventually it will have to be accepted that these procedures are no longer solving the problems that they are supposed to and that they have addressed successfully in the past. It is only when this is fully recognised that the search for new institutional ways to reconcile social and economic objectives in Europe will start in earnest.

Part 2

New visions of economic citizenship

4   Europe of the regions and the future of national systems of industrial relations

Introduction

One argument about the future of the European Union is that as integration deepens so the power of nation-states will atrophy. To avoid any governance gap emerging, new democratic structures and policy functions will have to be established at the European level, and at the local or regional level. Thus as national sovereignty withers away, a new symbiosis emerges between more decentralised forms of political decision-making and new supranational political structures. Perhaps the most coherent articulation of this view is the idea of a 'Europe of the Regions'. Paralleling this discussion is a debate in economic sociology that also suggests that the regional level is becoming an increasingly important strategic site for economic activity. In relation to labour market matters, two different arguments are normally presented in support of this view. The first is that the twin pressures of globalisation and productive decentralisation have weakened the labour market coordination capacities of nation-states. A frequent example given is the demise of corporatist bargaining. At the same time, marooning enterprises without extra-firm support structures in areas such as wage setting or training may be a recipe for new forms of economic distortions. As a result, regional institutions are required to help manage labour markets.

The second is that the regionalisation of economic life is bringing in its wake new ways to organise and regulate the employment relationship. In particular, it is argued that because firms are socially embedded in regional economic systems, trust relations are established between employers and employees in the absence of formal institutions (Lorenz 1993). This is a departure from the 'traditional' industrial relations approach which suggests that a web of rules and laws is necessary to bring order and stability to connections between labour and capital. According to this view, both the structure and form of national industrial relations systems in

Europe are being recast. Putting these arguments together we have a fairly coherent vision of the emergence of regional labour market structures in Europe. The purpose of this chapter is to assess the plausibility of this thesis. It argues that no matter how attractive this model of labour market organisation appears on paper, it suffers from a range of considerable shortcomings. In particular, it underestimates the huge transitional problems involved in the move from national to regional systems of industrial relations. Instead of ushering in a new benign system of labour market coordination, a programme of regionalisation could cause enormous fragmentation and disorder. A further problem is that the regionalists misinterpret some of the key dynamics operating within European integration and European labour markets. On the one hand, it is questionable whether the European Union is about to be reorganised in a way that will see greater powers going to regional-level administrations. A Europe of nation-states appears to be the logic that is driving integration at the moment. On the other hand, the insight that European industrial relations is changing, so that informal trust relations between management and workers are replacing the formal regulation of class conflict appears an excessive generalisation of specific regional practices. To the extent that there is a common pattern in European industrial relations, the pattern can be seen in the way in which different countries are diffusing the principle of flexibility into their labour market systems.

This chapter is structured as follows. The first part examines the key influences that are encouraging assessments that economic and political life in Europe are on the threshold of regionalisation. Three important influences – political, monetary and productive – are identified and these are outlined in some detail. Then the chapter highlights the reasons why regional labour market systems in Europe are neither feasible nor desirable. The conclusion suggests that current economic and political circumstances in Europe are not particularly propitious for the emergence of well-ordered regional models of labour market organisation.

Political influences

In recent years, several European countries have pursued programmes of administrative decentralisation which have resulted in sub-national tiers of government acquiring considerable new powers (Keating 1993). These initiatives have corresponded with the loosening of the political and social bonds that have made nation-states in Europe cohesive for more than a century, and with the growth of regional and ethnic identities. Virtually every member-state now contains some type of regionalist, even separatist, movement. For many of these movements, a constitutionally stronger EU represents an ideal route to further disconnect themselves from a national political formation with which they have little empathy. Thus, for some time the slogan of the Scottish Nationalist Party has been for a 'New Scotland in a New Europe'. The League Lombardi in Italy, the separatist group in Corsica and the Basque 'nationalist' movement in Spain are amongst others making similar demands. Other political parties which are not regionalist in character none the less support administrative decentralisation largely on the basis that it leads to more efficient and accountable forms of government.

Within the context of the EU, these rather disparate political forces have come together to demand a 'Europe of the Regions' (Scott *et al.* 1994). A central part of this project is to recast the EU along integrative federalist principles. Instead of being a tidy constitutional package, integrative federalism is a mixed breed, containing elements of two different intellectual traditions. One is Roman Catholic social teaching on subsidiarity. In some quarters the debate about subsidiarity has concentrated on whether the concept promotes decentralised decision-making. But traditionally the term has not been seen in such a narrow and administrative way. Instead it is regarded as a guiding principle for the social and political organisation of society, particularly with regard to creating a balance between the interests of individuals and those of society as a whole; or, perhaps more precisely, between liberty and authority (Adonis and Jones 1991).

According to Catholic social theory, such a trade-off can be secured by a society having a transparent combination of obligations and rights (Van Kersbergen and Kerbeck 1994). The main obligation constraining individual behaviour is the non-infringement of property rights. But a range of secondary obligations should exist encouraging individuals, amongst other things, to play an active role in society. In counter-balance to obligations there should be a body of political and social rights. Thus, individuals should have the right to free speech and complete freedom of association. In addition, they should enjoy a range of social rights, protecting them from poverty and allowing them civilised standards of health and education.

Catholic thinking on subsidiarity also focuses on the institutional provision of rights. Whereas the social democratic tradition suggests that the state should be the main provider and guarantor of rights, the Catholic perspective is that the central authorities should not have such a direct role (Hanley 1994). Instead, social protection should arise mainly from the activities of lower tiers of government as well as associations in civil society. Social intervention by the state is regarded as a policy of last resort –

a lifeboat operation to rescue local social safety nets. The American Catholic Bishops put it like this: 'Governments should not replace nor destroy smaller communities and individual initiative. Rather they should help them contribute more effectively to social well being and supplement their activity when the demands of justice exceed their capacities' (cited in Scheltex 1991: 39). Thus from this perspective of subsidiarity, social protection should be the outcome of rich and dense interactions within civil society, involving the family, community, and voluntary organisations and the Church, with the state prepared to intervene when necessary.

The other pillar of the integrative federalist project is that part of the fiscal federalist literature which emphasises the capturing of economies of scale and positive externalities (Centre for Economic Policy Research (CEPR) 1993). Capturing economies of scale normally relates to the administrative functions of government. In the fiscal federalist literature, there is a clear preference for decentralised policy-making especially in large political units. At the same time, it is recognised that it is inefficient for certain functions to be implemented at the local level: in some circumstances, centralisation allows for specialisation and less fragmentation. For the most part, it is the realising of such positive externalities or spillovers that justifies the assignment of policy functions to a higher tier of government. Within the EU context, the argument is that a number of positive spillovers may be captured if the EU centre were to have a stronger role in policy formation. Thus, for instance, benefits may arise if public investment in transport systems or public policies for the environment were coordinated by Brussels rather than by each European capital. Perhaps the most sophisticated and thorough articulation of this view was the 1977 MacDougall Report. More recently, it has gained political articulation through the development of the multi-level governance approach to European integration.

A mixture of Catholic thinking on subsidiarity and fiscal federalist principles is the substance of integrative federalism. To introduce such a system inside the EU would involve reorganising the present political structures to create a new institutional balance between the EU centre, national governments and regional administrations. Such a reordering would produce a new hierarchy of norms and a sharper delineation of competencies between the different tiers of governments inside the EU. As a result of these changes, the contestable character of the EU's political structure would be reduced. Instead of relationships between the member-states being embittered by disputes about whether or not the EU should have a presence in a certain policy area, a new legitimacy would be attached to EU-level interventions. Moreover, the weak institutional connections between the member-states and the EU centre, which in the past have reduced the impact of so many EU policies, would be replaced by new, more robust and stable support structures. All in all, integrative fiscal federalism is about copper-fastening the political connections between the different levels of government in a way that allows the EU to operate as a more effective political and economic entity.

Thus, the 'Europe of the Regions' project is about weakening national-level economic and political institutions, and about increasing the scope of local-level and EU-wide policy actions. Political reorganisation along such lines would have important implications for industrial relations arrangements. Under integrative federalism, individual member-states would not be totally free to determine their own system of labour market governance. Rather they would have to comply with certain employment policy interventions decided upon at the EU level, particularly with regard to the objectives of the proposed actions. Thus, integrative federalism could lead to a strengthening of EU social policy. At the same time, the new-found freedom of the EU to set down social policy objectives, and even obligations, would not automatically be a licence to introduce heavy harmonising measures. On the contrary, if the subsidiarity principle is adhered to, then an EU social policy based on 'continental uniformity' would be eschewed. An integrative federalist employment policy is more or less about ensuring that each member-state establishes a minimum level of social protection, with any member-state free to implement more advanced measures. In addition, it is about the EU centre having the capacity to *support* (as opposed to override) regimes of social protection and labour market regulation at lower tiers of government, particularly if they appear to be fragmenting.

An integrative federalist EU would also give considerable momentum to the already existing trend of local and regional governments expanding their repertoire of policy interventions. With new-found powers and competencies these local municipalities and similar institutions would sooner or later get involved in labour market matters by promoting training schemes, active labour market policies, better relations between unions and employers, etc. Thus, integrative federalism would create the political foundations or the institutional conditions for the regionalisation of certain industrial relations practices. With policies being pulled upwards and pushed downwards under such a political system, the notion of *national* systems of industrial relations would be punctured. But the state's involvement in labour market affairs would not completely wither away. Too many policies for the labour market presently organised at the national level could not be easily transferred to either local institutions or the EU centre. A good example would be social security systems. Thus, the nation-state would remain a presence in industrial relations under integrative federalism.

Although a popular political slogan amongst regionalists (and federalists) across the EU, it is unlikely that the 'Europe of the Regions' programme could win the assent of the European Council. National sovereignty is still a powerful norm in defining the outlook and behaviour of politicians and government elites in the member-states. As a result, it is doubtful whether they would agree voluntarily to a programme that would drastically modify their influence on political and economic life. Thus, the political front door appears firmly closed to a recasting of the EU along integrative federalist lines. But one calculation is that an economic back door may exist due to pressures arising from monetary union in Europe and moves toward productive decentralisation.

Monetary influences

At the heart of the Maastricht Treaty is a plan to establish monetary union in Europe (EMU). When this happens the monetary policy of the member-states will be passed from the national level to an independent European central bank. A single currency will be established and the control of inflation as well as interest rate policy will be the responsibility of the new bank. In addition, member-states will no longer be able to adjust their exchange rates unilaterally, either to offset differential inflation rates between EU countries or to deal with country-specific shocks.

Establishing EMU would almost certainly impinge on wage-setting institutions and behaviour with implications for the content of EU social policy. But the way this impact is felt, and by how much, is a matter of some dispute. One view is that EMU would remove any exchange rate illusion that may exist in the European economy (Spencer 1992). As a result, Spanish workers, for example, could demand Danish rates of pay even though their productivity levels are much lower. However, as trade union 'orbits of coercive comparison' in annual collective bargaining rounds continue to be national in character, such pressures are unlikely to emerge at least in the short or medium run (Teague and Grahl 1992). Thus, little weight should be given to this perspective.

An alternative, more subtle, view is that EMU would encourage fragmented and decentralised wage bargaining behaviour (Eichengreen and Frieden 1993). Over the years, central banks have played an important role in national bargaining systems, by deterring trade unions from pursuing pay claims that would have a damaging impact on competitiveness (Streeck 1994). Essentially, the central bank signals that it would appreciate the currency to offset the impact of high real wage increases. Trade unions regard this threat as credible and as a result constrain collective bargaining demands. With the powers of national central banks being effectively emasculated under European monetary union, this institutional sanction against unruly wage behaviour is removed. Accentuating this problem is that EMU changes the economic context in which wage bargaining takes place. In a coordinated bargaining situation, wage-setting is heavily influenced by prevailing economic conditions – unemployment and inflation rates, balance of payments and so on. But monetary union downgrades these national reference points, since the main macro-economic indicators will be European inflation rates and unemployment rates. Thus, by removing certain institutional constraints and eroding the economic and social parameters to coordinated wage bargaining, EMU may have a disruptive impact on established features of European industrial relations (Henley and Tsaksolotos 1994).

To compensate for the loss or weakening of wage coordination mechanisms at the national level, the EU could attempt to establish similar arrangements at the European centre. Institutionally, this would mean the European trade unions and employer bodies having a much bigger say in wage formation. It would probably operate along the lines of the European social partners in consultation with EU authorities determining norms for pay rises after examining European-level economic data. Then the trade unions and employers would use their institutional channels to diffuse these norms to lower negotiating tiers in the hope that they would be accepted.

Whether such a European system of collective bargaining could be established is open to question. Certainly, major changes would have to be made to the present social policy framework of the EU. The European social partners would have to be given more authority and resources and appropriate forms to establish credible European wage norms. Invariably, such a system would entail some centralisation of wage determination. But, again, a big doubt exists about whether national trade unions and employers, as well as member governments, would be prepared to transfer authority upwards with regard to wage formation even under monetary union conditions. However, queries about such an arrangement go beyond its institutional feasibility. Setting Europe-wide wage norms would be paramount to creating a form of transnational corporatism. Yet, problems of scale and of heterogeneity may themselves make EU-level corporatism impossible. Sweden, one of the largest countries to have adopted corporatist procedures, has a workforce of some 5 million people with a single language and a common culture. In the EU of twelve member-states, there are some 120 million employees in the most divergent economic circumstances, divided by language, cultural, ideological, national and regional traditions. In this situation, it would be very difficult for the EU to establish pay norms that would be credible at the ground level.

At the same time, Europe-wide uncoordinated and decentralised pay negotiations could lead to sub-optimal labour market outcomes. Thus, while a centralisation of wage formation may not be feasible at the EU level, some degree of pay coordination is nevertheless desirable. To resolve this conundrum, the idea of regional labour market systems or regional industrial relations systems is gaining currency (Sabel 1992). The functions of such a system would be more or less the same as present national arrangements. Thus, one dimension would be the absorption function, whereby the wage system is structured so that it helps to promote low unemployment. The region is potentially a more appropriate level for such unemployment/real wage trade-offs: employers ought to have a strong interest in preventing their competition for labour spilling over into higher wages, while unions should also have incentives to restrain wages to provide their members with alternative employment opportunities in the case of lay-offs. A second function of a regional industrial relations system would be to assist the drive to improve economic performance. A key part of this task is the development of extra-firm institutions, such as training and active labour market strategies, to assist skill formation by enterprises, etc. A third element is the promotion of equity within the employment system so as to reduce potential distortionary effects in the labour market. Norms of fairness of this kind are an effective challenge to opportunistic behaviour that reduces the ability of regional industrial relations systems to deliver wage restraint and provide collective productive goods.

Productive influences

The assessment that EMU will trigger a regionalisation of labour market structures reinforces a popular theme in economic geography and sociology that production is becoming more spatial in character. According to this literature, the 1950s and 1960s were the eras of the big corporation. At this time, large firms emerged to capture internal economies of scale in an effort to service mass, relatively homogeneous, product markets. But economic changes currently taking place are making this system of mass production, sometimes called Fordism, obsolete. For one thing, whereas economic life under Fordism was characterised by reasonably high levels of stability, the marketplace is now turbulent and volatile. On the demand side, there is increasing instability as the modern consumer continuously seeks new products and product variety. On the supply side, firms face intensified commercial pressures as a result of the globalisation of economic life. To succeed in this rather uncertain environment, firms must be flexible and adaptable. But the Fordist internal economies of scale model, which is predicated on inflexible and rigid production techniques, is inappropriate for these more volatile conditions (Sengenberger 1992).

In recent years there has been a significant shift towards productive decentralisation so that enterprises are more in line with the new patterns of consumption. Thus firms have become smaller and have acquired the ability to move in and out of market niches. New technologies are central to these developments. Widespread productive decentralisation has led to the creation or sharper delineation of regional economic systems. Firms have become increasingly dependent upon the spatial infrastructure of the market to which they belong for their competitive success. Put differently, productive decentralisation has in some instances given rise to external economies of scale (Romer 1994). In such cases, a range of dynamic commercial effects arises which are external to individual firms but internal to the economic system.

Just why such regional economic systems emerge and ensure that the collective commercial effort is greater than the sum of the individual parts is not at all clear. But there appear to be a number of factors at play (Saglio 1993). All the successful regional economies have dense connections between individual firms and strong linkages exist between external non-market institutions and these commercial networks. One benefit that arises from dense commercial relationships is a low transaction cost environment. Information is more fully available and better processed, thereby making enterprises more sensitive to market developments. As a result, firms are in a better position to do business. Another advantage of commercial collaboration is the creation of a high level of trust between firms. With the suspension of, or at least a reduction in, a self-interest calculation, opportunistic behaviour is reduced, allowing firms to pursue commercial strategies with each other, which they would not otherwise do. Cooperation and competition are set side by side rather than being brought into collision.

Perhaps it is unrealistic to believe that all regions can develop such virtuous economic arrangements. Nevertheless, those regions that do produce such effects gain a considerable competitive advantage. A common theme in the academic literature on this topic is that industrial relations practices and institutions play a key role in the formation of dynamic regional economic systems. Locke (1990) describes how Italian trade unions and employers in the textile industry have broken away from national sector agreements and are establishing geographically defined collective agreements, so that working conditions and practices are more closely tied to local circumstances. Moreover, in this new bargaining arena, trade unions focus on a wider range of issues than simply pay. Much importance is given to training, the organisation of working time and so on, which allows for more encompassing collective agreements.

Sabel (1991) pushes the point even further by arguing that industrial relations in successful regional economic systems depart from and even eschew the formalised and hierarchical forms of collective bargaining that have emerged in industrialised countries during this century. In particular, he suggests that such employee relations systems are based on informal deals and agreements in principle, rather than on elaborate and detailed rules or codes. These implicit social compromises produce a common understanding that employers will not pursue exploitative practices in return for employees agreeing to the flexible deployment of labour and machinery. The trust relations that sustain this social compromise are seen as arising from the *social embeddedness* of firms. By social embeddedness Sabel appears to mean the situation where the boundaries between the firm and the wider civil society or community become blurred. Dense harmonious interactions between citizens in a community spill over into firms, and help to establish cooperative social relations between employers and employees inside the firms.

The significance of Sabel's arguments is far-reaching as they depart from the traditional way the academy has approached industrial relations matters. Industrial relations have no widely accepted theoretical roots, but the text that is widely regarded as the pioneering work in the area is John Dunlop's *Industrial Relations Systems* first published in 1958. The two main arguments of this book are that the relationship between employers and workers needs to be governed by an institutional web of rules and laws, and that the state has an important role in the formation and operation of such a system. Sabel challenges these two assumptions by suggesting that the strategic site for much industrial relations decision-making has moved from the national to the regional level, and that the substance of the bargain between employers and employees has changed. No longer are industrial relations about how different (national) systems manage conflict between capital and labour, but instead they are about how such systems connect the world of work to wider society in a way that establishes trust relations between the social partners. Thus, for Sabel and others, the regionalisation of economic life is transforming the political and social foundations of industrial societies.

The potentially crushing impact of monetary union on national economic management, the growth of regional production complexes and the political calls for a Europe of the Regions are the main factors encouraging assessments that the traditional structure and conduct of industrial relations are under threat. At first glance, the idea of regionalised employment systems is attractive: decentralised political and economic structures more sensitive to local conditions, and an EU committed to promoting decentralised labour market practices and productive structures tied to wider social and community influences are fairly attractive images. But on closer examination, a number of significant shortcomings to this model of regional labour market systems can be found. In particular, questions can be raised about the feasibility and even the desirability of this model.

Towards regional labour market systems in Europe?

One problem is that it is not at all clear how regional forms of economic and labour market adjustment could be realised in the New Europe. Some clues to answering this puzzle may be gained from an assessment of the USA economy that has operated a single market for more than a century. In the USA there appears to be a well-developed pattern of regional adjustment to adverse economic shocks based on migration and not on movements in wages (Blanchard and Katz 1992). Thus, when an adverse economic shock occurs virtually immediately, people seem to respond by moving to more prosperous parts of the country. In the longer term, after about a ten-year period, the migration process allows the unemployment rate to move back towards the national average. However, employment does not recover to its initial level, indicating that the regional economy has shrunk and that the stock of jobs has fallen. At the same time, a negative employment shock has a negligible downward impact on wages and, in the long term, the regional wage level more or less coincides with the average national wage level. All this suggests a high level of convergence in terms of income between the various states of the USA.

Whether the European economy could adopt a spatial adjustment process based on migratory flows is doubtful, at least in the short term. Inside the EU there are extremely low levels of labour mobility. Only Ireland and Portugal have a sizeable share of their populations living in other member-states. Ironically, labour migration between European countries was higher in the early 1950s before the creation of the Common Market in 1958. Of course there *is* labour mobility in Europe but this tends to be confined to within member-states. Thus root-and-branch changes would be required before the EU could imitate the regional pattern of adjustment found in the USA. At present the European Commission is pursuing a number of programmes aimed at removing the obstacles to the free movement of people inside the EU. One initiative is to get the member-states to recognise each other's qualifications and diplomas in similar occupational categories to improve the labour market matching process across countries. Another measure is to bring the member-states' social security systems closer together, allowing portability of pensions inside the EU for the first time. Such schemes will undoubtedly make it easier to move from one part of the EU to another. But they are unlikely to trigger a big wave of Europe-wide migration. A range of formidable cultural and linguistic influences will continue to stand in the way of an open, fluid European labour market.

Marsden (1994) suggests that current developments are indicating a European labour market 'map' along the following lines. At the higher end of the occupational structure, he suggests that cross-border mobility is increasing. Much of this increased movement is the result of increased merger and acquisition activity inside the European market that is leading to more companies operating in a number of member-states. To improve company efficiency and to satisfy the demands of young skilled workers, many of these enterprises are developing Europe-wide internal labour markets. At the bottom end of the labour market, there is also some move-ment of unqualified labour inside the EU, particularly in the service-related occupations. But the vast majority of workers continue to operate within nationally delineated labour markets which can vary a great deal from country to country. For example, some member-states, most notably Germany, have occupational labour market structures which emphasise the merits of the economy-wide certification of training in order to encourage the transferability of skills between enterprises. Other member-states, such as France, promote firm-specific training that encour-ages workers to stay with one employer and develop their careers through internal labour markets. These distinctive national systems are unlikely to wither away, even if monetary union is established in Europe. As a result, regional patterns of employment adjustment based on migration are unlikely to emerge across the member-states in the foreseeable future.

Towards regional wage adjustment?

Another way regional labour markets could arise in the New Europe is by encouraging spatial forms of wage adjustment. It is neo-classical economics that most directly makes the connection between regional pay and employment, by arguing that unemployment can be kept low if the wage level is downwardly flexible. But in economics a virtual consensus has emerged that the wage level should be regarded as relatively sticky. Certainly this appears to be the case in Europe where nominal wages are fairly rigid and much less responsive to price changes than in North America. In North America, only 14 to 18 per cent of a price increase is passed through to nominal wage increases, but in Germany the transmis-sion is 75 per cent, in Italy 60 per cent and in the UK 50 per cent. Given this situation, it seems over-optimistic to assume that Europe would be able to contain the pressures created by monetary union by creating flexible regional wage systems (Eichengreen 1992).

One alternative possibility would be to encourage, in the aftermath of monetary union, regional collective bargaining structures so that pay setting could move in line with economic conditions. The big problem with this option is that relatively little collective bargaining, or any other industrial relations function for that matter, currently takes place at the regional level. As Chapter 2 emphasised, the general trend is for a certain amount of wage bargaining to take place at the sector or national level, supplemented by pay negotiations at company level. Thus many member-states continue to seek an interface between the macro and micro aspects of wage determination systems (Teague 1994). In many cases, the institutional practices created to make these connections represent formidable obstacles to the regionalisation of collective bargaining. Consider the notion of 'spread' in collective bargaining systems. In many north European countries, there are few workers that are not covered by bargaining agreements determined outside the enterprise. In other words, even in situations where trade union density is fairly low, collective bargaining coverage is high. This practice ensures that a degree of national uniformity exists to wage levels and terms and conditions of employment. Such arrangements are being reinforced by other institutional changes taking place. In several European countries, trade unions have been merging in response to declining membership and to occupational shifts in the workforce. Out of this process are emerging big conglomerate trade unions organised internally on national rather than regional lines.

Thus, much of the institutional architecture associated with European industrial relations still runs from the company to the sector and then to the national level. In this situation, root-and-branch institutional change would be required to create regional-level collective bargaining structures. Employers would be asked to withdraw from national wage determination bodies only to be obliged to re-enter untried regional industrial relations arrangements. Employees would be asked to give up national uniformity in employment systems and to accept regionally differentiated labour market outcomes. Industrial relations institutions such as trade unions would be asked to organise their internal structures on a geographical rather than an industrial basis, breaking with at least century-old traditions. Governments would in effect be asked to relinquish competence on wage bargaining matters that would be tantamount to forsaking macro-economic coordination. In other words, creating coordinated regional collective bargaining institutions would in reality require the reinventing of European industrial relations activity. Apart from the fact that few industrial relations actors in Europe appear eager to move in this direction, such a project could not be carried out without important relationships becoming embittered, and that would undermine the functionality of the new system. Existing industrial relations institutions in Europe are deeply embedded, even though they may not be functioning that well, and this creates enormous resistance to radical change. A regionalisation of industrial relations in Europe demands too much of a leap into the dark and underestimates the problems of path dependency associated with collective bargaining structures being locked into national institutional traditions.

Trust or flexibility? The current dynamics of European industrial relations

The proposition that decentralised or regional forms of production are encouraging the formation of sustainable trust relations between employers and employees can also be challenged. Streeck (1992a) describes this view of industrial relations as 'neo-voluntarism' since it downplays the roles of formal institutions and rule-making in the resolution of potential conflicts at work, and in the generation of consensus between the social partners. The neo-voluntarist vision is of workers and managers being bound together by informal social norms of reciprocity. Such social processes, which have the effect of suspending self-interest calculations, may exist in certain local communities, particularly in the much-researched Emilia Romagna district of Northern Italy. But it would be misleading to suggest that the generation of trust relations through informal procedures and mechanisms is the dominant pattern in European industrial relations (Hyman 1994). A more convincing thesis is that most European governments are busy attempting to introduce greater flexibility into their systems of labour market regulation. In other words, the search for labour market flexibility appears to be the overriding industrial relations issue across the EU (Brewster and Hegewisch 1994).

Of course, the pursuit of labour market flexibility can take a variety of forms. In Britain, a thoroughgoing deregulation programme has been enacted to curb the role of law in employee relations and to give managers greater freedom of action. Spain has also deregulated, although not in pursuit of a neo-liberal labour market, but simply to relax many of the complex and detailed rules governing the hiring and firing of employees. A more measured approach seems to be favoured elsewhere as other countries attempt to mesh flexibility with regulation. Although these various reform packages are different, all are concerned with the extent to which the European labour market should be governed by legal rules and formal institutions. Those who argue that legal interventions have gone too far and have triggered sclerotic tendencies in the European labour market are not overly concerned with how a symbiosis can be created between the interests of workers and employers. They are more eager to restore managerial prerogative in European industry and to allow market forces to work more freely. The agenda of those who seek to mesh flexibility and regulation is to recast and update the European 'social model' (Regini 1995). This camp accepts that some of the key assumptions that have underpinned labour legislation for decades are no longer applicable. As a result, there may be a growing incongruity between labour market institutions and newly emerging employment systems at the ground level. Thus, regimes of labour market regulation require modification to smooth out this asymmetry. This is a quite different project to the deregulation approach which seeks simply to roll back the rules governing the employment relationship.

Those who argue that European industrial relations are characterised by employers and employees seeking a new consensus in the absence of formal rules seem to have misinterpreted developments. They have simply exaggerated the significance of certain isolated and local moves toward industrial districts in Europe. The dominant trend in European industrial relations is the clash between labour market deregulators and modernisers. It is by no means certain that the modernisers will win. As emphasised in Chapter 2, if EMU goes ahead, it is feasible that economic and political circumstances may favour those arguing for labour market flexibility. In the absence of large-scale Europe-wide labour mobility, or a well organised coordinated bargaining system, governments may be obliged to turn towards employment flexibility as a mechanism for economic adjustment in a single currency area. This is an important point, for those who argue that a new milieu of co-operative and self-sustaining employer relations is near may actually be encouraging a move away from the idea that the labour market should be regarded as a social institution requiring formal rules and laws to hold it together. In the present political climate promoting a purely voluntaristic agenda for European employment relations around the theme of trust may have the unintended consequence of opening the gate wider for neo-liberal reform of the European labour market.

The problem of national systems of production

The US experience suggests that regional employment systems work better when productive activity is also organised on a spatial basis. But in Europe there is much less regional productive specialisation than in the USA (Begg and Mayes 1992). This difference reflects the fact that the USA has operated a single market for more than a century, whereas Europe is still mainly made up of separate national economies. A consensus has emerged that these separate national economies have caused the fragmentation and segmentation of the European market, causing industries to be less geographically concentrated relative to their American counterparts. Indeed, the programme for completing the European single market was sold on the basis that it would encourage more specialisation and the capturing of bigger economies of scale (Emerson 1988).

Thus, at the moment, the strongly national orientation of productive structures, or at least regional productive systems, housed within the boundaries of existing member-states is not particularly conducive to the creation of regional labour market systems in the EU. Deeper market integration between the member-states may trigger greater Europe-wide industrial specialisation. But reducing market segmentation may be at the expense of increasing regional income equalities in the EU, which could have a strong bearing on the type of regional employment systems established in Europe. This argument is worth exploring in greater detail. Currently there are considerable regional disparities in income levels and general economic performance inside the EU. European Commission figures indicate that those living in the ten poorest regions have an income level of about 45 per cent of the EU average, whereas people residing in the ten richest regions enjoy a standard of living 45 per cent above the average. Obviously the disparity eases when the sample is made less extreme, but nevertheless the gap is still large. Thus, when the top and bottom twenty-five regions are examined, the figures show that the less prosperous areas have an income per head of about 57 per cent of the EU average, while the richer areas are about 35 per cent above the median. All in all, then, the prosperity gap in the EU is quite large.

Standard integration theory suggests that such a gap would be reduced by the removal of all barriers to trade between the member-states (Buiges *et al.* 1990). A genuinely open internal market, it is assumed, would promote convergence by allowing each member-state to specialise in economic activity in which it has a comparative advantage, and by encouraging corporate movements to poorer regions to capture cost savings. But this conventional view of income equalisation through deeper market integration is being increasingly challenged. Krugman (1991), for instance, argues that rather than taking advantage of lower factor costs, firms in the New Europe may congregate in richer regions to reap the benefits of economics of scale and agglomeration. In other words, in the search for industrial specialisation, firms may abandon the less favoured regions and relocate in the European core. The likely outcome of such a scenario would be an accentuation of the economic divide between the richer and poorer parts of the EU.

Growing economic divergence would have far-reaching implications for the regionalisation of employment systems in Europe. On the one hand, the vision of regional labour market structures promoting productivity coalitions between employees and employers, giving rise to industrial relations practices in tune with local productive circumstances, is to some extent plausible for the richer parts of the EU. But such a benign view is not convincing for the poorer regions. On-going research into industrial performance in the peripheral regions of the EU suggests that many are trapped in low-skilled and low value-added forms of production. Moreover, the labour market rules that exist tend to reinforce this pattern of commercial activity. Thus, for example, few incentives exist to encourage firms to upgrade the skill levels of employees, and the labour market regulations that do exist on health and safety, equal pay and so on, are poorly enforced. If the extent of divergence inside the EU were to widen, then the prospects of poorer regions moving from labour market arrangements that emphasise the cost route to competitiveness to industrial relations systems that encourage quality-orientated commercial activity would be reduced. The reverse may actually happen, with the less favoured regions intensifying their drive to capture market share by lowering costs. It is this scenario that has fuelled the debate about social dumping.

Implicit in the Europe of the Regions thesis is a benign, positive sum, vision of local economies, embedded in high-value, high-quality, forms of production, co-existing cooperatively. But if deeper economic integration precipitates greater spatial bifurcation inside the EU, the reality could be much different. A negative sum game may emerge with certain regions winning at the direct expense of other regions (Bowring 1986). As a result, a head-to-head clash might be initiated, not only between the richer and the poorer regions, but also between the poorer regions themselves, as they vie against one another to catch up with the core. One argument is that the EU centre could reduce such an unseemly scramble for economic progress by operating a regime of fiscal transfers to compensate those areas losing from deeper integration. At the moment, the EU does not have the budgetary capacity to make such transfers. The structural funds would have to increase by about a factor of ten before they could become effective as a redistribution mechanism.

Should the EU be recast along 'Europe of the Regions' principles, then there would certainly be considerable pressure for the expansion of these funds. But a sequencing problem could arise here. Putting the EU centre in the position to be able to operate a fiscal transfer system would obviously be a protracted affair. In the meantime, the pursuit of industrial specialisation by enterprises at the market level may deprive certain regions of the capacity to grow endogenously (Barro and Sala-i-Martin 1992). As a result, by the time a redistribution mechanism is established at the EU centre, a transfer of funds runs the risk of simply raising income levels in beleaguered regions rather than improving productive performance. In other words, the depressed regions may become reliant on external subsidies rather than on their own internal capacities to secure a better standard of living. This is a problem of dependent development in which some regions in Europe, such as southern Italy and Northern Ireland, have become trapped. Thus, the presence of a fiscal transfer arrangement does not necessarily resolve the insider/outsider regional problem that may emerge in the wake of deeper integration. The basic point is that a convincing malign scenario can be developed for the 'Europe of the Regions' thesis. As a result, more balanced assessments of the merits or otherwise of 'regionalising' employment structures in Europe need to be developed.

Conclusions

The main conclusion from this chapter is that the economic and institutional conditions for the widespread enactment of regional systems of labour market governance across Europe do not exist. The continuing national orientation of many governments and other labour market actors, coupled with the highly uneven levels of economic development across countries, place formidable obstacles in the path of a regionalisation of European industrial relations. There is hope in some quarters that the creation of a single currency may sweep away these obstacles and allow for the emergence of a Europe of the Regions. But there is little convincing evidence to support this story. A more level-headed examination of prevailing economic and institutional conditions suggests that, if anything, monetary union is likely to intensify pressures for the relaxation of employment regulation. It is battles against the Americanisation of the European labour market and the adjustment of national labour market structures to new economic and social times that are the dominant trends in European employment relations.

Apart from the feasibility of regionalised industrial relations in Europe, the desirability of such a project can be questioned. In particular, a big shift to the regional level could break up important dimensions of existing nationally embedded systems of social protection. Another way of making this point is to say that the nation-state still matters for industrial relations. Too many advocates of the regional option offer little more than optimistic, even runaway, speculation in support of the claimed superiority of geographically defined employment systems. But governments and labour market actors cannot be expected to endorse an employment programme that is based on little more than an act of faith. At the same time, this does not mean that the 'regional issue' will disappear off the political agenda. The questions of administrative decentralisation, and giving greater powers to specific regional groups, will remain important issues for many European countries. But these matters are likely to be addressed within specific countries themselves by the creation of new political and economic relationships between the centre and the localities. New regional governments may open up linkages with the EU centre but these will be of secondary importance, only complementing the key power relationship between the local administrative tier and the national government. A Europe of the Regions, ushering in some form of multi-level governance inside the EU, is too ambitious a political programme to rescue economic citizenship in Europe.

5   New Keynesianism and active labour market policies in Europe

Introduction

High unemployment stands as the most visible sign that Social Europe is not working properly. With so many people unable to find a job, considerable strain is placed on the claim that Europe's brand of welfare capitalism is economically functional. Sooner or later, if Europe fails to reduce its jobless numbers, it is almost certain that social protectionist systems will be radically reduced, if not dismantled altogether. This chapter examines why European unemployment has proven to be so stubbornly high and assesses what is being done about it. In particular, it sets out and evaluates the dominant approach to explaining persistent unemployment in Europe, which can be called New Keynesianism. In addition to developing a diagnosis for widespread joblessness, New Keynesian economists have been exhorting governments to adopt employment measures that fall under the umbrella term 'active labour market policies'. This chapter also examines the extent to which such policies have been diffused, and evaluates whether these will be the remedy to the unemployment crisis.

The chapter is organised as follows. The analysis begins with an overview of the extent of the jobless crisis in the European labour market. Then the broad theoretical framework of New Keynesianism on employment matters is set out. Next, the active labour market policy agenda arising from this approach is outlined. The ensuing discussion assesses the extent to which such policies have been enacted by European governments. A further section looks at the Dutch model to see if that is the way ahead for Europe. After this discussion, the debate about the strengths and weaknesses of active labour market policies is reviewed. The conclusion brings together the key arguments of the chapter.

The European labour market: the sluggish job generation machine

Employment performance in Europe is unimpressive, if not poor. Currently, unemployment in the EU stands at about 10 per cent of the labour force. As Figure 5.1 shows, European unemployment is much higher than in other regional economic blocs. In the USA, reflecting buoyant economic times, the jobless figure is 5 per cent of the workforce, which is a twenty-five-year low. Even Japan, which has experienced acute economic difficulties for most of the 1990s, has been able to maintain unemployment at below 4 per cent. Thus in a comparative context, the European economy looks a genuine labour market laggard. Yet the enormity of Europe's unemployment problem at times seems to be downplayed, or, even more bizarrely, explained away. But the bottom line is that having 10 per cent of the workforce unemployed, and many more economically inactive, is not a healthy economic system. On the contrary, it shows that the European labour market is malfunctioning in a serious way. There can be no shirking this matter since labour market stagnation is a sure way of creating long-term unemployed and economic marginalisation.

A consensus exists that Europe's jobless problem goes beyond cyclical factors and has its roots in a lacklustre job generation process. Figure 5.2,

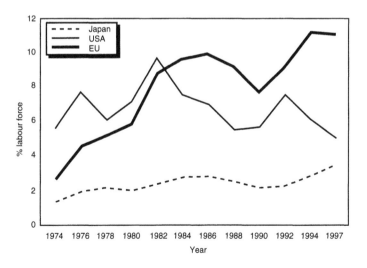

Figure 5.1 Unemployment rates in the EU (15), USA and Japan, 1974–97

below, contrasts employment rates in the EU, the USA and Japan. It shows that the EU employment rate has stayed more or less unchanged at around 60 per cent of the working age population for nearly two decades. In comparison, the employment rates in the USA and Japan are reaching postwar records with about 75 per cent of the population of working age in jobs. Lying behind these sharply contrasting unemployment rates are different job generation machines. In Europe between the early 1970s and the late 1980s, job creation in the private sector virtually seized up altogether. In fact, the numbers employed in this part of the economy fell continuously during this period. An expansion of public sector employment, particularly in the late 1970s and early 1980s, prevented the unemployment rate from looking even worse. But overall it seemed that the job generation process almost ground to a halt. By contrast, the private sector in the USA was able to create about 20 million new jobs in the period from 1974 to 1990. The difference in the employment records of Europe and the USA could hardly have been sharper. This trend has continued into the 1990s. For example, in 1996, the US economy created 2.5 million jobs while the EU managed less than 600,000 extra jobs most of which were part-time.

Of course a number of qualifications must be made to this story. First of all, the EU is a more open trading region than the USA, causing competitive pressures to be more intense on European companies than on American firms. For most of the 1970s and 1980s, the manufacturing

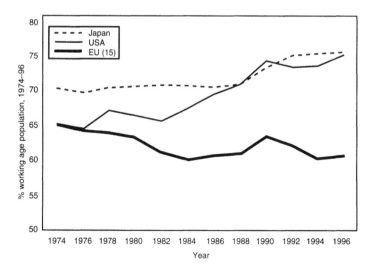

Figure 5.2 Employment rates in the EU (15), USA and Japan, 1974–96

sector in Europe experienced higher annual increases in productivity than its counterpart in the USA. In an era of relatively sluggish overall economic growth, this caused higher rates of job shedding and lower recruitment in Europe's private sector than in the US private sector. Second, many of the new jobs created in the USA are casual and located in low-grade areas of the economy. With the relative absence of good-quality employment, some US economists are querying whether the future is one of lousy jobs (Burtless 1990). Overall, however, even with these reservations, the US employment generation machine in the past twenty years has been quite impressive. In comparison, the European record looks rather tawdry. The magnitude of Europe's unemployment problem is put into perspective when we realise that the EU would need 20 million net new jobs to reach US or Japanese rates of labour market participation.

There are many dimensions to the European unemployment problem. Perhaps the most acute is long-term unemployment: nearly 5 per cent of the EU workforce has been unemployed for a year or more and this has been the trend since the early 1980s. The picture for youth unemployment is brighter, but far from rosy. On average, 20 per cent of young people are unemployed in the EU which, although still too high, marks an improvement from the scandalously high rates of the early 1980s. For the most part, falling youth unemployment is due to demographic factors and higher participation rates in education. As Chapter 1 highlighted, the number of women in the European labour market has continually increased since the 1970s – almost two-thirds of the net additional jobs in the EU between 1993 and 1996 went to women. Yet the unemployment rate for women is nevertheless about 3 per cent higher than for men.

An increasingly structural component is entering the European unemployment equation. Whereas unemployment is concentrated among the low skilled or those who have lost skills, virtually all the net additional jobs between 1994 and 1996 required labour with some type of formal qualification. A further problem is the wide disparity in employment performance between regions, which to some extent reflects the diversity between the member-states in terms of economic structure and living standards. Thus parts of Spain and Portugal have unemployment rates well over 20 per cent of the workforce, whereas parts of the UK, Denmark and Austria have unemployment rates as low as 5 per cent. Overall, with so many dimensions to the problem, it has been hard to develop a convincing theory for the rise and persistence of European unemployment (Bean 1993).

New Keynesianism and unemployment

Perhaps the most comprehensive and accepted explanation of the unemployment crisis is what can be called the New Keynesian approach (see Gordon 1990 and Romer 1993). As the label suggests, the approach shares many of the principles of traditional Keynesianism (particularly in terms of ideas such as sticky wages and non-clearing markets) but also has several novel characteristics. New Keynesianism is different from traditional Keynesianism in at least two important ways. First of all, each has its own assessment of the wage setting process. Traditional Keynesianism regards the real wage as exogenous. In other words, the real wage is derived from competitive markets and, therefore, is accepted and not determined by workers and managers. This formulation is significant for the standard Keynesian prescription for reducing unemployment. For Keynes, unemployment was essentially caused by deficient demand. Thus, expansionary monetary and fiscal policies are required to shorten the dole queues; but any reflationary strategy may require the wages of those in work to be controlled to prevent the economy overheating or hitting a balance of payments constraint caused by the purchase of too many imported goods. Since the real wage was assumed to be exogenous, government control or manipulation of pay settlements was regarded as a relatively straightforward exercise.

New Keynesianism approaches the question of wage formation rather differently. In particular, the modern perspective is to view the real wage, as well as employment and unemployment, being (jointly) determined within imperfectly competitive product and labour markets. In other words, wage setting is regarded as endogenous, with firms and other labour market institutions such as trade unions having considerable power in setting pay levels. This is a departure from the traditional assumption that the real wage can be manipulated (directly) to reduce unemployment. An important implication of the New Keynesian thesis is that the level of unemployment is highly sensitive to the behaviour of labour market actors in the wage bargaining process (Greenwald and Stiglitz 1993). When negotiating the level of pay increases, the bargaining system can set either conventions or contagions. A convention is when a going rate for pay settlements is consistent with what the New Keynesians call the non-accelerating inflation rate of employment (the NAIRU) – the rate of unemployment consistent with stable inflation.

Without entering into the technical details, a pay settlement is consistent with the NAIRU when the trade union wage claim (the target wage) corresponds with what the employer can pay (the feasible real wage) without passing on the cost to the consumer (Jackman *et al.* 1994). A convention is when the target wage and feasible real wage more or less coincide. Establishing a convention normally requires the labour market to be coordinated in one way or another. If the target wage and the feasible real wage do not correspond, then a contagion will arise. A contagion is when the going rate for any settlement is inconsistent with the NAIRU, causing unemployment or inflation or both to be higher than would be the case otherwise. Contagions usually occur when the bargaining process is distorted in one way or another. Layard and Nickell (1992), perhaps the most sophisticated advocates of the New Keynesian approach, give the example of leap-frogging – a process of bidding up wage rates in labour markets – as a bargaining distortion.

Thus, for the New Keynesians, labour market institutions, such as trade unions, can either contribute to disequilibrium unemployment or actually assist in its reduction. Whether they play a malign or benign role usually depends on how these labour market institutions are organised. Particular stress is placed on the degree of coordination in the wage bargaining process in helping to maintain equilibrium unemployment. Until recently, a virtual consensus emerged that either highly centralised or highly decentralised collective bargaining systems were more employment-friendly than hybrid regimes (Calmfors and Driffell 1988). Centralised bargaining is seen as assisting the job generation process by making the trade off between wage increases, inflation and unemployment more transparent, thereby reducing the scope for opportunistic or free-riding behaviour. As a result, trade unions are more likely to realise that, although excessive pay increases may benefit some workers, they may also damage others in terms of job losses or higher inflation (Mitchell 1993). The much-celebrated corporatist structures of the Nordic countries are held up as the prime example of such centralised arrangements.

The functioning of wage bargaining systems has been assessed in Chapter 4. We found that the institutional and corporate foundations to coordinated bargaining in Europe have narrowed in recent years. The economic functionality of the Nordic social corporatist model appears to have withered: the German 'decentralised coordinated' system is under grave pressure as a result of the aftershocks of reunification and the preparation programme for EMU; almost everywhere enterprises are seeking more and more control over pay levels. Many countries are 'reinventing' national bargaining to help them meet the Maastricht conditions for monetary union membership. But it is highly questionable whether such efforts can be described as programmes to secure labour market coordination. Thus, while the New Keynesian prescription that a well-organised pay determination system is an important tool to help reduce unemployment may have theoretical validity, it is unlikely to be feasible in practice.

Policy-makers will have to rely on other measures to reduce joblessness in Europe.

The second major innovation of New Keynesianism is the departure from a conventional demand and supply analysis of the labour market. Instead, it uses a framework partially based on the Beveridge curve, sometimes called the UV curve, which defines the relationship between unemployment and vacancies (Jackman *et al.* 1994). For the most part, this curve highlights the dynamic nature of labour market behaviour: the nature and extent of flows in and out of employment; the relationship between the skills of the unemployed and the skills demanded by enterprises when advertising vacancies; the restructuring intensity in the economy; and so on. In addition to the Beveridge curve, New Keynesians use a vacancy supply curve which attempts to capture the impact of optimal wage-setting on the part of workers, and the employment creation behaviour of firms on the relationship between unemployment and vacancies. Sidestepping much technical detail, the interaction of the Beveridge curve and the vacancy supply curve gives rise to three different types of unemployment as shown in Figure 5.3.

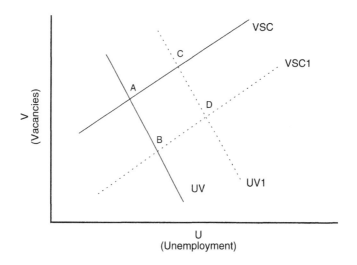

Figure 5.3 Different types of unemployment

Notes:
a   equilibrium employment
b   demand deficit unemployment
c   mismatch unemployment
d   hysteresis and long-term unemployment

When an economy experiences an economic shock, such as an oil price increase or an upsurge in worker militancy, the vacancy supply curve moves to the right (from VSC to VSC1), causing an increase in unemployment and a fall in vacancies. As a result, equilibrium unemployment, A, will be disturbed and a new equilibrium, B, will arise. This movement from A to B can be regarded as demand deficit unemployment. To a large extent, this type of unemployment is similar to the traditional Keynesian diagnosis of unemployment. According to the New Keynesians, demand deficit unemployment does not jeopardise the initial equilibrium rate of unemployment. When demand conditions improve, the unemployment rate will progressively move back from B to A.

New Keynesians do not rule out the use of active macro-economic policies to reduce unemployment, but this policy option is seen as closely constrained. Thus the modern version of Keynesianism is much more circumspect about the use of expansionary fiscal or monetary policies than the traditional approach. To some extent, a new consensus has emerged on the limited role of macro-economic policy, bringing to an end the extremely sharp monetarist/Keynesian polemics of fifteen years ago. The content of the new consensus is, however, mostly negative. Active fiscal and monetary policies are not seen as promising large gains because governments face balance of payment problems and public finance difficulties. In this situation, any widening of deficit positions is rapidly and directly sanctioned by capital markets. At the same time, if most economists see limited scope for the use of aggregate demand to tackle unemployment, they have become much more cautious in its use against inflation. This is essentially because of *unemployment persistence*: tight macro-policies can indeed control inflation (if not eliminate it), but the costs, in terms of lost output and employment, of a drastic restriction are no longer seen as transient. The negative consensus then might be summarised as maintain pressure on inflation, but avoid negative shocks to demand, even if this means some subtlety in the interpretation of monetary and other intermediate targets. Thus reflationary macro-economic action is a low priority for New Keynesianism, if it is on the policy agenda at all.

A movement of the UV curve towards the right (from UV to UV1) represents a simultaneous increase in the unemployment rate and vacancy rate. Such a shift indicates that unemployment is not due to normal business cycle fluctuations, but to structural factors such as industrial change. In this situation, a major gap is likely to have opened up between the skills composition of the unemployed and the skills requirements of advertised vacancies. Thus, the rise in joblessness caused by the shift from A to C is known as mismatch unemployment. Clearly this type of unemployment is most profound in geographical areas which contained traditional industries such as mining, shipbuilding or steel. Over the past two decades these industries have experienced deep cutbacks, causing thousands of redundancies. Because the skills of those made unemployed were so tied to the declining sectors, they could not transfer easily to alternative job opportunities, should they exist. They became displaced, and frequently discouraged, workers. As a result, the decline of industrial sectors frequently resulted in region-wide mismatch unemployment.

The concept of mismatch unemployment has been broadened to deal with other 'structural' characteristics of unemployment. For example, in the past twenty years, unemployment amongst the unskilled has doubled and sometimes trebled in many European economies. Gregg and Wadsworth (1996) show that whereas one in twelve unskilled males was unemployed in Britain in 1975, the figure in 1994 was one in three. Just what accounts for this fairly rapid fall in demand for unskilled (male) workers is the subject of widespread debate. Some argue that it is the result of increased exports from developing countries, while others point the finger at technological change. Whatever the reason, the result has been a gap opening up between the higher skill demands of employers and individuals without qualifications. This is a worrying development for it is virtually assigning the unskilled to a life without a job or to a job where pay is low and conditions are precarious.

Yet a further twist to the 'mismatch' unemployment theme is that the institutional organisation of the labour market could be responsible for the co-existence of high vacancies and high unemployment. For example, Kiel and Newell (1993) suggest stringent hiring and firing rules may lead employers to adopt stiffer recruitment criteria to increase the chances of attracting highly motivated workers. Alternatively, high levels of benefits may encourage the unemployed, particularly those with skills, to wait longer for a job which more closely meets their expectations with regard to pay and working conditions. In other words, institutional rules governing the labour market may encourage both employers and employees to be more selective, thereby causing tensions between the demand and supply sides of the labour market. Thus a variety of factors lie behind mismatch unemployment. Whatever the causes, it is more damaging than demand deficit unemployment because movement back to the initial equilibrium jobless rate (from C to A in the figure) is more difficult. For instance, mismatch unemployment cannot be successfully dealt with by expansionary macro-economic policies because increasing demand may increase the tension between unemployment and vacancies rather than ease it.

A rightward shift of both the UV and VS curves (from A to D) represents an economy experiencing at once an adverse shock and intense restructuring. Most European economies underwent such a shift in the

1970s as they reeled from large oil price increases and massive over-capacity in key industrial sectors. Such double shocks can severely rupture self-correcting forces in an economy, to the extent that point D could emerge as a new equilibrium position for unemployment. The term 'hysteresis', a word which has its origins in experimental physics where it describes the fact that when steady state relationships are disrupted they may not return to their initial equilibrium position, was borrowed to help explain such a process (Blanchard and Summers 1986). Thus, the initial rises in unemployment across Europe in the 1970s were seen to trigger additional problems that made it even harder for those out of work to obtain a job. As a result of this thinking, the notion of long-term unemployment was formulated. A consensus has emerged that long spells out of work have deleterious effects on the supply side of the labour market: the skills of people atrophy, they become demotivated and reduce their search for a job. All in all, they begin effectively to exclude themselves from the labour market. The spillover into the wider economy is also negative, as the numbers dependent on public support get larger, putting even more stress on the public finances.

Supporters of the New Keynesian view suggest that a comprehensive package of employment policies based on the thinking outlined above could make significant inroads into the jobless total of Europe. Table 5.1 outlines the 'active labour market agenda' arising from New Keynesian thinking.

Active labour market policies in Europe

The backdrop to active labour market policies

The foundation of active labour market policies in all member-states is an extensive and elaborate education and vocational training system. No detailed description or analysis of these systems can be given here, but a number of key points need highlighting. First of all, the institutional provision of education and training varies greatly across the member-states. This diversity is important because institutional design can have a key influence on the efficacy of the overall system (Calmfors 1994). For example, much of the literature stresses that it is the institutional framework that determines whether or not market failures are reduced in a vocational training system (Crouch 1993). Second, most member-states have substantially expanded their higher education systems. For the most part, this development reflects changing employment and occupational structures. With the expansion of service sector activity almost everywhere in Europe, employers are seeking to recruit people with computer and

Table 5.1 The New Keynesian employment policy agenda

ITEM	Description
Labour force skills and competencies	• Increase access to higher education • Increase off and on-the-job training • Align qualifications with current and future labour market needs
Labour market matching	• Reform job brokering techniques of public employment services • Relax restrictions on private sector employment services • Give the unemployed access to counselling and careers advice
Increasing labour demand	• Short-term job generation programmes • Youth employment schemes • Wage subsidies
Taxes, benefits and the labour market	• 'Passport' benefits to reduce the unemployment trap • Tighter benefit rules on availability and willingness to work • Lower non-wage costs for labour at the bottom end of the wage structure
Targeting labour market programmes	• Recruitment subsidies for employers to employ the young and the long-term unemployed • Early retirement plans • Training programmes for particular categories of labour
Labour market flexibility	• Relax regulations governing the use of part-time and temporary workers • Ease legal restrictions on the recruitment and dismissal of workers • Reduce constraints on the deployment of labour

Source: Author's own research

communications skills. Higher education is the best and cheapest method of equipping people with these attributes. Third, many member-states are recasting vocational training systems to reflect the changing nature of work. As Chapter 4 highlighted, a common trend is to move vocational training towards the teaching of competencies. In some instances, this involves modifying traditional apprenticeship schemes, but in other cases it has meant introducing new skill acquisition programmes. Overall, active labour market policies are sitting on a wide educational and training base that is undergoing considerable change

Expenditure on active labour market policies varies across the member-states. The Nordic countries tend to spend more than the other member-states: for example, Denmark and Finland spend about 7 per cent of GDP on such measures while the figure for Belgium, Italy and France is around 3.5 per cent of GDP. Behind these aggregate figures there is a big paradox in employment policy in the EU. Those countries with lower unemployment are able to spend more on active labour market policies than those with high jobless figures. Member-states with high unemployment are obliged to spend more on passive labour market measures – social benefits for income support – which tends to crowd out expenditure on positive programmes designed to get people back to work. Over the years, concerted efforts have been made to redirect expenditure from passive to active measures but with only limited success. Almost two-thirds of the 180 million ecu spent on employment policies in the EU is used to finance social benefits. Although the proportion going on active measures has increased in recent years, most member-states still believe that passive measures take too large a slice of employment policy budgets.

The long-term unemployment problem

Approximately 5 per cent of the EU's labour force has been out of work for more than a year and the figure is substantially higher for the poorer member-states such as Ireland, Spain and Greece. During the past decade, all the member-states have developed targeted measures for the long-term unemployed. Considerable convergence now exists across the EU on this matter, with measures falling into one of three categories: counselling and employment advice; basic training and education programmes; and short-term employment schemes. An EU-wide assessment of action programmes in this policy area concludes that whilst not solving the problem, most measures make a positive contribution (European Commission 1993). Counselling is regarded as a particularly useful and cost-effective measure. At the same time, there is a widespread view that more radical reform is needed to reduce the incidence of long-term unemployment.

Thus Layard (1995) argues that the problem of long-term unemployment cannot be effectively tackled unless the benefit systems in many EU countries are overhauled. His argument is that the unlimited duration of benefits encourages long-term unemployment. Countries such as Sweden, Japan and the USA, where benefits are stopped after six months or a year, tend to have fewer people in long-term unemployment than those countries where benefits are available for much longer. Layard suggests that after a year on the unemployed register, people should have their benefits stopped and automatically be offered a place on a training or temporary work scheme. But reforming the benefits system to bring the long-term unemployed back into the labour market is far from problem-free. Most European governments are in a catch-22 situation. On the one hand, if they reduce or in some way cap benefits to encourage the unemployed to take a relatively low-paying job, then they may be creating a poverty trap. On the other hand, if benefits are kept high, then the incentive to take up a job, particularly a low-wage, low-skilled, job, is weakened – an unemployment trap is created.

Despite its political sensitivity, many member-states are taking action on the matter. In a small way, the UK has introduced 'passport' benefits whereby the unemployed can continue to receive social benefits if they accept a job offer. More controversially, a new Job Seeker Allowance has been introduced, which provides the unemployed with a single benefits package provided they are available to take up work immediately and are actively seeking employment. In Sweden, the public employment services are also considering new tougher ways of enforcing availability and willingness to work requirements. Reforms have also been introduced to ensure that the (fragmented) system of social insurance does not create disincentives in terms of the unemployed searching for work. Germany has started to travel down a similar policy route. A selection of measures is being used to tighten up the job acceptability criteria for recipients of benefits and to widen the gap between social benefits and the average net wage. More and more, member-states are beginning to act in a similar vein, indicating that the interface between work and welfare will be a central aspect of employment policy in Europe in the next decade.

Experimentation and active labour market policies

A related issue receiving increasing attention is that of reducing the non-wage component of total labour costs (OECD 1997). Non-wage costs cover such things as employer social security contributions and in most member-states they amount to between 35 and 40 per cent of total employee costs. These high social charges are regarded as having a negative impact on the recruitment of unskilled labour. Because this group tends to consist of lower productivity performers, high non-wage costs makes them relatively expensive. Many member-states are attempting to address this problem. French labour market authorities have placed this matter at the centre of labour market policy. For example, a law has recently been enacted reducing employer sickness insurance contributions in respect of low-paying occupations. Italy too has reduced employer social security contributions in the hope that this will boost job generation. Other countries, such as Belgium, the Netherlands and Spain, have introduced more targeted reforms by which reductions in social security are linked to the recruitment of unskilled workers. Overall, however, improving the employability of low-skilled workers has not received the priority it deserves (International Labour Organization (ILO) 1996). Continuing and intensifying technological change will almost certainly make this problem more acute in forthcoming years.

Active labour market policies have sought to increase labour demand through a range of measures from short-term job creation or employment programmes to employer wages/recruitment subsidies (Calmfors and Skedinger 1995). Most of these initiatives have their origins in the 1970s. After the collapse of the golden age of economic growth, most member-states established short-term employment schemes as an ameliorative measure: in many cases the programmes were regarded as a stopgap until the return of full employment. However, the golden age failed to come back. As a result employment programmes have become a quasi-permanent feature of national labour market regimes. Indeed, the lion's share of expenditure on active labour market policies goes on such initiatives. Evaluations of such programmes were mixed. Separate assessments of training for unemployed adults in Italy, France, UK and Germany found that many of the participants failed to get jobs in the formal jobs market when the scheme came to an end. Short-term job creation schemes for the young are also widespread, but again evaluations are not entirely positive. Some surveys show that many of these schemes do not give young people 'marketable' skills to gain employment in the formal economy. As a result, many young people experience a revolving door syndrome of completing one scheme simply to join another. The French refer to this as 'employment parking'. Overall, the effectiveness of short-term employment schemes has yet to be proven.

Because of such lukewarm evaluations, a preference is emerging for recruitment and wage subsidies (Snower 1995). These initiatives are regarded as superior because they allow the unemployed to build up an employment record with a regular employer doing a regular job. Countries such as the UK, Germany, Finland and Ireland have all launched programmes of this type. At the same time, recruitment subsidies have not won universal support. Evaluations in North America suggest that a high level of dead weight and displacement is associated with such initiatives. Moreover, it is doubtful whether recruitment subsidies are a viable substitute for short-term job creation measures. Despite all the blemishes associated with such programmes, it is likely that the member-states will persist with them given the levels of unemployment across Europe. But the limitations of both recruitment subsidies and employment schemes have focused attention on the effectiveness of active labour market policies.

Appraisals are resulting in placement services gaining more prominence on the active labour market policy menu (Fay 1995). In most member-states, placement services play a lynchpin role in employment services. Sometimes they administer social assistance and employment placement schemes, but almost everywhere they carry out job brokerage and counselling activities. Counselling services in particular are attracting interest as they are seen as a cheap but effective method of preventing people falling into long-term unemployment. In recent years, the UK, Germany, Austria, France, Italy and Sweden have all introduced reforms to improve the counselling and careers advice that placement services give to the unemployed. While there is a consensus that these bodies are worthwhile, their role should not be overestimated. Mosley (1997), in an interesting study of public employment services in the EU, suggests that some of these bodies deal with only about a quarter of the unemployed when filling vacancies. One indication that the job brokerage role of public placement services is not operating optimally is the general move across the EU to relax restrictions on private placement services. Some accounts suggest these organisations are better at matching the demand and supply aspects of the labour market.

Increasingly, measures to promote employment flexibility are coming under the umbrella of active labour market policies. Greater employment flexibility is seen as one way of improving the job creation content of overall economic growth. Looser regulatory constraints on temporary and part-time contracts, for example, could encourage greater hiring by employers. Alternatively, weaker labour market rules may increase the geographical mobility of labour, thereby helping to reduce the problem of regional unemployment black spots. This increased focus on flexibility will probably lead to active labour market policies becoming more concerned with adapting institutional and legal structures for employment to new emerging patterns of work. To some extent, this is already happening. For example, the Netherlands enacted an innovatory programme in 1996 which attempts to combine flexibility with employment security measures for atypical workers.

Overall, it can be concluded that the vast majority of European countries are using an active labour market policy framework when addressing the problem of unemployment. This has resulted in greater convergence in employment policy priorities across national frontiers. Thus almost everywhere long-term unemployment and the employment consequences of the falling demand for unskilled workers are the main concerns of labour market policy-makers. Another common feature across countries is the emphasis placed on experimentation and innovation: governments are continually seeking new ways to improve their package of employment assistance for the jobless. At the same time, important national differences remain, not only in terms of the institutional delivery of employment measures, but also in respect of the policies themselves. Some countries have a preference for short-term employment schemes while others place more reliance on placement services backed up by recruitment subsidies. Thus, it is important not to over-emphasise the convergence amongst European nations toward an active labour market regime.

The EU and active labour market policies

The EU has thrown its weight behind the drive towards active labour market policies. Since it has few powers to launch independent employment policies, the EU's role is mainly one of coordination and exhortation. For some time now the EU centre has been encouraging the member-states to enact measures that improve the employability of young people. More recently, efforts have been made to obtain greater transparency and coordination on labour market initiatives across the member-states. For instance in 1993 the European Council agreed the Essen strategy that set out the broad economic policy objectives to be pursued to promote employment and growth in Europe. A number of employment reports have been presented to subsequent Council meetings on the back of this initiative. These have codified and clarified the type of labour market policies being pursued by individual member-states, thus enabling a more informed debate about employment measures in Brussels. As a result, a follow-on proposal was launched in 1996 under the title Action for Employment – a Confidence Pact. This report encourages the member-states to adopt a series of initiatives to improve job generation machines. Although this initiative does not have any formal legal status, it places informal pressure on the member-states to do more on the jobless problem.

More recently, mainly as a response to popular concern that the member-states had become too preoccupied with the monetary union project and were paying insufficient attention to the jobs problem, the EU has further revised its employment strategy. In particular, the European Council has adopted a strategy that rests on four main pillars. First is improving employability, which covers measures to prevent youth and long-term unemployment, and the adoption of a social partnership approach to labour market policy. Second is developing entrepreneurship, which involves such efforts as making it easier to start up and run a business, exploiting the opportunities for job creation and making the tax system more employment friendly. Third is encouraging adaptability in businesses and their employees, with particular emphasis on the promotion of employee participation and enterprise flexibility. Fourth is the strengthening of equal opportunities policies, which encompasses measures to reconcile work and family life, facilitating return to work and addressing gender and disability gaps in the labour market.

In addition to fine-tuning its employment programme, the EU has adopted a new, more formalised, system of coordinating labour market policies across the member-states. In particular, a benchmarking procedure has been introduced to improve the connection between different national labour market regimes as well as to improve the monitoring and evaluation of measures by the EU centre. The objective of the new procedure is to highlight best practice and to identify the initiatives that are successful in improving labour market outcomes. At the 1997 Madrid Summit, the member-states agreed that youth and long-term unemployment as well as equal opportunities should be priority areas for the new benchmarking procedure. Some work has started on this decision. Consider the area of equal opportunities. On the positive side, the benchmarking exercise has uncovered a number of best practice examples in Portugal and Spain with regard to promoting the return of women to work. On the negative side, the exercise has found large gaps in equal opportunity provision across the member-states. Belgium, Austria, Sweden and the UK were found to be the only member-states that had adopted a policy of 'mainstreaming' equal opportunities in employment policies. Moreover, wide variation was found to exist across the EU on public provision for child care and the elderly, which has a big bearing on whether or not women enter the labour market.

The early results from the benchmarking procedure have highlighted the lack of coherence to national labour market strategies and the lack of coordination across the EU on the matter. This supports the point made earlier in this chapter that most member-states are experimenting with active labour market policy in the hope of getting the right combination of measures that best fit their own circumstances. But the diversity that is evident in employment regimes makes it more difficult to operationalise the benchmarking exercise, as 'best practices' are hard to ascertain. Compounding this problem is the fact that because many policies have only existed for relatively short periods of time, it is difficult to make definitive judgements about their success or otherwise. At times, it is even hard to gauge whether or not the EU or individual member-states are on the right track. Thus, benchmarking, to the extent that it has occurred, has emphasised the need for the member-states to build a new framework for the understanding and evaluation of employment policies.

Overall, the EU has embarked upon an employment strategy that incorporates but also goes beyond active labour market regimes. In forthcoming years, the likelihood is that greater policy connections will be forged between the member-states to learn from each other in relation to labour market performance. This is an exciting new development, for, as Chapter 6 shows, the information and communication channels between the member-states are distorted in several important ways. The prospect of more transparent and purposeful linkages between the member-states and the EU centre is a positive development with potentially far-reaching implications for European political integration. Meantime, the search is on for appropriate benchmarks to monitor national public policies for the labour market. From the various 'national roads' to tackling high unemployment, the so-called 'Dutch model' has attracted the greatest amount of interest. Supporters of this model argue that it has produced impressive employment growth and allowed greater labour market flexibility to set side by side with social consensus. Certainly, it is worth investigating this employment regime since it is being held up as the future model for Europe as a whole.

The Dutch model

The backdrop to the Dutch model was the dismal economic performance of the 1970s. At that time, economists frequently referred to the 'Dutch disease' to highlight how a country can get trapped in a vicious economic circle. On all economic fronts, the Netherlands was performing badly. Real unit labour costs rose sharply, reducing profits, investment and the general level of international competitiveness. Inflation and unemployment increased steeply as did the tax burden. In the late 1970s, the property market dived and this foreshadowed the wider economic recession of the early 1980s. At this point the economic picture was nearly all doom and gloom. But, miraculously, since the early 1980s virtually all economic news has been good. Inflation and unemployment have fallen substantially and now appear firmly under control. International competitiveness seems to have been restored as the country has a thriving tradable sector. A fairly hefty fall in real labour costs appears to be the key to success on this score. All in all, by the early 1990s, the Netherlands looked as if it had one of the healthier economies in the EU. It is the scale of the turnaround in economic fortunes that has prompted people to talk of the Dutch model and even of the Dutch 'miracle'.

A number of factors lie behind the transition from laggard to relatively good economic performer. First of all, there has been a series of wage agreements, beginning with the Wassenaar agreement, which have kept a tight lid on pay increases. For most of the past fifteen years or so, wage increases have been lower than productivity rises. As Figure 5.4 shows, the fall in real unit labour costs was particularly sharp in the 1980s, although performance on this front has been less impressive during the 1990s. Overall, the national pay deals have been the single most important factor for improved economic competitiveness. For the most part, the operation of the national pay programmes is consistent with the analysis presented in

Chapter 2 regarding the new pay centralisation in Europe. On the one hand, because the Dutch authorities effectively tied the guilder to the German Deutschmark in the early 1980s, the pay deals can be seen as preparing the economy for deeper monetary integration in Europe. On the other hand, by accepting that centralised wage agreements are a key instrument to improve competitiveness, trade unions have accepted, or at least complied with, a shift from a traditional social corporatist bargaining agenda.

Second, high unemployment has been reversed largely as a result of a job generation process centred on the creation of part-time employment. Since the early 1980s, two-thirds of net additional jobs have been part-time. As Figure 5.5 shows, the share of part-time employment in total employment increased from 22 per cent in 1985 to 37 per cent in 1996. This trend contrasts sharply with the EU average, which has been on a gently rising curve for the past decade and now stands at about 15 per cent of the workforce. From the survey evidence that exists, it seems that part-time work is mostly voluntary and reflects positive social preferences. In choosing part-time work, many people appear to be making a statement that they want to combine a career with family responsibilities and leisure activities. Undoubtedly, this choice has been made easier by the compre-

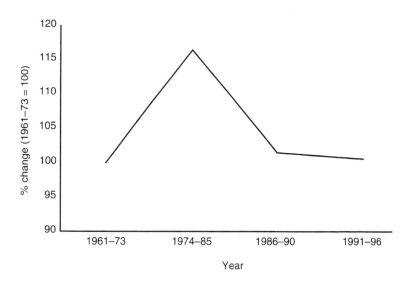

Figure 5.4 Dutch relative unit labour costs in common currency (against other OECD countries)

hensive social security coverage enjoyed by part-time workers in the Netherlands. At the same time, it would be wrong to paint a totally glowing picture of this type of work in the country. For example, Schmid (1997) highlights that many part-timers work fewer than ten hours per week, which reduces their legal protection and level of subsistence.

A third feature of the Dutch model has been large-scale labour supply reductions. For the most part, these have been secured by the early retirement of workers aged 55 or over. Only about 31 per cent of the population aged between 55 and 64 are actually in work. The Netherlands has the lowest participation rate for older workers in the EU. In addition to early retirements, a large number of people have withdrawn from the labour market by claiming disability allowances. At the moment about 11 per cent of the workforce is considered too sick or handicapped to take a job. To a large extent, these big labour market withdrawals have been fuelled by relatively generous social benefits for those who have either been declared sick or who are on early retirement programmes. Generally, people on these schemes receive a level of benefit equivalent to about 70 to 80 per cent of the average wage. Of course, the withdrawal of so many workers from the labour market calls into question the reliability of the 'official' unemployment figures. According to the government, as shown in

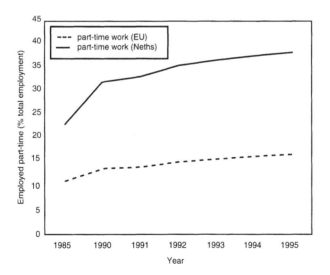

Figure 5.5 Part-time work in the EU and the Netherlands, 1985–96

Figure 5.6, the Dutch unemployment rate is about 5 to 6 per cent of the labour force. But if a wider measure is taken, so that all economically in-active people are included, then broad unemployment rockets to 27 per cent. In the short-term, this is not an overly serious problem, since many of the economically inactive enjoy high benefits. But if this situation were to change, particularly if deep cuts were to be made to welfare provision, the spectre of economic and social exclusion would be raised.

Another interesting aspect of the Dutch model is that the country's per capita GDP, a measure of the country's wealth, trails the EU average. For most of the 1970s and 1980s, this measure declined fairly steeply against the rest of the EU. Normally such a trend indicates economic inefficiency, but this is not the case with regard to the Netherlands. Measures of hourly productivity, for example, suggest the country is highly dynamic (Schmid 1997). What appears to be happening is as follows. Those in work are highly productive, but because the country's employment rate is fairly low, they have to share their efficiency with the economically inactive, which puts a drag on the overall wealth of the country. Neo-classical economists disparage this situation for distorting incentives in the economic (and social) system. On the other hand, it shows that the Dutch have opted for a strong programme of income and employment redistribution in a rela-

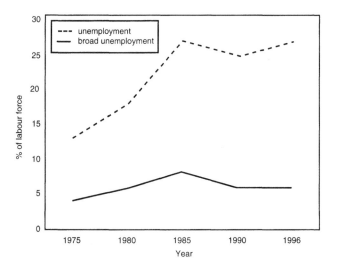

Figure 5.6 Dutch unemployment, 1975–96

tively cold economic climate. The big question is whether such social solidarity can be sustained in the longer term.

Recently, the Dutch government has introduced a number of labour market reforms designed to rein in the generosity of the social benefits system. In particular, the sickness benefits system has been 'privatised' – employers now run large parts of it themselves – and the level of subsistence has been lowered. In addition, government-sponsored early retirement schemes have been curbed. Thus the 'attractiveness' of life outside the formal labour market is likely to diminish in forthcoming years. At the same time, there is little reason to believe that these changes sound the death knell of the Dutch model. Ultimately, the sustainability of the labour market regime in the Netherlands is tied to the essentially political matter of the willingness of the Dutch people to fund the employment and income distribution programme by paying relatively high taxes. So far, there are no tangible signs that this commitment is waning.

Meantime, the Dutch government has been pushing ahead with new and innovatory labour market programmes, which seek to combine labour market flexibility and social consensus. A key theme is employability – a term much used nowadays. A life-long learning plan has been developed to give workers the opportunity to retrain and get re-skilled throughout their employment career. At the same time, the legal restrictions on the use of fixed-term contracts have been eased, as has the licensing system that regulates temporary work agencies. The logic behind the strategy is evident. Both greater labour market flexibility and wider access to educational provision are promoted, in the hope that individuals come to feel less threatened by the prospect of having to change jobs more than once in their careers. In addition to pursuing such new employment measures, the Dutch government has also overhauled the organisation of its employment services to create 'one-stop' shops where people have access to the full range of active labour market measures.

Overall, the Dutch model can be best described as a hybrid system, tied to 'old' features of Social Europe, but at the same time attempting to adjust to new economic times. On the one hand, traditional institutions and programmes associated with the European welfare state – comprehensive and generous social benefits – have facilitated large-scale labour market supply-side reductions. On the other hand, key aspects of the labour market flexibility agenda have been introduced, particularly with regard to the use of part-time and temporary workers, but usually accompanied with countervailing measures designed to provide some form of social protection. Attempting to link the past with the future and to balance flexibility and regulation are the key innovatory features of the Dutch model. Other European governments can learn a lot from this essentially pragmatic reform path. This is not to propose the Europe-wide implementation of the Dutch labour market regime. After all, a key lesson of the Netherlands' experience is that any social and economic modernisation programme that departs too abruptly or is not in some way connected to established social institutions could run into trouble. Moreover, question marks still hang over the efficacy and the long-term viability of the Dutch model. To some extent, this uncertainty has been fuelled by new doubts about the effectiveness of active labour market policies, and it is to this matter that we now turn.

The effectiveness of active labour market policies

At the beginning of the 1990s, there was a virtual consensus that active labour market policies would bring benefits both to individuals and society. But this common view appears to be fragmenting, as the effectiveness of such measures is being increasingly questioned. Robinson (1995: 4), for example, argues that 'it is time for active labour market policy to be seen as one of the more modest instruments of economic policy ... whose efficacy should not be exaggerated'. A number of factors are behind this verdict. First of all, although expenditure on active measures has increased in many member-states, unemployment has remained high, something which raises concerns about the cost effectiveness of such policies. Second, it is argued that there is a lack of convincing evidence about the beneficial impact of many specific employment programmes. Robinson cites research from the USA and Sweden, which found that people who received training were not greatly more employable than those who obtained no assistance. These findings are in line with other evidence collected by the OECD suggesting that some broadly targeted training programmes yield small returns.

Doubt is also cast on the potential impact of recruitment subsidies. The ground for scepticism here is that too much dead weight, and too many substitution and displacement effects are associated with such programmes. In other words, employers use recruitment subsidies when they would have hired somebody anyway; or they 'lose' staff so that they can take on new workers covered by the subsidy; or they favour those eligible for assistance over other job seekers. It is also argued that short-term job creation initiatives can displace regular work in the formal economy. This is particularly true for construction-related activities. A further criticism is that many training and employment programmes deliver poor-quality skill formation and do not give participants transferable qualifications. Finally, Robinson asserts that measuring the economic effects of active labour market policies is so laden with methodological and technical difficulties that a fair amount of scepticism should be attached to those studies claiming big gains for such measures.

Shackleton (1995) makes more far-reaching criticisms of active labour market policies. He suggests that the current policy-talk about the need for a skills revolution is misplaced, largely because the acquisition of qualifications does not greatly improve the lot of the unemployed or enhance the competitiveness of companies. The following reasoning lies behind Shackleton's argument. First, the rise in unemployment across Europe during the past twenty years cannot be attributed to a declining demand for unskilled labour. As a result, increasing the skill levels of the unemployed will not ensure that they will get back into regular work. Second, increasing investment in training is unlikely to translate into higher economic growth rates. For the most part, this view is based on the observation that many people are already over-qualified for the jobs they are doing. In this situation, increasing financial resources to training is not seen as the best use of (scarce) public money. Third, the heavy emphasis placed on training and active labour market policy overestimates the potential of supply-side measures alone to reduce the problems of joblessness and unimpressive economic performance. Demand-side policies, such as boosting corporate investment and expanding job creation in the public sector, are also required to address the employment deficit in Europe.

Thus, there is now greater equivocation about the benign effects of active labour market policies. Not all economists are persuaded by the above criticisms. Layard (1995; 1997), a doyen of New Keynesian thinking on employment matters, has strongly defended this approach. He regards the argument that active labour market policies simply help some people to get jobs over others (the dead-weight, displacement and substitution effects) as a variant of the wrong-headed lump-of-labour fallacy, which suggests that the total number of jobs in an economy is somehow fixed. Layard rejects this argument on the following grounds. Consider measures designed to help the long-term unemployed back into work. After receiving training or financial assistance, a long-term unemployed person becomes more attractive to an employer. As a result, the employer may decide to recruit the person in preference to somebody else who is on the jobless register but who has not yet slipped into long-term unemployment. In this singular case, the active labour market policy has allowed the long-term unemployed person to 'capture' a job from another jobless person. But the key point is that the disappointed person is still attractive to employers even though he or she did not get that particular job. Thus, enhancing the employability of the long-term unemployed person does not diminish the attractiveness of others who are unemployed, but rather increases the total number of employable people in the economy.

Greater numbers of employable people in the labour market trigger informal supply-side pressures for higher overall employment. One way in which this informal pressure works is by keeping wage inflation in check. Most countries now have an inflation target. If active labour market policies increase the number of employable job seekers then employers will face less pressure to increase wages. As a result, inflationary pressures will be lower, probably causing the actual inflation rate to be below the target level. In such circumstances, the monetary authorities are likely to reduce interest rates, thereby giving a boost to investment and jobs. Thus active labour market policies can have the effect of increasing job creation at a given level of inflation. Layard regards critics of active employment measures as guilty of overlooking such dynamic effects.

He also suggests that the sceptics underestimate the wider social benefits that can arise from active labour market policies. Consider the social implications of reforming benefit systems. As already pointed out, Layard believes that giving those out of work for a year or more the option of retraining or a place on an employment programme may drastically reduce the incidence of long-term unemployment. One spillover from this choice may be the creation of a social norm that encourages the unemployed to strive to remain connected with the labour market proper: the option of adjusting to a life on benefits may become a social stigma. In making this point, Layard is dusting down a central point made by Beveridge in his 1944 Employment Report, that a successful employment policy involves balancing the rights and responsibilities of both government and citizens.

Two cheers for active labour market policies?

Layard is right to argue that active labour market policies may have dynamic effects: improving the supply-side of the labour market can release pressures that increase the overall stock of jobs. But one legitimate query concerns the size or degree of such dynamic macro-economic effects. Clearly, this question cannot be answered precisely as social and economic conditions differ across countries. But it is doubtful that they would be of the order to solve the unemployment problem in some member-states. Consider Spain, admittedly an extreme case, with an unemployment rate of 22 per cent. It would be nothing less than heroic to claim that active labour market policies and associated positive spillovers alone would make large-scale inroads into the jobless total. One report on Spanish unemployment came to the conclusion that in *addition* to supply-side employment policies, the country needed to enact measures that would stimulate growth and investment (Blanchard *et al.* 1985). Active labour market policies by themselves were regarded as too weak to address the high unemployment problem. This diagnosis is as valid for other member-states as it is for Spain. Thus Layard may be placing too much reliance on narrow supply-side measures.

As a result, while his rebuttal of the critics of active labour market policies may be persuasive, his own position is not foolproof. For the most part, the shortcomings of his own analysis are due to his downplaying of the importance of the demand side of the labour market, and his failure to connect employment policies to the wider battle against social exclusion. A one-sided supply-side view is surprising from Layard, for previously he was the champion of the two-handed or 'scissors' approach to reducing unemployment. From the 'scissors' perspective, unemployment in Europe needed both supply and demand policies (Blanchard *et al.* 1985); increased investment and expenditure were required as much as training and employment policies. It is a measure of the extent to which active demand management policies have fallen out of favour with mainstream economists that Layard feels unable to endorse any kind of demand-side agenda. Of course, a small band of economists argue that a big Europe-wide reflationary programme is the only way to get unemployment down in Europe. But this essentially traditional Keynesian view is not taken seriously: the EU has neither the financial instruments nor the political will to embark upon a radical inflationary programme.

While traditional Keynesianism may be a non-starter, the demand side nevertheless remains important for two reasons. One is that the scope appears to exist for a limited fiscal stimulus. Dreze and Malvinaud (1994) suggest that the share of public investment in GDP has fallen from 3.9 per cent in the 1960–73 period to 2.7 per cent from 1985 onwards. Thus the macro-economic environment is probably overly disinflationary, which indicates that some room exists for fiscal activism without triggering inflationary pressures. The European Commission seems to hold this view. In 1994, following on from the Growth, Competitiveness and Employment White Paper, it proposed that the member-states increase public expenditure on a range of productive investments such as a trans-European transport network. The actual amounts involved were relatively small beer; overall the Commission was seeking the public and private sectors in Europe to spend 30 billion ecus. Yet the member-states refused to endorse the plan, reflecting a deep reluctance to sanction any level of pan-European fiscal programme. But such obduracy is misplaced and overly cautious. As a result, the chance of giving a boost to supply-side oriented active labour market policies is being missed.

The second reason why the demand side is important is subtler. Layard's argument that active labour market policies can generate economy-wide dynamics largely rests on the assumption that such measures will genuinely give the unemployed competencies to compete with traditionally more employable people in the labour market. Thus, employment programmes must be meaningful so that they genuinely upgrade the skills and competencies of participants. But such programmes are costly, requiring a big public expenditure commitment from government. Trying to run these programmes on the cheap invariably reduces the quality of the schemes. Therefore, developing an effective, comprehensive range of active labour market policies will almost certainly worsen the fiscal situation of a given country. As a result, governments must accept that active labour market policies will be a significant drain on public coffers. In a period of tight budgets almost everywhere in Europe, whether governments take this message on board is open to doubt. In many European capitals the unspoken view still appears to be that active labour market policies are a way of not spending large quantities of money on the unemployment problem. Such a perspective is excessively short term and ultimately self-defeating.

Thus many European governments are on the horns of a dilemma. On the one hand, they need to enact comprehensive employment measures to make inroads into jobless figures. On the other hand, budgetary circumstances are extremely tight, reducing scope for policy innovation. One idea to get out of this conundrum is to use green taxes to boost employment in Europe. The thinking behind this proposal is straightforward: the tax system should be reorganised so that environmentally harmful activities are fiscally penalised and the revenues collected are used to promote jobs. For example, the extra public money could be used to reduce taxes on unskilled labour; the European Commission estimates that a reduction of labour taxes on low-paid jobs equal to 1 per cent of GDP could cut the unemployment rate by about 2.5 per cent over four years. Alternatively, increased resources could be directed at active labour market programmes. Whatever option is chosen, the basic message is that to be genuinely effective, active labour market policies require governments to reorganise fiscal regimes radically. Layard and other New Keynesians do not give sufficient attention to this point.

Another matter raised by Layard, but not fully addressed, is the social implication of active labour market policies. New Keynesians tend to view employment policies simply as a way of building up the competencies of individuals or making them behave as good citizens. But the types of employment policy governments pursue speak volumes about the political and social systems they are trying to promote. Without being placed in a wider social framework, active labour market policy regimes could easily be misinterpreted as souped up neo-liberalism – a smaller version of

American-style workfare programmes. Thus making the connection between active labour market policies and the fight against the spread of social exclusion in Europe may pay dividends. Although a term frequently invoked nowadays, 'social exclusion' is actually hard to define (Silver 1994). Broadly, however, it can be taken to mean a set of processes within the labour market and the welfare system by which individuals, households, communities or even whole social groups are pushed towards or kept at the margins of society. It encompasses not only material deprivation but also, more generally, a lack of opportunity to participate fully in social life. It is associated with stigmatisation and stereotyping but, at the same time, it highlights the responsibility of wider society to show solidarity with its marginal members. Associating active labour market policies with the wider drive to prevent social exclusion has a number of benefits. First, it would put clear blue water between New Keynesian and neo-liberal economic strategies. By more visibly connecting active labour market policies with the fight against social exclusion, the social and political support base for such programmes would widen.

A second benefit is that a more encompassing and integrated approach may be taken towards the plight of the unemployed. Active labour market policies become a comprehensive package of support measures designed to stop economic and social bifurcation, rather than a range of narrowly focused programmes to improve the lot of particular individuals. An all-embracing approach of this type encourages innovatory thinking on the organisation of the labour market. For example, a theme gaining currency is that of the 'third' economic sector or the social economy. The basic idea is that a new intermediate economic area should be developed between the public and private sectors, which is largely devoted to activity centred on social and environmental concerns. Governments would legitimise and make acceptable such activity by ensuring: (1) that the projects or work tasks were purposeful; (2) that those engaged in the sector were covered by acceptable wages and working conditions; and (3) that opportunities existed for training and educational advances. The notion of a social economy has considerable merits. It forms a buffer zone around the formal labour market so that those who lose jobs do not fall into unemployment. At the same time, it offers a pathway for those that have been out of work, particularly the long-term unemployed, leading to meaningful economic and social activity. In addition, it could prove an effective public policy instrument to improve the circumstances of disadvantaged areas such as inner city neighbourhoods.

Viewed in the broader context of the fight against social exclusion, the significance of active labour market policies becomes more transparent. They are an attempt to get away from dead-end approaches to the problems of unemployment and economic inactivity, such as empty sloganeering about the return to full employment. Instead we are challenged to see present levels of unemployment as not arising simply from the actions of nasty employers or governments, but as much the result of a transition to a new economic and social model of development. We are encouraged to ask uncomfortable questions. For example, can the principle of universal social benefits, embedded in so many welfare systems in Europe, continue for much longer? In short, active labour market policies should be seen as central to the drive to reform welfare states and labour market governance structures in Europe. They are part and parcel of the recasting and remodelling of economic citizenship across the member-states. Creating programmes that genuinely promote the employability of individuals and increase social inclusion will be a litmus test of the extent to which European governments have been able to modernise their social systems.

Conclusions

New Keynesianism has advanced understanding of the operation of labour markets in Europe. In theoretical terms, it has delivered a big blow to the narrow neo-classical analysis of labour markets, which uses a demand and supply framework to explain movements in and out of employment. At the same time, it lays bare some of the deficiencies of the traditional Keynesian perspective on the labour market. Emphasising that labour market performance has its roots in the micro-economic behaviour of firms and workers as well as institutional rules and social norms, it escapes the overly macro-economic focus of orthodox Keynesianism. In terms of policy-making, New Keynesianism is not nearly as innovatory as some of its supporters would have us believe. Many of the remedies proposed for reducing unemployment have been around for some time. The achievement of New Keynesianism has been to revamp and integrate the various initiatives into a more coherent whole. At the same time, its proposals, usually put forward under the catch-all term 'active labour market policies', have been highly influential across Europe. Unquestionably, this is the dominant policy framework used by most European governments to reduce unemployment.

Will the New Keynesian policy agenda succeed in reducing high unemployment in Europe? Recently, the trend has been to suggest that active labour market policies will have a limited impact on joblessness. This chapter suggests that these criticisms are overdone and in some instances based on faulty economic analysis. At the same time, it argues that the effectiveness of active labour market policies could be thwarted by two factors. One is the tendency to think that employment measures to reduce European unemployment can be done relatively cheaply. This line of thinking is specious: improving labour market performance requires properly funded, comprehensive programmes. To tackle unemployment properly involves a big fiscal commitment. New Keynesianism pays too little attention to, or at least has to little to say on, this matter. The other potential shortcoming is that the development, design and implementation of active labour market policies are not given enough consideration. But it is such matters that will usually determine the success or otherwise of employment programmes. Moreover, these matters cannot be fully addressed by some type of 'institutional fix'. The social and political foundations of active labour market policies also have to be brought into the equation. In particular, greater effort is needed to connect active employment measures to the wider battle against social exclusion in Europe. Active labour market policies should be seen as part of the project of reinventing economic citizenship in European society. New Keynesianism has not provided all the answers to this big project, but it has certainly made a positive contribution.

Part 3

Economic citizenship and the EU

6   EU social policy

Between constitutionalism and
neo-voluntarism

Introduction

EU social policy-making is knee-deep in controversy. One argument
concerns the efficacy of EU interventions in European labour markets.
The supportive view is that EU social policies are required so that citizens
of the member-states are properly integrated into economic life. By
contrast, advocates of neo-liberal Europe suggest that EU labour market
rules only intensify the already big rigidities in national employment
systems. Another disagreement relates to the characterisation of EU social
policy. Some argue that the EU is slowly building a social constitution,
which in the end will establish a Europe-wide floor of employment rights.
Others are less upbeat, regarding the social policy regime in Brussels as
weak and fragmented, unable to meaningfully restrain the action of either
employers or trade unions. Thus, an ill-sorted set of views exists about the
form, impact and future direction of EU social policy.

This chapter outlines the evolution of EU labour market policy and
carefully analyses its exact political significance. The first part of the
chapter examines the development of EU employment laws and assesses
whether or not it is valid to regard them as supranational forms of labour
market regulation. In the second part, attempts at establishing a social
dialogue between employers and trade unions in Brussels are analysed to
see whether they represent a nascent form of corporatist decision-making.
Finally, the analysis touches upon the wider political debate about the
significance of European social interventions. The conclusions offer some
comments about the future.

The evolution of EU social policy

Phase one: from negative to positive social policies

Virtually no clause of an interventionist kind on social policy was included in the Treaty of Rome (1957). Big aspirational objectives were laid down for the participating countries to increase the living standards of their citizens and to work towards closer economic and social systems. But no specific programmes or policies were tied to these objectives, thus ensuring that the various countries were not shackled to unrealistic or over-ambitious commitments. Most social policy measures contained in the Treaty were concerned with promoting the free movement of labour. For instance, a Social Fund was established to ease the problems of social integration when people moved from one national labour market to another. An obligation to maintain broad equivalence in holiday entitlements and to guarantee equal pay for equal work, as well as proper health and safety standards, were the only explicit positive social policies set down. All in all, the Treaty reflected the consensus at the time that market integration alone could bring prosperity and employment.

In the following decade, until 1968, employment policy played a marginal role in the integration project. Initiatives were launched on issues such as health and safety, and training provision, but these were small-scale and mainly concerned with increasing communication between national labour market bodies. Regulation of the employment relationship continued to be firmly embedded in the national context. At the end of the 1960s, however, the integration agenda began to change. By this stage, the Common Market had reached a turning point. On the one hand, the experiment of creating a new pan-European economic arrangement had been quite successful. Most of the 'negative' integration objectives of the Treaty of Rome had been achieved. But on the other hand, the Common Market was widely regarded as a remote institution, unrelated to the general economic and political affairs of the member-states. Important political leaders such as Willy Brandt regarded this situation as undesirable. As a result, they started to argue for a Common Market with a 'human face'. In order to achieve this goal, more 'positive' integration programmes were deemed to be necessary. The development of European-level social policies was seen as a particularly important way to deepen the political and social foundations of the Union. At the 1972 Paris Summit, the now nine member-states officially endorsed this view by declaring themselves as committed to a social union as to an economic one.

Thus in the 1970s, the Commission attempted to expand the EU's role in social policy in a number of ways. Probably the most important dimension has been efforts to introduce EU legislation on employment relations topics. A list of some of the main labour laws that were passed by the member-states during this period is given below. The nature of the Directives reveal that the EU was attempting to respond to the more pressing concerns in the European labour market at the time. Thus, the statutes on equal opportunities reflected the growing social consensus that legal penalties should be incurred by employers who discriminated against women. In addition, the workers' rights legislation was a response to the large-scale redundancies and industrial restructuring programmes occurring in almost every member-state. By developing employment initiatives that were in line with ground-level labour market conditions, the EU was attempting to establish itself as a legitimate actor in national systems of employment regulation.

EU employment protection legislation (excluding health and safety), 1975–80

Equal opportunities

1   *Equal Pay Directive 1975* Obliged member-states to abolish all discrimination between the pay of men and women arising from their laws, regulations and administrative provisions, and to take the measures necessary to ensure the principle of equal pay for work of equal value is applied.
2   *Equal Treatment Directive 1976* Promoted equal treatment for women with regard to access to employment, vocational training and working conditions.
3   *Social Security Directive 1978* Designed to eliminate from social security schemes all discrimination based on sex, either directly or indirectly, by reference in particular to marital or family status.
4   *Social Security Directive 1986* Established for the first time international social security standards for private sector occupational schemes.

Workers' rights

1   *Collective Redundancies 1978 (amended 1991)*   Obliged companies who were enacting redundancies to give workers and their representatives, at least 30 days' notice of a proposed closure plan.
2   *Transfer of Undertakings Directive 1979*   Obliged companies involved in mergers and takeovers to inform workers in advance of any agreement. It also protected existing employment conditions and rights.
3   *Insolvency Directive 1980*   Required institutions to be set up at the member-state level to pay workers' outstanding claims which arose from their employment relationship before the employer ceased to meet his or her obligations.

Overall, the 1970s were a relatively good decade for those who wanted to see social legislation being enacted by the EU. But it should be pointed out that the Commission had failures as well as successes. A proposal to introduce a common model of employee involvement was rejected by the member-states as seeking too much harmonisation. The inability of the member-states to agree to any proposal on this matter after more than two decades of negotiations suggests that real limits exist to increasing the uniformity of industrial relations systems inside the EU. Another proposal – the infamous Vredeling Directive – to establish information and consultation procedures inside multinational corporations also ran aground after a highly effective worldwide campaign against the initiative.

Phase two: legal activism and intergovernmentalist immobilism

Few new labour market Directives, and none of any consequence, were passed during the 1980s, which was the clearest sign that a deep stalemate had crept into EU social policy. To a large extent, the unrelenting opposition of successive British governments to Europe-wide employment measures caused this *immobilisme*. For instance, in the early 1980s, the Commission brought forward a family of initiatives on the reorganization and regulation of working time, but Mrs Thatcher and her ministers, by either using or threatening to use the UK veto inside the Council of Ministers, prevented their passage. This blocking strategy was highly effective because it brought the EU social policy-making process to a virtual standstill. By the middle of that decade Commission officials responsible for labour market measures were a pretty dispirited bunch.

At the same time, the legal authority of the EU on labour market matters did increase during the 1980s due mainly to specific rulings by the European Court of Justice. Clauses of the Treaty of Rome and subsequent amendments are automatically interpreted as primary EU legislation, which means that they take precedence over the national laws of the member-states. Throughout the 1980s, Article 129 of the Treaty, which committed member-states to the principle of equal pay, was used by both the Commission and equal opportunities organisations to challenge perceived shortcomings of equality legislation in particular member-states. In many cases brought before it, the Court of Justice adopted a fairly broad interpretation of the Article, thereby obliging most member-states to toughen anti-discrimination legislation.

Other changes to the legal architecture of the EU also increased the legal capacity of Brussels to Act in the social policy field. In 1987 the member-states adopted the Single European Act to give the single market programme a legal base. This Act contains a number of important, although confusing, clauses relating to social policy matters. On the one hand, Article 100A (2) made the rights and interests of employed persons clearly a matter for unanimous voting only. On the other hand, Article 118A, which covers issues open to majority voting, specified that 'member-states shall pay particular attention to encouraging improvements in the working environment as regards the health and safety of workers'. This sub-clause manifestly made health and safety a matter for qualified majority voting. Less clear was whether the reference in the clause to the 'working environment' allowed the Commission to propose initiatives on other aspects of working conditions for decision by qualified majority voting. Considerable legal uncertainty remains on this issue even though the European Court of Justice touched upon it in its ruling against the UK government on the 'Forty-eight hour Working Week' Directive.

In an important article, Weiler (1994) argues that in the 1980s EU decision-making was marked by a dualism between successful supranational European law and unsuccessful intergovernmentalist policy formation. On the one hand, the European Court of Justice busied itself with developing a European legal order, standing above and in many instances taking precedence over national legal regimes. On the other hand, many arenas of policy formation in Brussels were gridlocked by a blocked intergovernmentalist decision-making process. Together, over-ambitious goals on the part of the Commission, disagreements among the member-states about the content of EU initiatives, and fault-lines between EU-level and national-level policy regimes prevented the adoption of a series of proposed initiatives. Social policy was particularly badly affected by this slow and cumbersome decision-making system. Thus, although legal activism on the part of the Court of Justice increased EU interventions in the European labour market, the formal policy-making route remained blocked. Intergovernmental impasse alongside legal activism is the best way to describe EU social policy for much of the 1980s.

Phase three: social policy and the single European market

Like almost every other part of EU decision-making, social policy was uplifted by the spontaneous increase in support for European integration in the wake of the 1992 programme. On the back of this popular support for Europe, the Commission proposed a Social Charter that would commit the member-states to a range of fundamental employment rights. Predictably, the United Kingdom resisted this proposal, which once again resulted in heated political exchanges in Brussels. In the end, no accommodation was reached on the matter and, without the UK, eleven member-states adopted the Social Charter at the December 1990 European Council. By adopting the Social Charter, the member-states had committed themselves politically to guaranteeing a range of economic and social standards. Very quickly, the Commission published a social action programme to put into effect the labour and social rights listed in the Charter. Although the programme set out forty-seven separate proposals, including seventeen for new Directives, it would be a mistake to describe it as an agenda to deepen EU employment regulation. Most of the proposals for the new legislation were in the health and safety area that commanded wide agreement among the member-states. Other proposals relating to employment conditions and working time were to prove more controversial. However, for the bulk of member-states these did not represent new supranational labour law, but only the codification of existing national employment legislation at the European level. The proposals are outlined in more detail on the next two pages.

EU social action programme proposals, 1991

Regulating atypical employment

Part-time workers

1 Sets out minimum procedures for firms to follow when recruiting part-time workers.
2 Part-timers should be included in statutory or occupational social security schemes on the same basis as full-timers.
3 Proportional rights to full-timers with regard to pay, holiday pay, redundancy pay and retirement benefits.
4 Provision for the transfer to full-time work.

Temporary workers

1 Limits on the operation of temporary work agencies.
2 Temporary workers should enjoy the same pay, benefits and conditions as comparable permanent workers in the enterprise.
3 Limits on the length of time for short-term contracts.

Short-term contracts

1 Employees on short-term contracts should enjoy the same benefits as comparable permanent employees.
2 Restrictions on the duration of such contracts.

Atypical work and social dumping

Restrictions on the use of atypical workers to obtain unfair competitive advantage.

Atypical work and health and safety

Restrictions placed on the use of part-time and temporary employees for job tasks normally requiring close supervision.

Regulating employment contracts

Obligation on employers to supply employees with written information on the terms and conditions of the employment relationship.

Organisation of working time

Rules to govern working time arrangements:

1   Minimum daily rest period of 11 hours in 24 hours.
2   At least one rest day in a 7-day period.
3   Annual paid leave related to national practice.
4   Night working confined to 8 hours per 24 hours.
5   Maximum working week of 48 hours, with employees having the right to work longer if they so choose.
6   Limited overtime by night workers.
7   Arrangements in place to allow night workers to transfer to day shifts.
8   Rotating shift and night workers to have frequent breaks and to have regular health checks.

Equal opportunities

1   Protection of pregnant women at work and women who have recently given birth. Provision of maternity leave of at least 14 weeks with at least 80 per cent of their salary.
2   Removal of health and safety hazards from working conditions.
3   Protection of employment rights against dismissal during maternity leave.

The decision by the eleven member-states to sign the Social Chapter without Britain did not end the controversy about EU employment policy. Disagreements resurfaced at the 1991 intergovernmental conference charged with writing a new treaty for the EU. The Commission and many of the member-states wanted a Social Chapter, more or less based on the 1990 Social Charter, in the new treaty, but this move was opposed by the British government. The dispute came to a head at the Maastricht European Council in 1992. Attempts at negotiating a compromise failed, resulting in eleven member-states signing a Social Protocol to the Maastricht Treaty and the UK opting out of this arrangement.

Social policy and the Maastricht Treaty

The Social Protocol to the Maastricht Treaty on European Union is significant in four important respects. First, it introduced the principle of subsidiarity into the formulation and implementation of EU social policy. Although a vague and contested term, 'subsidiarity' can be defined as the EU centre making an intervention only when a proposed action cannot be fully achieved by a member-state or another lower tier of government. Second, the Social Protocol allowed qualified majority voting on some aspects of EU employment policy. In particular, it sanctioned qualified majority voting on activities to improve the working environment; information and consultation of workers; equal opportunities; and the integration of people excluded from the labour market. At the same time, the Treaty maintained unanimous voting for the more central aspects of the employment relationship including social security; termination of employment; the representation and collective defence of the interests of workers (including co-determination); employment conditions for third-country nationals; and financial contributions towards job creation.

Third, the Protocol focused mostly on the sphere of individual rights and not on collective rights. For example, the important matters of strikes and lock-outs as well as pay determination remain outside the scope of EU action. Heavy intervention in such areas is seen as inappropriate since it may disrupt well-established and finely tuned power relations between national employers and trade unions. Fourth, the Protocol formalised the long-held ambition of the Commission to have a European-level social dialogue between trade unions and employer organisations (the social partners). Thus, it is now an obligation for the Commission to consult the social partners when preparing a social policy proposal. In addition, a procedure has been created for the conclusion of European framework arrangements between management and trade union representatives, with the possibility of them being enforced by the use of EU law. Furthermore, the Protocol permitted the implementation of EU Directives through national collective bargaining systems rather than via normal legislative channels. Some of these developments are more contentious than others. A number of the changes simply represented a benign and uncontroversial tidying-up exercise. From the mid-1970s, a sizeable gap had emerged between the sparse social policy clauses of the Treaty of Rome and the actual content of EU social policy. By adopting a range of laws on equal opportunities and worker protection, the EU gained a presence in the area of labour market regulation without directly sanctioning clauses in the Rome Treaty. Equally, the Rome Treaty made no explicit mention of an EU-sponsored social dialogue, yet an evergreen in EU employment policy has been the promotion of institutionalised relationships between employers and trade unions. The Social Protocol was an attempt to end this anomaly by giving EU labour market initiatives a clearer legal base.

Another goal of the Protocol was to establish a decision-making process on social policy which was free from institutional bottlenecks. In particular, the extension of majority voting in the field of social policy was an attempt to end the ability of any one member-state to block proposed labour market initiatives. On paper, this change appeared to open the door to a big increase in the number of EU social laws. But this prospect was held in check by the Treaty clause on subsidiarity. Some confusion exists about the relationship between the new system of majority voting and the legal rule confining EU interventions to situations where a lower tier of government cannot respond adequately to an employment policy matter. One relatively benign interpretation is that whereas the subsidiarity principle lays down the rule for deciding if a particular matter falls within the scope of EU social policy, the majority-voting clauses of the Protocol simply establish the procedures to be followed once such a decision is reached.

But this assessment is not fully convincing and leaves many unanswered questions. For instance, would the subsidiarity clause encourage a sharper and even more formal delineation of competencies between different tiers of government inside the EU on labour market issues? If not, then the question is just how would the member-states decide whether a labour market matter was within or outside EU social policy competence? A further uncertainty is the extent to which the EU would be able to enact genuinely supranational labour laws that imposed new obligations on the member-states. In other words, even though the Maastricht Treaty addressed some of the shortcomings associated with the making of European social laws, it by no means resolved the controversies surrounding this area of EU policy-making.

Social policy in the 1990s: the move to soft laws

Amidst the debate about the legal and political significance of the Maastricht Social Protocol, the European Council continued to pass employment laws. Most of the new legislation has been in the health and safety field which continues the pattern set in the 1980s. However legislation relating to other labour market areas has also been adopted. The 1991 Employment and Remuneration Directive promotes greater transparency in the employment relationship by obliging enterprises to provide a document which informs employees of the nature of employment, the duration of the contract, the system of protection provided and references to any relevant laws and collective agreements. The 1992 Equal Treatment for Men and Women Directive was widely supported. Its purpose was to remove from national legislation laws that prohibited the employment of women in night work. Another equal opportunities Directive enacted in 1994 related to pregnant workers, and laid down health and safety guidelines for their protection. Another Directive passed in 1994, concerning young workers, focused largely on health and safety measures but also restricted the working hours of those under 18. These various measures proved relatively uncontroversial and were supported by all member-states.

More controversial was the Improvement of Living and Working Conditions Directive, which aimed at limiting the working week in the EU to 48 hours. When the Commission first published the draft Directive, the UK Conservative government immediately signalled its disapproval on two grounds. One was the legal basis on which the Directive was proposed: the British objected to it being introduced under Article 118A of the Single European Act, which allows for qualified majority voting mainly in the health and safety area. The second objection was their standard British line that such initiatives only increase rigidities in the European labour market. In a round of negotiations the British were able to secure important concessions. The main amendment was the ability of workers and employers to elect to work more than 48 hours if they so wished. Although the changes made the Directive more palatable to the British government, it still voted against the initiatives. However, because the initiative was proposed under the majority voting procedure the Directive was passed nevertheless. Immediately, the British brought the case to the European Court of Justice, arguing that the Commission had misused the Single European Act and that the Directive had no sound legal base. But the British lost the case as the Court ruled in favour of the Commission.

Perhaps the most significant new EU employment law passed in the 1990s has been the European Works Councils Directive. For nearly three decades, the Commission had attempted, without success, to get a

Directive enacted in the broad area of information and consultation rights for workers. Thus, the adoption of this new law represented something of a breakthrough, but it was only accomplished by the Commission using the qualified majority voting procedure set down in the Social Protocol. Given its distinctly transnational character, some regard the Directive as the first building block to a pan-European industrial relations area. However, in a hard-hitting analysis, Streeck (1997a) suggests that the information rights in the Directive fall short of those already enjoyed by workers in many member-states.

For example, he points out that the law contains none of the co-determination rights that exist in many of the member-states and which oblige management to consult with workers before enacting a particular corporate plan. Thus, the Directive is not regarded as an effective institutional constraint on how management organises the information structure of the enterprise. A further criticism is that the law is not genuinely European as it applies only to a small group of firms, causing the relationship between the national and European levels with regard to information and consultation to be fragmentary and uneven. Overall, Streeck concludes that the works councils are pretty weak bodies that will not act as a countervailing force to managerial decision-making. He concludes that it is premature to regard the Directive as representing a radical departure in European employment systems.

For the most part, it is doubtful whether any of the Directives passed since 1990 represent substantial or far-reaching social legislation; the Social Protocol is not metamorphosing into an EU Social Constitution. The Commission appears to have opted for relatively modest labour law proposals rather than the promotion of genuinely supranational initiatives. Some of the Directives are aimed mainly at bringing existing national labour law regimes more closely together, not through harmonisation but through approximation. Other Directives, such as the European Works Councils law, are designed to provide a modicum of legal support to national legal regimes in an era of deeper economic and political interdependence in Europe. But EU laws of this type are not heavy regulations that impose tight constraints or obligations on national employment systems. Few of the Directives require root-and-branch change, although most require the introduction of modest reforms. Sciarra (1995) has got it about right when she suggests that the EU has resigned itself to passing 'minimal labour law' backed up by the increasing use of soft laws.

Snyder (1994: 63) describes soft laws as 'rules of conduct which, in principle, have no legally binding force but which nevertheless may have practical effects'. More specifically, soft laws relate to the use of Recommendations and Opinions – forms of EU decisions which morally commit governments to a particular policy or action without imposing legal obligations – in relation to social policy. Two recent examples of the use of these instruments are the 1991 Recommendation and Code of Practice on Sexual Harassment and the 1993 Opinion on the Equitable Wage. Soft laws also cover other non-legal initiatives of the Commission in the labour market field. For example, the Commission is increasingly promoting action programmes on a wide range of employment topics – equal opportunities, disability, poverty, social security, training and so on. These programmes are designed to encourage greater synchronisation and coordination of labour market policies across the member-states.

The preference for minimal and soft labour law has delivered a body blow to those who favour a European Social Constitution that would set out a raft of supranational employment rights. Under a social constitution, national labour market regulation would be subservient to EU employment law, and as a result individuals and interest groups would be more likely either to challenge aspects of domestic labour law or to call into question the specific employment practices of individual companies. Inevitably, this would lead to the European Court of Justice playing a central role in EU social policy, since it would not only decide whether or not a social right had been breached, but also, through its rulings, give operational meaning to particular clauses of a constitution.

Thus, to a large extent, the effectiveness of a social constitution would be tied to the operation of the Court of Justice and its willingness to oversee the creation of an effective pan-European plinth of employment rights. But there are signs that the Court is adopting a more cautious approach in social policy cases. For example, in the *Kalanke* judgement, the Court of Justice ruled that the regulation operated by the City of Bremen in Germany which gave preferential treatment to women in certain cases was illegal. The Court concluded that the principle of preferential treatment conflicted with the 1976 Council Directive of equal treatment of men and women in the workplace. Although the Court did not set out the arguments behind its decision, it has been widely interpreted as a setback to equal opportunity campaigners, who see affirmative action as the only way to redress the labour market imbalance between men and women. It has also been interpreted as an indication that the Court is retreating from the legal or judicial activism of the 1980s. As a result, it can no longer be assumed that the Court of Justice will act to strengthen EU social policy interventions, thereby deflating the notion that some type of constitutional arrangement would be good news for employment regulation.

It can be convincingly argued that the Commission too is becoming more equivocal on the merits of heavy labour market interventions. In the 1993 White Paper, *Growth, Competitiveness, Employment*, the Commission argued that the EU needed to pursue a three-pronged labour market strategy. First, better education and training provision to reduce the problem of youth unemployment, to meet the demands of the new technologies and to increase the adaptability of the employment system. Second, lower social charges on labour to encourage enterprises to recruit new employees. The White Paper estimated that about 35 to 40 per cent of total labour costs in the European economy consist of non-wage commitments such as employer social security contributions. Third, although the White Paper rejected the British model of 'labour market deregulation', it called for a 'remodelled and simplified national systems of regulation and incentives' for employment (European Commission 1993: 14). One legitimate interpretation of this argument is that the Commission is shying away from making any new full-blooded commitments on labour market regulation.

Certainly the medium-term social action programme for 1995–7 gave credibility to this interpretation, for it stated that the Commission would not be bringing forward any fresh labour law proposals. Instead, the emphasis would be on tidying up EU employment legislation and bringing to completion those proposals already inside the decision-making system. Moreover, the programme stated that in the future more time would be spent encouraging dialogue, debate and research on the role of EU social policy. The Commission said it was particularly interested in encouraging new thinking about solving Europe's unemployment problem (see Chapter 5). The reaction to this action programme was interesting. On the one hand, UNICE, the European employers' organisation, and long-time critic of Commission social policy initiatives, gave the document a warm welcome. On the other hand, the reaction of ETUC, the European Trade Union Confederation, was somewhat muted, and it declared that it would campaign to have the programme toughened up. There can be no doubt that the programme was a big disappointment to supporters of a full-fledged social Europe.

This shift towards minimal labour law and a greater emphasis on the reduction of European unemployment was embodied in the Amsterdam Treaty. Four changes occurred to the EU social policy regime. One was the inclusion of a new employment chapter in the EU's legal base. For the most part, the clauses in this chapter commit the member-states to trying to secure high employment and to coordinating efforts to reduce joblessness. A second change was a new clause on non-discrimination. In light of the multi-racial character of many member-states, it has long been seen as an anomaly that the EU was legally silent on combating discrimination outside the sphere of sexual equality between men and women. The new clause goes some way to rectifying this shortcoming without creating a strong Europe-wide regulatory regime on the matter. The third change is the incorporation of the provisions of the Social Protocol into the main body of the Treaty. The only significance of this revision is that the UK once again becomes a fully paid up member to the EU social policy regime. A fourth change is the incorporation of the European Convention of Human Rights into the legal base of the EU. An optimistic view is that this represents the first steps towards a social constitution. An alternative, more sober, view is that this move amounts to little, since most of the member-states are already signatories of the Convention. Overall, the Amsterdam Treaty leaves the soft social policy regime intact.

The evolution of the European social dialogue

Alongside the development of EU employment legislation, the Commission has attempted to build an EU-level dialogue between trade unions and employers. In the 1960s and 1970s, a number of joint sector committees involving the social partners were established in Brussels, mostly in the areas of agriculture and transport. These bodies were given a fairly open-ended remit, although the unspoken hope was for them to evolve into some type of European collective bargaining institutions. In the absence of a transparent mandate, most of these bodies busied themselves writing reports on their industries and occasionally giving expert advice to the Commission. However, virtually no progress was made towards concluding European collective agreements which would have laid down EU-wide rules on working conditions and practices. Only the agricultural sector committee managed to conclude an agreement, but this was relatively innocuous since it only codified existing national arrangements. In addition to the sector committees, the Commission also set up a Standing Committee on Employment and a Tripartite Committee. These two bodies were to encourage an exchange of views between employers and trade unions on economic and social matters with a view to reaching common positions on what the EU should do to promote employment, growth and equity. But, once again, actual deliberations fell short of initial expectations.

This unimpressive record gave rise to an essentially liberal intergovernmentalist explanation of the relative failure of the early social dialogue experiments. Stripped of much of its wherewithal, liberal intergovernmentalism suggests that it is the preferences and behaviour of political parties, interest groups and others at the national level that have a decisive influence on the direction and scope of EU actions. From this perspective, a European social dialogue remained stillborn because national trade unions and employers were unenthusiastic. With only a lukewarm commitment from the national social partners, the institutional structure necessary to house the social dialogue failed to emerge in Brussels. For example, ETUC and UNICE, the main organisations representing trade unions and employers respectively at the EU level, were not given authority to enter into collective agreements. Moreover, both organisations were put on a tight rein by national affiliates to prevent them from developing into strong, independent bodies. In the language of the corporatist literature, they were not peak associations and had neither the capacity nor the mandate to enter into collective negotiations.

A further problem was that the various committees set up never really developed the characteristics of a policy community. According to Wright (1989) well-functioning policy communities have two main features: (1) policy norms which shape and guide the outlook and actions of the participants; and (2) behavioural norms which establish the code of conduct and the pattern of personnel interactions. Together these two features create the institutional and normative structures for a policy community. But these remained stunted with regard to the European social dialogue: no transparent, widely agreed policy and behavioural norms emerged. When the sector committees were established in the late 1960s, for instance, each side of industry was highly suspicious of how the other would attempt to use the bodies. As a result, the behavioural traits of successful policy communities – trust and cooperation – did not emerge.

Yet a further drawback was that the EU's political system made the creation of an ordered institutional framework for a social dialogue that much more difficult. The French are fond of saying that the EU is *un object politique non-identifié*. Being neither a fully-fledged federation nor a narrow intergovernmentalist body such as the United Nations, the EU defies established political categories. Because of its hybrid character it does not have the authority to create a neat functional distribution of competencies inside the EU on labour market matters. Nor does it have the capacity to confer a representational monopoly on certain interest associations to help manage particular policy areas. In Streeck and Schmitter's (1991) terms, it cannot build and maintain associative orders whereby the representatives of capital and labour are given public status, and placed at the centre of democratic decision-making. In other words, corporatist arrangements that were the hallmark of many European countries in the 1970s and 1980s cannot be replicated at the EU level. The EU simply lacks the political and institutional conditions to put such a system of governance in place.

Those who hope that a European social dialogue would be a conduit for the building of corporatist structures in Brussels do not give due weight to this point. Contrasting institutional configurations exist at the national and European levels and these effectively rule out the transfer of political arrangements from one to the other. Consider the character of interest group representation at the European level. Although the EU has not enough authority to sustain corporatist structures, it has, nevertheless, more decision-making capacity than most run-of-the-mill international organisations. It has the potential to regulate business activity, write the competitive rules for particular markets, manage industrial adaptation, and allocate public money. This ability to formulate and implement economic rules has encouraged the formation of highly specialised and functional employer groups, which Traxler and Schmitter (1995) call business associations. Streeck and Schmitter (1991) estimated that more than 400 business organisations operate in Brussels. Some of these bodies are purely lobbying organisations, pressuring the EU decision-making institutions to adopt particular policies. Others have a more technical function, feeding expert advice into the Brussels bureaucracy. Overall the structure of interest group representation is fragmented: Streeck and Schmitter (1991) call it transnational pluralism. In this system, business group activity is product market-related rather than labour market-focused, which makes it difficult to generate a generalised identity inside the political system. With the EU centre unable to order and codify the different groups, important legitimation and cohesion structures that exist inside most of the member-states to support corporatist structures are absent at the European level.

The social dialogue after 1985

Although the near consensus in the academic literature was that efforts to enact a full-fledged social dialogue in Brussels would prove fruitless, those at the heart of the EU decision-making process kept faith with the concept. When Delors became President of the Commission in 1985 he regarded a dialogue between the social partners as a possible way of resolving the impasse on EU social policy. His calculation was that if the Commission transferred the initiating role for EU employment measures to the social partners, the British government might become less hostile to European-level labour market initiatives. Thus despite a lacklustre track record, Delors was prepared to hand over the policy initiating role on employment matters to the social partners; agreements between employer and trade union representatives in Brussels would become the basis of EU social policy.

To a large extent, the strengthening of the social dialogue process in the Single European Act can be attributed to Delors' strong support for the concept. Giving employer–union exchanges a stronger legal base was an attempt to give added legitimacy to the renewed social dialogue that had got underway under the title of the Val Duchesse talks. But before these talks commenced there was nothing to suggest that trade unions and employers were treating the initiative as a new beginning. For example, to get the two sides round the table, the Commission had to provide UNICE, the employers' organisation, with a commitment not to use any agreements that might be reached as the basis for new EU social legislation. This concession effectively scuppered the Delors' plan of turning the social partners into policy initiators. Thus, although the social dialogue had been given a firmer legal base, it was in practice still bedevilled by many of the pre-existing shortcomings. In the end, a number of Joint Opinions emerged from the Val Duchesse talks, but none had any significant impact on either EU social policy or national collective bargaining.

Perhaps the most positive feature of the Val Duchesse talks was the reactivation of the various EU tripartite bodies, particularly the sector committees, that had been set up in the 1960s to promote an exchange between the social partners. Many of these bodies had either fallen into abeyance or were functioning in name only. In a relatively short period of time, about eight sector committees had been reconvened and were giving advice to the Commission as well as writing reports about their industries. When the Val Duchesse discussions came to an end in 1989, the Social Affairs Commissioner, Vassa Papandreou, moved quickly to keep the social dialogue alive by sponsoring two new working parties, one covering education and training and the other prospects for the European labour market. Six Joint Opinions emerged from these two working groups, although none were particularly influential. Nevertheless, the increasing ability to reach agreements of sorts was a good sign for the future.

With trust relations between the trade unions and employers steadily improving, the member-states used the writing of the Maastricht Treaty to create a new institutional framework for a European social dialogue (Bercusson 1993). In particular, the Treaty set out new procedures for the dialogue and gave it greater status. First of all, the new arrangements oblige the Commission to consult the social partners when preparing a social policy proposal. If the trade unions and employers so choose, they can conclude a European collective agreement on the subject, thereby making the Commission proposal redundant. Member-states are required to implement the agreement either through the legal process or by a collective bargaining mechanism. A time frame of nine months was set down for the social partners to decide whether or not they wanted to use the procedure. Should they opt not to make an agreement, they would nevertheless still be able to convey their views to the Commission. Another change formalised the right of management and labour to make agreements that could then be turned into EU social legislation. All in all, the Treaty made the social dialogue part and parcel of the EU legislative process, even though a number of ambiguities exist about its exact role (Bercusson 1992)

Despite the new *de jure* situation, uncertainties continued about whether the result would be a more purposeful social dialogue. At the end of 1993, UNICE signalled that it was prepared to enter negotiations with a view to concluding a collective agreement on the vexed question of European Works Councils. After difficult negotiations it appeared that an agreement on the matter was all but concluded. However at the last moment, the Confederation of British Industry (CBI) got cold feet and stated that it was unwilling to be party to the agreement. With such a powerful dissident in its ranks, UNICE had no alternative but to walk away from the negotiations. Once again the organisational shortcomings of the social partners in Brussels had prevented the conclusion of a collective agreement. The Maastricht changes to the social dialogue had got off to an inauspicious start.

But significant improvements have been made since then. In particular, at the end of 1995, after a year of negotiations, the social partners concluded a collective agreement on Parental Leave. The main clauses of the agreement are that: (1) both male and female workers should be given the right to unpaid leave of at least three months to take care of a child up to the age of 8; (2) workers are also entitled to time off work for urgent family reasons; and (3) member-states are obliged to enact measures that protect workers who apply for or take such leave. In January 1996 the Commission adopted a draft Directive based on the agreement and the member-states subsequently ratified it at the European Council in June of that year. Some reservations can be expressed about the Directive. For example, the important question of income during leave is not addressed by the legislation. Moreover, the law does not lay down penalties if the Directive is not properly implemented by the member-states; this responsibility is delegated to the member-states. Questions can be also raised about the effectiveness of the negotiations between the social partners on the matter. The agreement that emerged after a year's dialogue closely resembled the text first sent to them by the Commission.

Nevertheless, the agreement must be considered a landmark not simply because it was the first time that the Maastricht social dialogue procedure was successfully used but also because it represents the first substantial agreement to emerge from the social partners at the European level. The trade union and employer organisations moved on and concluded another agreement on the contentious matter of flexibility and the organisation of working time. Overall the contents of this agreement are not far-reaching, but important concessions were made on both sides during the negotiations, which suggests that the social dialogue is entering a qualitatively new phase. Another sign of a warmer climate for social dialogue is that both ETUC and UNICE have been modernising their internal structures. For instance, in 1991 ETUC introduced a limited form of qualified majority voting to improve its decision-making capacity. Other administrative changes were made in 1995 to address a number of coordination failures inside the organisation. Although UNICE is moving at a slower pace, it too is embarking upon internal change to enhance its effectiveness. Thus, the prospects for a European social dialogue look as bright as they have ever been.

Although it is still early days, the Maastricht Treaty appears to have released institutional and legal incentives for a more ordered social dialogue. At the same time, Falkner's (1996) assessment that the Treaty 'has encouraged developments towards "Euro-corporatism"' is perhaps too sanguine. Many of the barriers towards corporatist decision-making remain intact. Trade unions and employers' associations at the European level can hardly be described as all-encompassing institutions and the EU centre still does not have the capacity to allocate resources in the labour market authoritatively. Such is the gap between theory and practice that it is even questionable whether corporatist literature should be used at all to explain European social dialogue in Brussels. Relations between employers and unions in Brussels are better interpreted as part of the ongoing search for legitimacy on the part of the EU centre. Practically since its establishment in 1957, the EU has striven to shake off the tag of being a remote and distant bureaucracy. The Maastricht social dialogue clauses are perhaps best seen as part of a continuing effort by the EU centre to show a human face. In other words, the social dialogue is more about serving the needs of the institutional dynamics of European integration than creating a new governance structure for the European labour market.

Thus, the new social dialogue begun by Maastricht is an attempt to obtain a more coherent and smooth functioning EU decision-making system in the social policy sphere. Connecting the social dialogue with the EU's legislative process is an attempt to upgrade the status of exchanges between trade unions and employers. Furthermore, the new arrangements oblige the EU centre to address important issues, which it has either overlooked or sidestepped. For example, for the first time the Commission has to set out criteria for the selection of those organisations that are eligible to be part of its consultative exercise when devising EU legislative proposals. The innovations are an attempt to turn the social dialogue into a more effective policy community, thereby improving EU decision-making.

By operating more effectively, the social dialogue may make a positive contribution to shaping the character of European polity. Bercusson (1992) argues that the new social dialogue can be used to enact EU-wide fundamental social and economic rights, and should be seen as an important institutional component of a European social constitution. This maximalist interpretation is over-optimistic since it can be persuasively argued that a number of legal hurdles stand in the way of European collective agreements being transformed into fundamental rights. Kenner (1995) points out, for example, that adopting agreements arising from the EU social dialogue as Council Decisions may not be sufficient to allow them to gain the status of primary legislation. He goes on to argue that the new social dialogue procedure is consistent with the 'soft law' model of EU social policy. From this standpoint, discussions between European trade unions and employer organisations would be designed to lay down general principles or norms for European industrial relations rather than enforceable social rights. Thus EU-level deliberations will, for the most part, only complement existing national collective bargaining structures. This is probably what Lord Wedderburn (1990) had in mind when he suggested that the EU social dialogue should conclude framework agreements to act as 'signposts' for national action by trade unions and employers.

The future of EU social policy

Discussion about EU social policy tends to be fairly polarised between those who argue it places additional burdens on business, thereby causing higher unemployment and reduced competitiveness, and those who claim it is necessary to promote equity in the European labour market. Common to both positions is the belief that EU employment measures represent a body of policies that has a meaningful impact on national industrial relations systems. Overall, the analysis presented here goes against this view. For the most part, it has been argued that neither EU labour laws nor the European social dialogue impact decisively on the governance of national labour markets. This assessment is in line with the consensus in the academic labour law literature which suggests that, taken as a whole, EU social legislation falls short of a body of supranational employment rules. It also coincides with the results of a large-scale survey of human resource managers in Europe, by Cranfield School of Management and Price Waterhouse, which found that the vast majority are untroubled by EU employment directives (Teague 1994). Thus, the role of EU social policy is not as great as is sometimes suggested by the big political controversy on the matter.

This is not to completely write off the importance of EU social policy, but simply to point out that the political and economic configuration of the EU does not lend itself to the enactment of a large body of supranational labour market regulation. At the same time, by adopting social measures, the EU has the potential to interact positively with the member-states on employment matters. By promoting a social dialogue, for example, the EU centre can send a strong signal that employment policy should be underpinned by social consensus. In other words, standing once-removed from direct labour market governance, the EU is well placed to encourage new thinking about the employment relationship. The argument of this chapter is that the EU centre has sought to perform such a role: it supports neither a maximalist nor a minimalist EU social policy, but some type of hybrid arrangement that allows for a degree of national autonomy within a generalised European social regime. The objective is to establish a symbiosis between EU labour market measures and national industrial relations systems.

A symbiotic EU social policy would influence national industrial relations systems in three main ways. One would be through approximation measures that encourage the member-states to pursue broadly similar employment policies within their own particular national institutional structures. The goal is to establish a degree of policy uniformity in the context of institutional diversity. Another would be by policies aimed at reducing spillovers that arise from the integration process. Certain political and economic interactions between the member-states may produce tensions which EU intervention might be required to resolve. For example, EU measures may be necessary to reduce the potential conflict between the principle of the free movement of labour and national employment rules which reduce mobility. Most initiatives in this category are fairly benign, but some proposals to reduce 'negative spillovers' are likely to be contentious. The third way would be through what might be termed orientation agreements (Wedderburn 1990). The thinking here, as set out earlier, is that since the EU is removed from the day-to-day pressures of ground-level employee relations or employment policy formation, it may be better placed to promote strategic discussions about the future character of the European social model.

'Obscuration' effect

For some time now the Commission has been attempting to enact a symbiotic social policy. But this strategy has not been fully successful since EU employment policies are not meshing properly with national labour market systems. An important reason for this is the haphazard and untidy relationship between the EU and the member-states on employment matters. The result has been the obscuration of EU social policy. A number of factors account for this obscuration effect. First of all, the essentially intergovernmentalist decision-making process of the EU makes it difficult to develop coherent labour market policies. In the absence of supranational decision-making, EU policies normally take the form of package deals between the member-states, so that an initiative is not vetoed by a recalcitrant member-state (Wallace 1990). Thus EU social policies are likely to be hard-wrought compromises between competing positions held by the member-states, which is hardly propitious for the development of coherent labour market measures.

Second, the legal system of the EU contributes to the shortcomings of EU social policy. Most EU social legislation takes the form of Directives so that the member-states can introduce an EU law in a manner that accords with their own legal custom and practice. In many instances, this procedure has failed to ensure that the contents of Directives are incorporated within national law either correctly or comprehensively. Evidence suggests that some member-states use control over the ports of entry through which EU law is implemented domestically to change or distort the contents of Directives. A further problem is that uncertainties exist about whether or not Directives have, in Euro-legal jargon, 'direct applicability' – the extent to which they can be seen as primary legislation of the EU. These fault-lines have served to reduce the impact of EU labour legislation on national industrial relations systems.

A third obstacle is that the support structures for a symbiotic EU social policy are underdeveloped. Institutional linkages between the EU and the member-states are not properly organised, making collaborative efforts between the two levels difficult. Many of the member-states have not got the labour market institutions that could maximise the impact of EU employment laws. For example, the UK is one of the few member-states that has an independent equal opportunities body which ensures the effective enforcement of European equality legislation. Thus, a series of institutional weaknesses stand in the way of the enactment of a symbiotic EU social policy. As a result, the EU presence in the European labour market is fragmented and disjointed. In the areas of equal opportunities and health and safety legislation, EU labour legislation has a direct influence on national industrial relations systems, even if it has not reached its maximum potential. In other spheres, EU measures merely parallel national labour market provision and it is hard to decipher how one level relates to the other. Yet another group of EU social policies, particularly those relating to training and employment, are really best described as symbolic, since these have not yet had any real impact on national arrangements. Thus, although there is a symbiotic intent behind EU labour market policy, the effect is one of obscuration.

Conclusions

Perhaps, the strongest conclusion of this chapter is that EU employment policy is not travelling down a route that will eventually lead to a social constitution. Those who hold this position over-stress the significance of EU labour laws and the Brussels-based social dialogue. Much of EU social legislation cannot be regarded as supranational nor can the exchanges between trade unions and employers be seen as important with regard to the organisation of the European labour market. Moreover, the proposal for a social constitution sits uneasily with the political architecture taking shape inside the EU. To be fully effective, a social constitution requires the EU to be a federal political arrangement. In a federal Europe, a sharper delineation of competencies would probably emerge between different tiers of government on social policy matters. In addition, a more transparent legal order would presumably develop, leaving behind the opaque and entangled judicial relationships that currently exist between the national and European levels with regard to employment legislation. But the political and legal structures of the EU are a far cry from such a federal configuration. Nor does there appear to be any big enthusiasm amongst the member-states to move towards federalism. If anything, the trend is in the other direction. Attached to the Amsterdam Treaty, for example, is a document that connects subsidiarity to EU decision-making. This document can only be described as a code to prevent the EU centre from gaining further political authority. Thus, the social constitution project is out of step with the current dynamics of political and economic integration in Europe, and as a result cannot be regarded as credible.

This assessment touches upon an argument that has recently gained prominence. According to Streeck (1995), it is moonshine to talk about EU social policy evolving into some form of supranational arrangement with strong regulatory powers. For him, EU labour market measures add up to a weak and fragmented policy regime that reflects a deep reluctance on the part of the member-states to engage in meaningful institution building at the European level. At the same time, he argues, they have been prepared to act cooperatively to launch market-deepening initiatives. As a result, a big mismatch has been created between a thin Europe-wide institutional structure and far-reaching market interdependence between the member-states. EU social policy is seen as one manifestation of this incongruity: laws or policies are adopted for particular labour market areas, but invariably these are not strong enough to act as a countervailing force to the hypertrophy of market and commercial activity inside the European market. Believing that the European market can be effectively governed without massive institution building at the EU centre is dismissed as neo-voluntarism; that is, the idea that employers will adopt worker-friendly employment practices of their own volition. In short, Streeck regards EU social policy as not worth a penny candle.

Parts of the Streeck analysis have validity. His scepticism about a social constitution, or some similar type of supranational arrangement, being established at the EU level is in line with the analysis presented here. Moreover, his diagnosis that an imbalance has opened up between European markets and institutions is persuasive and is a point that is further developed in the next chapter. But there are also parts of the Streeck argument that can be disputed. First of all, his blanket dismissal of EU social policy is much too sweeping. Various EU labour laws, particularly in the areas of equal opportunities, health and safety and the transfer of undertaking, have had an important impact on national employment systems, which cannot be regarded as negligible. Second, his characterisation of the asymmetry between markets and institutions inside the EU is faulty. Though he views this asymmetry as the failure of institution building, it can also be regarded as a macro-economic problem. For example, many of the constraints that have been placed on national welfare systems could be eased if a proper form of monetary union were established by the member-states,something which does not require large scale institution building in the social field.

In many ways, Streeck is overly binary in his approach to European integration: if the member-states do not create structures that embed welfare capitalism on a Europe-wide basis, then the result will be neo-liberalism. In this binary world, the EU faces the stark choice of becoming either like the USA or a greater Germany. Thus the misinterpretation of what is called in the next chapter the 'coordination deficit' leads Streeck into a political dead-end: while the Americanisation of European economic life is not particularly desirable, the construction of a greater Germany is not feasible. The analysis of this chapter takes us down a different route. Throughout, it has been argued that the EU defies established political categories and that it falls halfway between an intergovernmental and supranational entity. For years, the Commission has been attempting unsuccessfully to establish an ordered relationship between the member-states and the EU centre on social policy measures. A number of institutional and policy failures are the cause of the lack of symbiosis between the two levels, and these could be corrected by a range of reforms. The task is to be neither overly sceptical nor overly ambitious, but to pursue an agenda that will allow for a more organised framework for EU social policy-making. For the most part, the reforms that are envisaged, for example new national bodies that would make more effective use of existing EU employment laws, do not involve excessive centralisation of social policy. Rather, national employment systems remain the institutional fulcrum of the European labour market. But there can be no hiding the fact that the efficacy of a symbiotic social policy will depend a great deal on the EU closing the coordination deficit that has opened up between the member-states. This is a matter addressed directly in the next chapter.

7 Monetary union and Social Europe

Introduction

European monetary union is imminent. Few other economic integration initiatives will have a more decisive impact on the economic and social governance structures of the member-states. Because monetary union is indivisible, the creation of a Euro-zone will involve a huge transfer of power from the national to the EU level. If such a shift takes place, one of the most potent signs of national economic sovereignty will have been punctured. Without French francs, Dutch guilders or Italian lira, it will be made clear to everyone that national governments have given up managing a large part of their own macro-economic affairs. Thus the creation of a single currency involves the EU crossing an economic and political Rubicon. The exact fallout of this constitutional and financial journey remains uncertain, but few aspects of economic policy-making will be left untouched. One area that is likely to be deeply affected is Social Europe.

Perhaps the most common position is that monetary union will impact negatively on Social Europe. For the most part, the cutbacks in welfare budgets across the EU, made so that the member-states can meet the Maastricht criteria for single currency membership, are the basis for this view. Although valid, this is only a partial account of the relationship between monetary union and Social Europe. A more comprehensive assessment is required to get a fuller picture of the social implications of a Euro-zone. This chapter attempts to provide such an assessment. It makes three key arguments. First, the road to monetary union set out in the Maastricht Treaty represents a big threat to European social systems. Second, in the absence of the monetary union agenda, prospects for Social Europe are not particularly bright, as the mismatch between deep market integration and 'thin' EU institutional structures is destabilising labour markets across the member-states. Third, closing the coordination deficit that has been created between markets and institutions inside the EU would go a long way towards putting Social Europe on a firmer footing, but this may require the Maastricht monetary union agenda to be complemented by more interventionist policies.

This chapter is organised as follows. The first section outlines the social consequences of national efforts to reach the Maastricht criteria. Then the likelihood of a deflationary macro-economic environment emerging in a new Euro-zone is assessed by examining the credibility of the Stability Pact signed at the 1996 Dublin European Summit. The following section shows that it is not simply the monetary union agenda that is placing constraints on national welfare systems and that the cold macro-economic climate for Social Europe has existed for some time. Next, it is emphasised that the problems faced by European social systems are accentuated by the coordination deficit that has emerged inside the EU. The following section explains how this coordination deficit not only limits autonomous national action on social matters, but also reduces the possibilities of creating a stable European monetary system that is a precondition for the European social dimension. The final section analyses the viability of various reform paths. The conclusions bring together the arguments of the chapter.

Adjusting to the Maastricht criteria: the social implications

The squeeze on public expenditure

During the 1990s, meeting the Maastricht criteria for entry into a European monetary union (EMU) has been the top economic priority of virtually every member-state in the EU. These criteria set down testing macro-economic targets for individual countries to reach before they can qualify for the single currency club. In expert economic circles, the consensus has been that little rationale exists for the Maastricht rules: there is no technical reason to believe that a monetary union established without the conditions being met would be any less robust or credible (Buiter *et al.* 1993). Another more focused criticism has been that the criteria relate only to nominal economic variables and not to real ones such as employment and output. This has led to concern about the ground-level economic foundations of a monetary union in Europe (Arrowsmith and Taylor 1996). These pretty far-reaching reservations have counted for little in policy terms. An almighty scramble broke out amongst the member-states to rein in government deficits and to keep inflation and interest rates low so that they would not be excluded from a monetary union.

Yet realising the Maastricht criteria has proved far from pain-free

(Bovenberg and De Jong 1997). Some member-states such as the Republic of Ireland and the Netherlands have found meeting the monetary and fiscal qualifiers for a monetary union easier than others – mainly due to pursuing tight macro-economic policies over a relatively long period. Consider Ireland, hardly an automatic candidate for division one Europe. Since the early 1980s, the Irish authorities have tied the fortunes of the punt to those of the Deutschmark. In addition, public finances have been managed extremely prudently, partly to reduce a large overhang of government debt and partly to improve the country's fiscal position in relation to monetary union membership. Invariably, those member-states that struggled to meet the Maastricht criteria did not adopt such a long-term policy stance, particularly with regard to fiscal policies. A good case in point is Belgium. In the late 1980s, the government responded to harsh economic times not with fiscal rectitude but by allowing government borrowing to increase. As a result, the country found itself some way off the Maastricht rules and meeting the criteria was an uphill battle.

Overall, securing the admission fee for monetary union involved almost all member-states enacting economic retrenchment policies. In particular, most took action to curb fiscal deficits, which usually consisted of cutting welfare and social expenditure. Some of the austerity packages were quite severe. In France, an initial 'Juppé' plan hoped to better place the country to join monetary union by cutting social security payments and other public expenditure programmes, but it had to be radically revised due to large-scale opposition. Although the recently elected socialist government introduced higher taxes on corporations and reduced expenditure on defence, it did not abandon the 'Juppé' plan altogether. This was a strong signal that membership of the single currency was as big a priority for the French socialists as it was for the previous right-wing administration.

Germany had to resort to more drastic action to meet the Maastricht rules. Its austerity programme (*Sparpaket*) was the biggest single fiscal entrenchment in economic history. Altogether, the authorities slashed public expenditure by £30 billion (70 billion DM). A large number of social programmes were cut back while unemployment benefits and other entitlements were frozen. Once again, the plan was met by strong hostility, but this opposition was not as successful as in France. Similar stories can be told about other member-states. The new right-wing government in Spain introduced welfare cuts in an attempt to reduce the government's fiscal deficit from 5.8 per cent to 4.4 per cent between 1996 and 1997. Italy faced a huge task to meet the convergence criteria by the 1999 deadline. Nevertheless, the 'olive tree' coalition government introduced a harsh budget to reduce the state deficit from 6.7 per cent of GDP to 3.6 per cent in two years.

The rise of competitive corporatism

In addition to squeezing public expenditure, many member-states, as shown in more detail in Chapter 2, attempted to reorient the functioning of labour market institutions in a way that was consistent with membership of a European monetary union. Particular emphasis was placed on promoting wage bargaining behaviour that assists the transition to a single currency and participation in the new Euro-zone. In most cases this involved using national- or sector-level pay bargaining structures to control the rate of wage increases. Moderate pay settlements for government employees ease pressure on the public finances directly. On the other hand, low wage rises in the private sector improve competitiveness by keeping in check, if not reducing, unit labour costs. The Netherlands and Ireland were the forerunners of this strategy. Since the mid- to late 1980s both these countries have operated national pay agreements designed to constrain wage rises, both in nominal and real terms, so that the economy would be better placed to live with a European single currency.

Other member-states soon began following a similar strategy. In 1996, a social pact was agreed in Belgium between the employers, trade unions and government. Its central feature was an agreement on the part of trade unions and employers more or less to shadow wage increases in the core countries of the EU, particularly France, Germany and the Netherlands. Two unions – the CSC and FGTB – are actually calling for a 'European social pact' for the new 'Euro-zone'. In Germany part of the *Sparpaket* involved imposing a pay freeze in the public sector whilst unions in the private sector accepted relatively moderate pay increases. Portugal has operated a social agreement since 1990, with the twin objectives of modernising the institutional framework of the labour market and promoting ordered wage bargaining behaviour. Preparing the country for EMU has been widely seen as the economic backdrop to these institutional changes. In Italy, national sector-based collective bargaining has been restored as part of a widespread revamping of the industrial relations system. Across industries, the social partners are approaching bargaining sessions with a view to reaching agreements that strengthen Italy's ability to live inside EMU. Greece, long regarded as the dishevelled cousin of the European industrial relations family, has been making important, even far-reaching, reforms to its collective bargaining system. Again, the looming EMU deadline has played a big part in triggering these institutional reforms.

Connecting wage bargaining to the EMU project has been an important innovation. In recent years it has been fashionable to argue that extra-firm pay determination institutions in Europe are on the wane due to the remorseless advance of economic decentralisation. Not everybody was comfortable with this argument, since these national collective bargaining structures represented the institutional articulation of social Europe (Crouch and Traxler 1995). On the surface, the renewed importance of national pay determination institutions seems to point to the continued resilience, if not vitality, of corporatist arrangements. This view appears plausible but, as pointed out in Chapter 2, it looks less convincing on closer examination. The wage pacts that have emerged recently in some countries are not the same as the classic social corporatist systems found in the Nordic countries in the 1970s and 1980s. Economic and political differences separate the two (Rhodes 1997). In economic terms, most social corporatist arrangements have an equity or redistribution function. Recent national pay agreements have had a weaker social agenda: they are more concerned with helping the member-states meet the Maastricht criteria or to improve domestic competitiveness by capturing real devaluations through reducing unit labour costs. Figure 7.1 shows how on an EU-wide basis, compensation has dipped below productivity trends. This decoupling contrasts sharply with an important aspect of the wage relationship during the golden age of economic growth – the close symmetry between pay and productivity.

In political terms, corporatism has traditionally represented the institutional embedding of a social bargain between capital and labour in *national* economic systems. But the bargain at the centre of the recent tripartite agreements is different and in many ways more profound. It is about the shape and texture of the economic and political relationships between the nation-state and the EU centre under a monetary union in Europe. Even though the recent social pacts offer little to organised labour other than narrow pay increases or a better 'social wage' – enhanced expenditure on health and education for example – many trade unions nevertheless strongly defend them. This is so because they are seen as the best strategy for ensuring that trade unions remain important economic and political institutions in a single currency Europe. Thus, far from signalling the vibrancy of corporatism in Europe, the new social pacts ironically highlight the weakness of this model of economic and political organisation. They are better regarded as a defensive, even survival, strategy to ensure that trade unions continue to play a role in the new Euro-zone.

Thus, member-states responded to the Maastricht criteria in two ways. One was the introduction of public expenditure cutbacks that in some instances almost amounted to emergency macro-economic stabilisation programmes. Fiscal retrenchment of this sort can have a damaging impact on welfare systems. On the one hand, it results in many social programmes experiencing a cash crisis. On the other hand, it obliges governments to

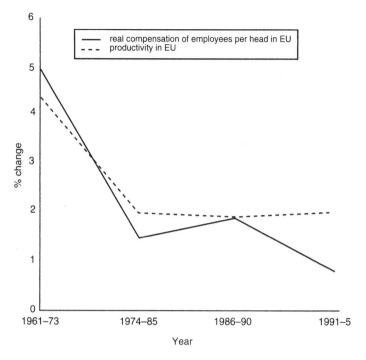

Figure 7.1 Percentage change in real compensation and productivity per head in the EU (averages for four periods, 1961–95)

make hasty, ill-considered and ill-prepared reforms to social security and welfare arrangements. In some member-states, such as France, the result has been mass unrest, but in others, where opposition has been more muted, the legacy may be new distortions in social policy regimes. The other response has been to reorient the behaviour of labour market institutions to the prospect of EMU so that wage bargaining systems are connected to the drive towards a single currency. Far from reinvigorating old-style corporatist institutions, the new social pacts are a sign of the fragility of these arrangements. To a large extent, they reflect efforts on the part of organised labour to secure a place in the new single currency area. Overall, the run-up to monetary union has imposed new constraints on Social Europe.

Nevertheless, this twin-pronged macro-economic strategy gave a green light to eleven of the member-states to join a monetary union. Denmark and the UK decided to opt out while Sweden and Greece were not considered ready for single currency membership. The decision to allow eleven to go ahead was mainly based on a Commission assessment of their success in meeting the Maastricht criteria. This 'convergence' report showed that most of the member-states have made enormous attempts to strip fit for monetary union. Inflation rates everywhere are low, averaging at 2.7 per cent, and are considered to be sustainable. Major improvements have been made to government deficits, with only one country registering a deficit above the 3 per cent benchmark. On the other hand, only four member-states – France, Luxembourg, Finland and the UK – recorded a government debt level below the Treaty reference value of 60 per cent. But for one reason or another, this benchmark has been overlooked and most member-states have been given the benefit of the doubt on this matter. Credibility with the financial markets has been deemed robust, as most of the member-states enjoyed exchange rate stability as well as gradual interest rate convergence over the previous two years. Thus, the Commission concluded that most member-states were ready for EMU. With most countries also willing, it is now certain that a new Euro-zone will be established inside the EU by 2002.

The stability pact and Social Europe

But one matter that is not fully settled is the form of the new Euro-zone. Whether macro-economic austerity will persist inside the single currency area or whether member-states will enjoy greater fiscal freedom is a particularly contentious matter. One argument sometimes put forward is that the fiscal straightjacket imposed by the Maastricht criteria is only temporary and that once monetary union is actually established it will be removed. From this point of view, the negative impact of the single currency project on the European social model is only short term (Allsopp and Vines 1996). For the most part, this view is based on the belief that monetary and fiscal regimes do not have to go hand in hand in a particular currency area. In other words, EMU can be established without developing Europe-wide rules on tax and public expenditure. Mini currency unions that have operated in Europe during the past century, particularly the UK/Ireland currency union and the Benelux economic union, are usually invoked to sustain this argument (De Grauwe 1996a). In each case, the monetary union placed few constraints on the operation of fiscal policy. As a result, quite contrasting public finance regimes co-existed in the one currency area. In the Benelux economic union – that still prevails – Luxembourg meets the Maastricht criteria whilst Belgium is amongst the worst performers. One implication of this line of argument is that monetary union in Europe could well remove some of the financial constraints that many member-states currently experience when operating macro-economic policy, thereby easing the fiscal pressures on Social Europe.

This 'loose' interpretation of fiscal policy in a monetary union looks somewhat suspect when we consider the Stability and Growth Pact that was signed at the 1996 Dublin Summit. Pushed through by Germany in the face of reservations from other member-states, the pact is designed to secure fiscal prudence in a future Euro-zone by levying automatic penalties against members running excessive deficits. In particular, the pact sets down that governments with budget deficits greater than 3 per cent of GDP will be immediately fined. A number of exceptions to this rule were established, but it is questionable whether these amount to much. Members will be exempt from an automatic fine should they run an excessive deficit due to their encountering a natural disaster or if they experience a fall in GDP in excess of 2 per cent in one year. Additionally, where national GDP has fallen between 0.75 per cent and 2 per cent, EU finance ministers will have some discretion on whether or not to impose penalties. Some of these 'let-out' clauses do not add up to much in reality. For instance, the waiving of fines for members experiencing a 2 per cent drop in GDP appears to be a paper tiger since that situation very seldom occurs in Europe. As a result, the consensus view is that the pact would tie member-states to tight fiscal policies under a single currency (Goodhart 1996).

A strict enforcement of the stability pact in a monetary union could result in the operation of a pro-cyclical fiscal policy. When countries enter an economic recession, budget deficits normally increase due to the tax base shrinking and public expenditure rising to cover extra unemployment and social benefits payments. Traditionally, the convention has been for countries to run higher budget deficits in economically hard times. But the stability pact changes all this by removing any scope for fiscal flexibility. Instead, countries experiencing a recession could find themselves in the position of having to raise taxes and cut public expenditure, either to avoid breaking the fiscal rules of the new Euro-zone or to pay fines imposed upon it by EU authorities. In such circumstances, the initial economic downturn is compounded and the member-countries are plunged into an even deeper recession. Thus an unbending application of the stability pact means bad news for Social Europe, as it would place further restrictions on national welfare systems.

Yet in the 'smoke and mirrors' decision-making process of the EU, it remains uncertain whether the stability pact can be made operational in any effective way. First of all, a number of prior stages of conciliation have been established to make it less likely for a member-state to be fined. Moreover, as De Grauwe (1996b) points out, the Maastricht Treaty stipulates that fines can only be imposed on member-states by a two-thirds' majority vote in the Council of Ministers. The stability pact does not alter this requirement in any way. As a result, the imposition of fines on a country for fiscal laxity will not be a straightforward affair since financial history shows that a third or more of the member-states run budget deficits in excess of 3 per cent of GDP at any one time. Overall, the member-states have signalled their preference for a series of preventive procedures, and checks and balances to stop a member-state ever being put in the dock for breaking the fiscal rules associated with the Euro-zone. Nevertheless, the exact role of public expenditure in a Euro-zone remains, for the most part, an open question. In this context, both overly optimistic and dire predictions about government finances under a single currency appear out of place. Equally, assessments that the European social model will either flourish or flounder in a monetary union cannot be given much weight. The truth is that the Euro-zone is a step into the unknown and it would be premature to predict the exact course of macro-economic policy before the new system is actually up and running.

The macro-economic environment for Social Europe

So far our assessment is that it is too early to make a definitive judge-ment about the possible social repercussions of the new Euro-zone, but that member-states' efforts to reach the Maastricht convergence criteria have constrained welfare budgets and impinged on the institutional architecture of European labour markets. Thus the Maastricht monetary union agenda represents a tightening of the macro-economic situation behind Social Europe. But the collorary of this observation is certainly not that the macro-economic environment for European welfare and employment systems has been either lax or problem-free up until now. Perhaps the overriding concern of macro-economic policy in Europe during the past two decades has been the control of inflation. From the mid-1970s until the mid-1980s, as shown in Figure 7.2, the key objective was to get inflation rates down from two-digit figures. Having succeeded in this task, the goal from the mid-1980s has been to maintain price stability at around 2 to 4 per cent each year. Almost all member-states have participated in the crusade against inflation, producing consider-able policy convergence on macro-economic matters. For the most part, monetary instruments, particularly interest rates and exchange rates, have been used to keep a lid on prices. As a result, it is not surprising to find, as indicated in Figure 7.2, that unit labour costs have also been on a downward trend since the start of the 1980s: tight monetary policies invariably oblige firms to increase productivity and keep wages in check to remain competitive.

Restrictive monetary policies, then, have been the norm in Europe for some time and they have delivered a low inflation, relatively good, unit labour cost economic environment. At the same time, they have done little to curb government debt or expenditure. While fiscal policy in the EU can hardly be described as profligate, gross government debt, as shown in Figure 7.3, has risen sharply during the 1980s and 1990s. In 1980 gross debt on the part of governments stood at about 38 per cent of GDP but by 1997 it had increased to 72 per cent. Thus an imbalance exists in the European macro-economic environment. On one side, monetary stability has been achieved through cautious financial policy-making. On the other, most member-states have been grappling with excessive budget deficits. A key factor behind the relatively poor fiscal performance of European economies has been the enormous strain on the public coffers of high unemployment in the EU. Comprehensive safety nets have prevented this job crisis turning into a social catastrophe. But the price has been a massive increase in public expenditure. Financing social security budgets is a huge drain on government resources almost everywhere in the EU.

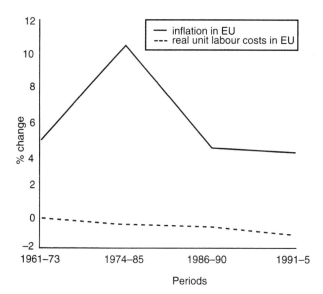

Figure 7.2 Percentage change in inflation and unit labour costs in the EU (averages for four periods, 1961–96)

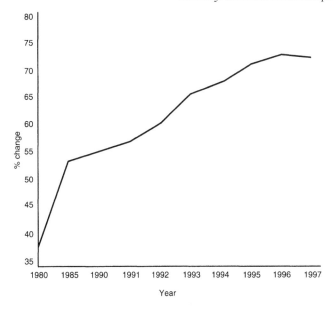

Figure 7.3 Gross government debt in EU, 1980–97

Thus welfare systems have come to play a prominent role in European economies largely as a result of massive under-performance in the European labour market. At the same time, bigger welfare systems have generated additional economic problems for many member-states, mainly in the form of large budget deficits. Social Europe has prevented the EU from hitting the unforgiving rocks of widespread poverty and inequality, but it has not been a cheap strategy. Of course other factors have been at play, such as the increased demand for health care and educational provision. But the key point is that financing social security schemes for the large numbers of unemployed people has made managing government expenditure that much more difficult.

On the horizon, other aspects of Social Europe are threatening to accentuate this budgetary problem. Consider the matter of pensions. With Europe's baby-boomers gradually getting older, the demographic structure of many member-states is changing significantly. Almost everywhere the old-age dependency rate is increasing. Invariably, this process will create extra pressure for more public expenditure, particularly in terms of pensions and health. The exact impact on government budgets remains uncertain, but the most reliable projections suggest the following scenario (Franco and Munzi 1996). Expenditure pressure from public pension schemes is likely to stay more or less under control until about 2005. Then the situation is expected to deteriorate progressively. After about 2015, when most of the baby-boomers retire, the pension burden increases sharply. By the year 2025, the ratio of pension expenditure to GDP in several member-states, notably France, Germany, Italy, Belgium and the Netherlands, is estimated to be about 15 to 20 per cent. If no ameliorative action is taken, the consequences for public budgets – and deficits – will be dramatic. Little wonder this matter is frequently dubbed the pensions time-bomb.

The key point from the above discussion is that the fiscal foundations to Social Europe are looking precarious. The Maastricht agenda for monetary union did not cause the problem, but has merely thrown it into sharp relief. In other words, even if the convergence criteria were somehow to disappear, the member-states would still face the public expenditure dilemmas of operating Social Europe. The uncomfortable truth, becoming more and more apparent, is that European welfare systems are proving exceptionally expensive to sustain. At the same time, as mentioned earlier, the Maastricht rules have hurried many member-states into making deep cuts in public expenditure. These actions have proved widely unpopular amongst European citizens, causing a conflation between the monetary union project and the problem of reducing government budget deficits. As a result, for some, the defence of Social Europe involves opposing the creation of a single currency.

But this conclusion is a big simplification of the conundrum Europe faces about the continuation of its social protectionist arrangements. On the one hand, the Maastricht convergence clauses and the 'hard' Euro-zone promoted by Germany spell bad news for Social Europe. On the other hand, prospects for the social model are not particularly bright without monetary union. In many ways, reform and modernisation of Europe's welfare capitalism would be easier in a monetary union that did not impose a straightjacket on public expenditure. But creating such a monetary regime will be exceptionally difficult in light of the current economic and institutional make-up of the EU. Resolving this dilemma is the central political economy question for the member-states.

Why monetary union is necessary

Europe's coordination deficit and the social model

Although the decision to set up a Euro-zone has been made, there remains considerable unease, if not complete opposition, to the project across the member-states. One argument frequently raised by those lodging in traditional Keynesian stables is that since the Maastricht convergence criteria involved a huge exercise in deflation, the plan for monetary union should still be resisted. Instead, the member-states should revert to national methods of economic and social management. Perhaps the biggest drawback of this argument is that it fails to take full account of the changed political and economic circumstances in Europe. After forty years of building closer economic ties between its members, the EU can be best described as a super-regional trading bloc. A defining characteristic of this bloc is the high level of market interdependence between the member-states. Decades of negative integration measures, such as the single market programme, have deepened trade interconnections in the EU. The typical member-state now sees 70 per cent of its exports going to other parts of the EU, while these in turn make up about 70 per cent of that country's imports. The hypertrophy of trade relations between the member-states has weakened Europe's external economic linkages with the rest of the world, resulting in a massive internalisation of economic activity inside the EU.

At the same time, this new European economic area is only weakly governed from the EU centre. Over the years, the institutional architecture of the EU has developed in a number of important ways. Bodies such as the European Parliament and the Committee of the Regions have been established and new policy competencies in areas such as regional and social affairs have been secured. Yet in spite of these developments, the EU remains an essentially intergovernmentalist political system: the member-states are still firmly in control of the good ship EU. Streeck (1996) argues that a persistent feature of intergovernmentalist decision-making in Brussels has been member-states coming together and acting cooperatively to implement market-oriented policies. Less frequent has been the adoption of EU policies of a more positive kind aimed at regulating and supervising the new European economy. Thus the member-states have shown little appetite for institutional building designed to create new Europe-wide forms of economic and social governance. Greater emphasis has been placed on market-making: intergovernmental decision-making has been used mainly to deepen competitive interdependence between the member-states.

Dense market connections between the member-states alongside weak policy structures in Brussels have produced a coordination deficit inside the EU. At one level this situation gives rise to market and government failures. For example, the European internal market would operate more effectively if a Europe-wide integrated transport system were in place. But as the member-states persist in planning their road and rail networks separately, this goal has proved elusive. At another level the repercussions from the coordination deficit are more far-reaching. The blurring of national market boundaries in Europe, for instance, has made traditional Keynesian demand policies a virtual non-starter. Any member-states embarking upon an autonomous reflationary programme would very quickly hit a balance of payments constraint as imports flooded in from other EU countries. In addition, market interdependence promotes competition between different national regulatory rules which puts pressure on domestic social systems.

Scharpf (1997) argues that regulatory competition has begun inside the EU. With the relative success of the 1992 liberalising programme, particularly the enactment of the mutual recognition principle, the EU is now an economic zone with few legal and administrative restrictions on the movement of capital. As a result, the 'exit' threat on the part of firms is more credible. In this situation, independent national economic action becomes less likely, since governments are reluctant to develop interventionary governance structures. The prospect of capital flight has brought about a more chastened and cautious policy elite in Europe. With financial prudence being the policy norm, the size of government comes under threat because raising taxes is virtually off the political agenda. And as the tax base gets smaller, so the scope for redistribution becomes narrower and narrower. Thus the gales of competition whipped up by the cumulative process of negative integration inside the EU have compounded the problems of maintaining national welfare regimes in Europe. Member-states are now in a highly dysfunctional position. On the one hand, the operation of national welfare systems in Europe has been squeezed by market integration. On the other hand, the EU does not have the competence or authority to compensate for this loss of national economic and social capacity by organising Europe-wide forms of collective or public action.

Being in no man's land between a collection of independent nations and a full-fledged federation reduces the scope for domestic action on the part of the member-states to rescue Social Europe. The consequences of this situation are far-reaching: in the words of Scharpf (1997: 28) 'at the national level, democratic self-determination has lost its effectiveness'. One desperate response is to argue for member-states to withdraw from the EU in an effort to reclaim national economic and social sovereignty. But such a political project does not have wide appeal and can be discarded as a non-starter. All that a member-state would achieve by following such a course would be political isolation in the context of continued deep economic interdependence with the rest of Europe. The uncomfortable reality is that Social Europe cannot be protected by national action alone.

The social model and the monetary system in Europe

Another frequently raised question is why does it take full-blown monetary union to stabilise the macro-economic situation in Europe? Why not improve monetary and exchange rate coordination without going all the way down the road and establishing a single currency? The plain answer is that the coordination deficit inside the EU makes the creation of a stable monetary system in Europe exceptionally difficult. A longstanding concern in economic integration theory has been the potentially dysfunctional effects of member-states maintaining control over their currencies in the context of deeper market interdependence. In the 1980s the EU appeared to have resolved the problem with the operation of the Exchange Rate Mechanism (ERM). The ERM appeared to be an effective tool not only for the management of currency relations between the member-states, but also for the control of domestic inflation. By the start of the 1990s, it was widely assumed that the ERM would be the launching pad for full monetary union in Europe. Yet virtually overnight the arrangement fell out of favour with the international financial system. As a result, big speculative attacks were mounted against the currencies of several member-states, which in the end effectively broke up the mechanism. Only a mild form of currency coordination between the member-states survived this episode.

Opinion differs as to why the ERM collapsed (Cobham 1994). The negative macro-economic spillovers from German reunification are certainly implicated. To finance the reunification project, Germany was obliged to increase public expenditure substantially. To counter-balance this loosening of fiscal policy, the Bundesbank tightened monetary policy by increasing interest rates. This hike in German interest rates played havoc with currency parities inside the ERM, thereby opening the door for financial speculation. While German reunification was an important conjunctural factor, Padoa-Schioppa (1994) highlights a structural tension inside the ERM that may have ultimately led to its demise. In particular, he argues that the EU was storing up trouble for itself by pursuing four conflicting economic objectives: (1) deep trade integration; (2) complete capital mobility; (3) managed (or semi-fixed) exchange rates; and (4) the continuation of national monetary regimes. This 'inconsistent quartet', as he called it, was sooner or later going to create distortions in Europe's monetary system and thus be the source of macro-economic shocks. The presence of such an 'inconsistent quartet' was nothing if not a manifestation of the coordination deficit in Europe. In other words, the virtual collapse of the ERM can in the end be traced back to the co-existence of tight-knit trade integration between the member-states alongside weak EU-level governance structures.

In the absence of a well-functioning system of exchange rate coordination, national social systems are exposed to a number of potential pressures. One is the essentially internal problem of exchange rate dumping. If exchange rates are not in any way managed in the EU, then the prospect of one or more of the member-states gaining market share from others as a result of currency depreciation increases. This problem actually arose in the wake of the ERM turmoil in 1992, particularly with regard to the lira and sterling. Consider the Italian case. After the lira was forced out of the ERM due to a huge bout of speculation, the currency depreciated, causing a sharp fall in Italy's real exchange rate and a sharp appreciation of the real exchange rates of France and Germany. Italy benefited from this situation in terms of increased exports, but the cost competitiveness of German and French industry increased virtually overnight. At the time, the EU Commissioner for the internal market warned that the lira's depreciation was giving Italian companies an unfair advantage over other European products. Moreover, he argued that the European internal market could not withstand unpredictable exchange rate fluctuations (*Financial Times*, 28 February 1995: 6).

In this case, the Italian authorities did not deliberately engineer the depreciation of the lira. Nevertheless, other member-states, particularly France, were quick to call foul. They were concerned that the lira's depreciation would jeopardise domestic jobs and place further pressure on beleaguered welfare systems. Clearly there is widespread anxiety that a single European market in which currencies move freely against one another will impact negatively on Social Europe. Certainly exchange rate dumping can have an immediately adverse effect on employment systems because it alters nominal cost and price structures between nations very quickly. In many ways its impact is more dramatic than social dumping, which is essentially about manipulating real cost differences (unit labour costs and productivity levels, for example) between member-states. Unpredictable currency movements are likely to have damaging consequences for the European social model.

Compounding this problem is the lack of a well-ordered global financial system. Relatively volatile international money markets can generate *external* pressures on exchange rate relations between the member-states. One feature of the unmanaged global monetary system is the close (inverse) association between the Deutschmark and the dollar. When confidence wanes in the dollar, financial institutions rush to buy Deutschmarks and vice versa. This hectic two-way monetary traffic between Frankfurt and New York has a spillover effect on the exchange rate status of other member-states.

Consider the situation where the money markets are moving out of dollars and into Deutschmarks. The effect of this switch is to cause the appreciation of Germany's currency against the USA's. But since most of the other member-states are closely tied to the Deutschmark, they too experience a rise in the value of their currency *vis-à-vis* the dollar. Thus, the competitive position of France and Austria, for example, with regard to the USA worsens, even though direct economic and commercial connections between the countries have not changed. The rollercoaster financial relationship between the dollar and the Deutschmark can put jobs and commercial performance under threat. In other words, not being inside a robust monetary zone exposes member-states to potentially harmful, externally generated, monetary shocks (Aglietta 1988).

The key point in the above discussion is that the coordination deficit has created an unfavourable monetary backdrop to Social Europe. Member-states could hardly be coping with a more inclement climate in which to organise employment and welfare systems. The present direction of political and economic integration has created a vicious circle with regard to the future vitality of Social Europe. Not only has the coordination deficit intensified pressures on social systems, but it has also heavily constrained the possibilities of remedial action at the national level. At the same time, the imbalance between market integration and 'thin' EU institutional structures makes the building of European macro-economic support arrangements for Social Europe more difficult. The debacle surrounding the ERM shows how problematic it is to create a credible monetary arrangement inside a EU that is an essentially hybrid political system. But without an ordered monetary system in Europe, the pressures on Social Europe arising from economic integration become even more acute. Thus, in dealing with the problems of Social Europe, member-states cannot retreat into purely national strategies, nor will they be able to develop coherent European solutions within the present economic and institutional design of the EU.

In theory, monetary union may offer a way out of this conundrum, since it represents the most effective way of closing the coordination deficit. Yet pursuing the Maastricht plan for monetary union, as we have seen, has meant hard times for social and welfare expenditure in Europe. Thus, while the status quo is hardly acceptable, the proposed road ahead, paved by Europe's political elite, is equally unattractive. This is the strategic dilemma facing supporters of the European social model. On this front, not all developments are discouraging.

Flexible integration and Social Europe

One piece of good news is the EU's decision to allow the majority of member-states to go ahead and form the single currency club. Without that decision, the possibility of the emergence of a two-speed Europe, which would have been calamitous for Social Europe, was very real. This point needs to be explained fully. It is now widely accepted that, as a policy-making body, the EU is too cumbersome and hidebound. Inefficient decision-making structures have resulted in European integration experiencing a legitimacy crisis. For the most part, institutional sclerosis inside the EU is due to the heterogeneity of interests between existing member-states. With the number of member-states set to grow, the policy log-jam in Brussels is likely to get even worse. Under existing institutional rules, the EU could become totally impotent to address the huge economic and social problems facing the member-states. The upshot will be a further deepening of the legitimisation crisis.

One proposal to rescue the EU from this impending problem is the notion of flexible integration. Dewatripoint *et al.* (1995) presents the most coherent and detailed exposition of this model. They suggest that the EU should be recast so that a common base is created which every member-state must join; participation in particular integration schemes would then be voluntary by signing up to open partnerships. Included in the common base would be all policies and programmes associated with the European single market and a select group of other measures, such as the Structural Funds. Open partnerships on the other hand would be designed for particular policy areas in which a group of member-states was eager to deepen integration. The authors set out a procedure for open partnerships to become part of the common base so that the two levels would be in some way connected with each other. Overall, the thrust of flexible integration would be to make the EU's decision-making process less rigid whilst maintaining certain bonds of cooperation and obligation between all the member-states. Interestingly, however, neither a single currency nor a strong social policy is considered as appropriate for the common base.

Under such a scheme, it would be easier for those member-states that enjoy a high degree of real and nominal economic convergence to go ahead and form a single-currency open partnership. Just which member-states would be involved in such a project is unclear, but it would undoubtedly include the bulk of north European member-states. Whatever the exact combination, if some member-states were to choose to go down such a route, the impact both on the EU and also on the European economy would be far-reaching. In particular, a sharp delineation would open up between an inner and an outer Europe.

To some extent, such a divide already exists. A number of reports have highlighted the disparity in incomes and living standards inside the EU (Dunford 1995). In terms of productive systems, Lipietz (1997) argues that the member-states are separated according to those that have orientated themselves to what he terms 'negotiated involvement strategies', which emphasise high-skills and high-quality commercial activities, and those that rely primarily on flexibility and low wages. A mini monetary union would reflect, but at the same time sharpen, this divide, with the 'negotiated involvers' being the 'ins' and the deregulators the 'outs'.

Monetary regimes have an important impact on labour market behaviour. For example, labour market adjustment was faster under the gold standard than under monetary regimes characterised by greater exchange rate variability (Bayoumi and Eichengreen 1996). Thus the 'ins' and 'outs' of a monetary union in Europe would develop different patterns of labour market action. For example, the 'ins' might move from national responses to economic shocks, to more integrated and cooperative regime-wide adjustment mechanisms, particularly as they would have similar product and labour markets as well as employment policy priorities. Moreover, as Jacquemin and Sapir (1996) point out, a core group of countries inside a restricted single currency club would be likely to establish new institutional structures to promote internal cooperation and coordination. Such developments would not only formalise and widen the divide between the core and periphery, but also increase the entrance fee for the 'outs' to join the 'ins', perhaps even to a prohibitive degree.

Thus a mini monetary union would deeply fragment Social Europe. On the one hand, an advanced European economic zone would be created, ensuring future prosperity for a select group of member-states. Monetary union would bring them greater macro-economic stability while the new bonds of reciprocity and cooperation created would allow them to solve welfare and labour market problems in a mutually supportive way. Outside this zone of advanced social and economic activity, Europe would look pretty tawdry. Economic and social chaos would most likely rule. Without any basis for collaboration, outer Europe would be characterised by national beggar-thy-neighbour policies. Countries trying to steal a march on their rivals in the periphery would become more and more reliant on low-cost economic strategies. As a result, pressure on welfare systems and labour market protection regimes would intensify, thereby worsening the crisis of Social Europe in these countries. Allowing such contrasting models of development to sit cheek-by-jowl with one another would hardly be an acceptable reform scenario for Social Europe. Thus flexible integration designed to end institutional *immobilisme* inside the EU would be the nadir for the European social model.

The way forward

The maximalist solution: an alternative Social Europe.

Preventing a two-speed Europe centred around a mini monetary union can be viewed as a defensive strategy to stop social fragmentation between the member-states. But what are the possibilities for a more positive agenda designed to make monetary union and Social Europe compatible. One proposal is what Lipietz (1996: 378) calls 'an alternative Social Europe'. This regime would have four key functions. First of all, the reduction of social dumping practices by the enactment of Union-wide common labour market ground rules and more tightly coordinated national employment policies. Second, the control of fiscal dumping which entices the member-states into a Dutch auction of attracting mobile international capital by offering minimal taxation. Addressing this practice would require a much higher degree of fiscal harmonisation than currently exists. Lipietz suggests that the EU should impose a regime of uniform taxation of capital at source. The third function would be lowering high unemployment through the launch of a Europe-wide recovery plan. For the most part, this plan amounts to a traditional Keynesian recovery initiative, involving the member-states running loose monetary and fiscal policies. Finally, the regime would involve the reorganising of the European labour market so that social equity, ecological demands and economic performance are made compatible. This objective would partly involve the EU centre lending support to national and regional efforts at developing a 'third' economic sector that would be heavily focused on ecological and social matters. But it would also involve the centre being at the forefront of employment policy innovations; one example given by Lipietz is job-sharing.

The 'alternative Social Europe' is a bold and radical plan. Although, Lipietz and others play this matter down, it would almost certainly lead to root-and-branch change to national welfare systems. Unquestionably, the EU centre would have to gain new fiscal and social policy competencies before the plan could be made possible. Indeed, it seems only reasonable to ask whether such a scheme would be workable without the building of a full political federation inside the EU. Without a supranational EU it is hard to see how this new Social Europe could be democratically controlled. Moreover, the plan places big economic demands on the member-states. They would be asked not only to ditch the Maastricht and Amsterdam Treaties, but also to jettison completely the macro-economic policies they had been following for a decade. In addition, they would be asked to accept the transfer of huge areas of economic and social governance from the national to the European level. There are few, if any, signs of member-states seeking to sign-up for such an agenda for economic and social integration in Europe. Only the wildest optimist or the most fool-hardy would say that the political conditions exist for an alternative Social Europe. It appears to be too out of line with the emerging institutional architecture of the EU.

Pragmatic reform

With radical change to protect Social Europe unlikely, pragmatic reform appears the only feasible way forward. The objective of the pragmatic path would be to introduce various reforms to make the new Euro-zone more 'socially friendly'. A number of possible revisions could be listed, but three key reforms would be: (1) ensuring that Maastricht does not dismantle Europe's automatic stabilisers; (2) making it permissible for member-states to spend a certain share of GDP on welfare matters; and (3) the prevention of wage undercutting as a form of social dumping. In times of economic downturn, almost every member-state has reverted to a counter-cyclical fiscal stance: to compensate for the decline in economic output and employment, government has allowed public expenditure to increase. In other words, built into the macro-economic regime is a high degree of automatic stabilisation. As already pointed out, the Maastricht rules for a single currency as well as the envisaged stability pact threaten these automatic stabilisers by tying the member-states to pro-cyclical fiscal policies: stringent fiscal restrictions would have to be pursued irrespective of prevailing economic conditions. Such a tight fiscal stance runs the risk of making the macro-economic environment in Europe excessively defla-tionary. Welfare expenditure would be the first to suffer under this regime. Thus an important reform would be to permit greater fiscal flexibility in the new Euro-zone.

Eichengreen (1997) sets out a possible way in which this could be done. He proposes that attempts by the EU centre to peg member-states to a 3 per cent budget deficit rule should be replaced by a new benchmark: the constant employment budget. Without going into the exact technical details, this criterion would allow the member-states to pursue loose fiscal policies in recessions, in order to maintain a pre-designated equilibrium unemployment rate. At the same time, the member-states would be obliged to shrink budget deficits when good economic times returned so that the constant employment budget balance rule was not violated. Such a proposal would not only introduce greater fiscal flexibility into the single currency area, but also make the question of unemployment a more central policy matter. Other related proposals have been made, but all seek to give member-states greater freedom to pursue automatic stabilisation strategies. The main intention is preventing the EU from enveloping itself in a deflationary fiscal environment – a prerequisite for the survival of Social Europe.

Other interesting reform proposals have been put forward by Scharpf (1997). First of all, he argues that to check the slide into Hobbesian forms of competition between different national social rules, the member-states should commit themselves to EU-level regulations that establish multi-level social standards. The idea is that linking the level of the social protection floor to a country's level of economic development minimises some of the harmful side effects of crude harmonisation. Second, he argues that member-states should adopt a European directive that binds them not to push total welfare expenditure below a mutually agreed share of GDP. The attraction of this policy measure is twofold. One is that it does not commit the member-states to any institutional harmonisation. The other is that it would place a floor beneath the levels of national income that should be spent on welfare and social matters, and which would be broadly the same across the EU. Embedding this informal consensus within an explicit EU regulation would send an important signal to the citizens of the member-states that national governments are acting in defence of Social Europe. Moreover, it would limit the opportunities for any member-state to pursue an aggressive social dumping strategy.

Ideally, the above reform measure ought to be accompanied by a policy designed to prevent wage determination being used as a mechanism for social undercutting. A number of the chapters in this book emphasise how deeper economic integration has had a disciplining effect on national collective bargaining. Monetary union could further change the way agreements are concluded. One possibility is that a form of European pattern bargaining would arise, with the German unions – IG Metall for instance – setting the going rate for wage settlements in other countries, particularly in surrounding north European member-states. Whether European trade unions have the strength to realise such a scenario is a moot point. An alternative, perhaps more plausible, scenario is that wage bargaining would stay national in character, which would increase the temptation for trade unions and employers to undermine German collective agreements in pursuit of competitive advantage. In other words, European concessionary bargaining might take off in the new Euro-zone. But concessionary bargaining is an ill-disguised form of social dumping. Setting European rules to address this problem is much more difficult than in the case of welfare expenditure. Nevertheless, establishing mechanisms to prevent wage determination being used as an aggressive competitive tactic should be a top priority for trade unions.

Overall, the thrust of these pragmatic reforms is to prevent the European integration process from placing excessive macro-economic and market constraints on national social systems. The objective is not to build a European-level welfare state or industrial relations system, but to give member-states the scope to introduce reform in a manner that is sensitive to their own institutional and structural circumstances. In other words, the aim is to ensure that European integration operates in a way that is conducive to the modernising of Social Europe and economic citizenship, rather than in a way that threatens its very existence. The extent to which this pragmatic reform agenda will succeed is an open question. A number of small but positive steps were taken at the 1997 Amsterdam European Council. In particular, a specific chapter on employment was introduced into the Treaty, including a clause that commits the member-states to attaining a high level of employment in the EU. Furthermore, the new British government has signed the Social Chapter, thereby allowing its incorporation into the main body of the New Treaty. More generally, the political context for Social Europe has improved, with the return of left of centre governments in Britain, France and Germany. These are all favourable trends, but they have yet to be translated into tangible EU-wide policy reforms that would prove beneficial to national welfare and employment systems.

Conclusions

The EU has got itself into a big predicament. By deepening market inter-dependence between the member-states it has placed further constraints on the region's already ailing brand of welfare capitalism. Member-states are presently caught in the unenviable position of finding it difficult to manage national welfare systems yet being unable to launch compensating initiatives at the EU level. In one sense, the hard Euro-zone proposal, as embodied in the Maastricht Treaty and the Stability Pact, represents a way out of this dilemma. It would resolve the tension between market integration and Social Europe by allowing the former to triumph. Obliging the member-states to keep a tight control on public expenditure and to become ultra-competitive would almost inevitably mean the enactment of huge reforms to existing European social systems. This would not add up to the complete dismantling of welfare provision, but it could involve large-scale cutbacks. Europe would probably experience a decisive shift towards a US-type economic system where the social safety net is loosely woven and the private insurance sector plays an important role.

But the hard Euro-zone scenario is by no means certain to happen. Across Europe there is still a big political commitment to the idea of meshing market and welfare principles together. These political forces may yet be able to subdue the potentially deflationary bias of the envisaged monetary union. It is important to stress, however, that if positive reforms are introduced, this will not amount to a complete triumph for Social Europe. All this would do is create a warmer macro-economic climate for the modernising of welfare and employment protection rules. That reform is required should not be a contentious observation. Independent of the single currency project, virtually every member-state is investigating strategies to update and renew social and employment regimes. Part of the motivation is to find ways of curbing the escalating costs of welfare and to remove distortions that have crept into specific programmes, but it is also an attempt to align public provision with new forms of economic and social life (for example, by developing innovatory forms of labour market regulation that more effectively meet the needs of atypical workers). Thus, a more benign monetary union does not obviate the need for social reform, but allows it to be carried out in a way that respects European traditions.

8 Remaking economic citizenship in Europe

Introduction

On any balanced view, the success of Europe in the period of postwar expansion was supported by social settlements – in a variety of national forms – that allowed equity and efficiency to feed positively off one another. This constructive commingling of economic and social structures propelled the rapid modernisation of European society. The main argument of this book is that the employment relations institutions and processes associated with this model of development are under strain. On the one hand, they are implicated in the generally unimpressive economic record of Europe during the past two decades or more: they suffer from a crisis of economic functionality. On the other hand, they are increasingly out of line with new emerging patterns of economic and social life. In present form, they are unable to operate as mediating mechanisms to interlock social and economic structures positively. Thus, economic citizenship in Europe is at once suffering from the problems of economic functionality and social coherence.

At the same time, it would be a mistake to believe that we are on the threshold of the Americanisation of European industrial relations. Influential political forces reject the dismantling of social Europe and its associated model of economic citizenship, and are likely to inspire continuing efforts for its reconstruction. Thus Europe is not yet a case of 'embedded neo-liberalism'. But while the political forces that identify with the underlying values of the European social model are formidable, there is a tendency stubbornly to defend inherited institutions rather than move towards the construction of new forms of social solidarity compatible with the complexity of modern economic life. Part of the problem is that although the existing model of economic citizenship may be dysfunctional, there remains no clear alternative to it. Being caught between the old and the new has slowed down reform. Bitter disputes exist between those committed to Social Europe about what should be preserved and what should be abandoned in the search for a new settlement. It is instructive that the return of centre-left governments in some European countries has not improved this situation greatly. Beyond increasing hope (and confidence) that the neo-liberal programme for labour market flexibility and deregulation can be blocked, little progress has been made with regard to the strategic articulation of economic and social programmes.

It may be that there is no big reform package and that the renewal of Social Europe will arise from the unintended consequences of a series of discrete, pragmatic changes. While this view has merits, the analysis of this book suggests that any innovations need to address three important themes – the democratisation of the EU; the future association between the nation-state and economic citizenship; and the institutional reform of labour market governance. In this concluding chapter some arguments are developed on all three points. The intention is not to set out a blueprint for reform, but to delineate the contours of the debate that needs to take place regarding the political shape of a modernised Social Europe.

A democratic agenda for the EU

Closing the coordination deficit

It is widely accepted that the EU suffers from a crisis of political legitimacy: the institutions of the EU are frequently seen as too remote from the citizens of Europe, and as failing to adequately address everyday concerns such as unemployment, health and education. Whether some of these concerns can be fully resolved is an open question given the institutional distance between Brussels and ground-level economic and social activity. Nevertheless, to improve on the EU's relatively poor standing thorough-going reform is required across the broad sweep of economic, political and social policy-making. In the realm of economic affairs, the most pressing matter is closing the coordination deficit that has emerged in the European economy as a result of deepening commercial interdependence between the member states. Far-reaching market integration alongside weak institution building in Brussels has only tightened the constraints on national social governance structures. The process threatens to get worse if the Union creates a 'hard' Euro-zone. Under such a regime, monetary and fiscal policy would be exceptionally tight and centralised. In practice, the member-states would be without any effective macro-economic instruments to adjust to economic shocks. Moreover, as labour mobility between the member-states would remain relatively insignificant, the only feasible path open to member-states in response to bad economic times would be to increase the flexibility of the employment system. Thus, the almost inevitable consequence of the Maastricht plan for monetary union would be a substantial reduction in the intensity of labour market protectionist rules in Europe.

Any democratic agenda for the EU must address this destabilising co-ordination deficit in the European economy. In particular, the programme for a single currency should be enacted in a way that allows the member-states greater flexibility in the use of fiscal policy in economic management. Saving Europe's automatic stabilisers, in Eichengreen's (1996) terms, appears to be the only effective way to avoid a collision between the monetary union project and the institutions of social Europe. If such a clash were to occur, the only winner would be the single currency. Looser fiscal policy, however, is not the full answer. To avoid excessive competition between national social rules, EU-wide obligations need to be established for social and welfare expenditure. In particular, Scharpf (1997) suggests that the EU should adopt a regulation putting a floor under national social budgets. This is not a particularly sophisticated proposal, but it does have the merit of avoiding excessive policy harmonisation or centralisation. But the basic point is that new EU policies are necessary to avoid social budgets being used as a 'negative' competitive tactic inside the open European market.

For some time now the member-states have turned their backs on a Europe-wide coordinated reflation programme to help reduce unemployment. At the same time, they have rejected proposals for the EU centre to gain more financial resources or new macro-economic instruments which would allow some type of independent pan-European employment initiative. In the absence of any effective policy mechanisms, the Brussels bureaucracy has fallen back on policy coordination, and occasionally on exhortation, to get the member-states to do more on joblessness. Relative to the scale of the European unemployment problem, these actions appear tame. As a result, the image of the Commission and other EU bodies standing by in the face of a badly malfunctioning European labour market only comes into sharper focus. Thus, for both economic and political reasons, the EU needs to do more on the problem of unemployment. To some extent, the insertion of a new employment clause into the new Amsterdam Treaty creates a warmer climate for EU initiatives. At the same time, it is unlikely that the member-states will have a change of heart about giving Brussels a more direct role in improving the European job generation machine. One possible way forward is for the EU to establish employment/unemployment targets which do not formally commit the member-states to any particular policy action, but nevertheless create informal obligations on the member-states to do something about the plight of the jobless. In other words, the EU role would change from policy coordination to policy mobilisation. This shift might not solve the EU legitimacy crisis, but it would be a positive step towards making European unemployment a higher economic priority among the member-states.

Taking subsidiarity seriously

The second part of a democratic agenda is taking subsidiarity seriously. Included in the new Treaty on European Union signed at Amsterdam is a detailed catalogue of procedures on how to operationalise subsidiarity as a legislative and policy-making instrument. The Commission now has to show that the Union has the competence to act on a particular matter, explain why EU intervention is preferable to national action in solving the problem, and ensure that the envisaged action is proportional or commensurate to the problem that is being addressed. It is hard to see how this new decision-making audit can do anything other than constrain the Commission's role as a policy entrepreneur. For the first time, a preference for local decision-making is embodied in a European Treaty, thereby giving legal force to the preservation of national identities and political flexibility. At one level, holding true to these two principles should ease the problem of policy overload in Brussels, which has long blighted the EU's decision-making machinery. At the same time, it might scupper proposals for a more dirigiste EU social policy that is predicated on a fundamental realignment of EU political structures.

Although much of the evidence points in the counter direction, subsidiarity is still discussed in terms of creating a quasi-federalist structure in the EU. Moreover, it is frequently assumed, for reasons that are not always clear, that federalism will be supportive of stronger Europe-wide employment regulations. But this view is deficient on two accounts: on the one hand, it underestimates the difficulties with building federalist structures inside the EU; and, on the other, it misinterprets the meaning of subsidiarity. An important feature of federalism is the vertical division of powers between different tiers of government. Many discussions about the character of EU policy arenas, actual or preferred, are strongly influenced by this perspective. Social policy is no exception. Jacobi (1997), reflecting a widely held view in the European industrial relations academy, argues that monetary union will necessitate a new EU-wide system of collective bargaining. A distinguishing feature of this system will be a neat division of bargaining activity between company, economic sector and European levels. Jacobi even suggests that subsidiarity is the organising principle behind this proposed arrangement.

Although popular, this is a flawed interpretation of subsidiarity, at least as it has been introduced into the legal base of the EU. Subsidiarity is a more thoroughgoing decentralising political and economic concept than is often appreciated. When grafting the concept onto existing Treaties, the main concern was not with meeting the niceties of constitutional federalist principles such as the enumeration of federal powers, preemption of state law and implied law. Rather the imperative was to signal to the member-states that their distinctiveness would be respected and not threatened by EU-level activity. One manifestation of this decentralising logic was the new Article 3b inserted into the Maastricht Treaty. This states that the EU should seek to refrain from policy interventions even in areas in which it has competence, particularly if action at a lower tier of government could effectively address the problem. As Bermann (1994: 453) remarks, this article 'systematically places the burden of proof on the proponents of Community action'. This is unlike federalism, particularly as it is practised in the USA, where the emphasis on maintaining a balance of powers between the federal and state levels of government creates a tolerance for higher-level policy interventions.

Thus the notion of creating a multi-tiered governance structure for the European labour market, in which there is a neat division of competencies from the EU-level downwards, fits uneasily with the politics of subsidiarity inside the EU. In many ways, the legal and institutional orientations of the EU are at odds with any plan to build a quasi-federalist structure inside the EU. As Chapter 6 emphasised, some social partnership procedures exist in Brussels, but these are not robust enough to engage in multi-tiered collective bargaining activities. Another reason to be sceptical towards proposals for the federal reorganisation of European industrial relations is the role of labour market institutions in countries such as the USA, Canada and Australia. None of these big federalist countries have highly coordinated systems of employment relations in which functions are neatly divided between levels of government. The reality is disorganised and disjointed employment relations processes, and in all three countries there is a strong movement toward the greater decentralisation of industrial relations activity. Over the years, it has been assumed that building a social dimension to the EU is simply a sub-part of the wider political programme of creating a federal Europe. But there is little evidence that federalism is a reliable piece of political architecture for the renewal of economic citizenship in Europe.

Throughout this book, big programmes aimed at rescuing the European social model have been treated with scepticism. To be credible, any progressive agenda for social policy must be broadly in line with the political system of the EU. In an interesting article, Schmitter (1996) argues that the political system of the EU is hard to define as it defies established political categories such as federalism or confederalism. The fallout from this situation is threefold: (1) although there is a European 'public space', there is no EU style of collective or public action – only in a limited number of areas does the EU have exclusive competence and in many others there is no neat vertical division of powers between different levels of government; (2) the European public space is diverse and fragmented largely because no one member-state, including Germany, has the hegemonic capability to impose its will or policy style on the others (in this regard the EU is unlike the North American Free Trade Area, NAFTA, where the USA does exercise hegemonic power); and (3) while the EU centre operates in a policy entrepreneurial role, it has only the resources or capacity to implement distinctive policies in a limited number of arenas. These factors make Schmitter (1996: 35) conclude that 'national and subnational administrations will continue to determine the style of face-to-face authoritative interactions with individual firms and citizens'.

The relationship between the member-states and the EU centre on employment-related topics presented in the preceding chapters more or less corresponds with this view of the EU polity. Over the years, as a result of legal mutation, policy activism on the part of the Commission, and policy opportunism by interest groups on the ground, the EU has developed an institutional presence in European labour markets. But the interface between the EU centre and the member-states on social policy is far from being well-ordered and coherent. It is more accurately portrayed as a contested terrain. Political disagreements have been rife in virtually every sphere of EU social policy: the extent to which the EU should have competence to make labour market interventions has been continuously challenged; the purpose and goals of particular strands of EU social policy have been interpreted differently; the status and impact of EU legislation is a matter of controversy. All in all, the connections between the EU centre and the member-states lack coherence. Political exigencies rather than a fully worked out employment or integration logic are behind most developments in EU social policy.

Promoting learning by monitoring

Thus, a third aspect of a democratic agenda for Europe should be to introduce more stability and order into national and EU interactions on employment and labour market affairs. As Chapter 6 highlighted, a number of fault-lines between national and EU administrative bodies have resulted in an 'obscuration effect' creeping into social policy. Placing EU social policy on a firmer footing means addressing these fault-lines. Part of this reform will involve making changes to national governance systems to maximise the impact of EU legislation. For an instructive example, consider the EU equality laws. The UK has consistently made more effective use of these laws than any other member-state by virtue of it being one of the few countries with a quasi-independent Equal Opportunities Commission. Thus, for EU labour law to have a meaningful impact, new national procedures, if not agencies, are required for the promotion and enforcement of gender equality policy. But the flip-side to any innovations to national policy systems must be a renewed commitment on the part of the EU centre to a method of law-making that reflects the reality of divergent national industrial relations regimes. In particular, EU social legislation must set out broad principles or frameworks that can be implemented in a manner consistent with the distinctive traditions of each member-state. To some extent, the recent Davignon Report on information and consultation reflects this approach. This document suggests that in drawing up legislative proposals, the EU should set out a menu of different employee involvement schemes, so that the member-states can devise an arrangement that best suits their own circumstances. The key point is that allowing national diversity to reign in the context of an overall Europe-wide policy framework is the only way that European social measures can be made consistent with the political system of the EU.

Obtaining a better balance between unity and diversity among the member-states must be accompanied by change to the formalisation and socialisation mechanisms surrounding EU social policy deliberations. Some sub-parts of EU employment policy-making are a hive of activity, but it is not always clear whether they are founded on fully developed policy norms. For example, a lot of EU-wide information exchange has taken place on employment policy without any explicit or well-defined objective. At times, the process seems to have been little more than national labour market institutions meeting an administrative obligation to furnish the Commission with information. Frequently, the opportunity for national employment policy-makers to use EU-level discussions to learn about each other's portfolio of labour market measures is forgone. But it is precisely this type of problem-solving and mutual learning that best fits with the location and character of the EU as a decision-making body. Not only that, Dorf and Sabel (1997) argue that such activity is becoming a decisive part of public policy-making.

As it is likely to prove influential, their argument needs outlining more fully. According to Dorf and Sabel, enterprises are becoming quasi-federalist organisations, consisting of semi-autonomous teams and working groups. Moreover, the boundaries between firms are becoming blurred in the search for a blend between competition and cooperation. To prevent organisational fragmentation, enterprises frequently use a form of benchmarking to connect the decentralised parts. Mechanisms are put in place to monitor the performance of each sub-unit and promote discussion about productive failures and successes. Dorf and Sabel call these processes learning by monitoring and argue that sooner or later public institutions will be obliged to revert to a similar type of activity when designing policies. This is so not only because governments are strapped for cash but also because many mainstream public policy programmes are not solving the problems they were created to address. In the area of employment policy, for example, no government in Europe, apart perhaps from the Netherlands', has come up with a menu of measures that effectively tackles issues such as long-term unemployment or the declining demand for unskilled workers. As emphasised in Chapter 5, many labour market programmes are experimental and provisional in character. In this situation, it seems appropriate that the member-states should be creating institutional procedures at the EU level to learn from each other about the design, implementation and outcomes of active labour market measures. But the current fault-lines between the nation-states and the EU centre have held back the formalisation and socialisation mechanisms that would underpin this cross-country learning activity.

But some encouraging signs are emerging that suggest change may be on its way. One important revision made to the European Treaty at Amsterdam, which has received virtually no attention, is the new Article 118. This clause stipulates that the European Council can encourage the member-states to adopt initiatives aimed at improving knowledge, developing exchange of information and best practice, promoting innovative approaches and evaluating experiences in order to combat social exclusion. This new article gives the EU a firmer legal base to build learning by monitoring institutions not only in Brussels, but also across the nations, regions and even the firms of Europe. The vision is not only of removing the policy fault-lines between many European capitals and Brussels, but also of intensified horizontal information and communication flows across the member-states. Some may regard this idea of mutual learning as a fairly anodyne policy departure, but if introduced correctly, it could have far-reaching consequences.

Consider three examples: the Europe of the Regions Committee, the European Works Councils Directive and EU employment policy. The Europe of the Regions Committee established by the Maastricht Treaty has the potential to initiate and orchestrate cross-national information and learning about the variety of regional economic development experiments taking place in Europe. Yet it is running the risk of becoming just another institutional artefact of the Brussels bureaucracy, since it has been caught up in the administrative toing and froing between EU institutions. As a result, the chance to promote and facilitate decentralised exchanges about the performance of regional economic initiatives is being lost. The second example is the European Works Councils that have been established in recent years following the 1995 Directive. Streeck (1997a) is right to argue that these arrangements fall short of existing co-determination procedures in some member-states. Moreover, his gloomy assessment that these bodies may not become effective tools for employee involvement cannot be totally dismissed. Many of them meet only once a year and are seldom properly integrated into the information structure of the enterprise.

At the same time, these councils may have more potential than he suggests, even given their restricted powers. Lord Wedderburn (1997) gives the example of the Danone Agreement which permits negotiations between trade unions and management at the European level to create broad framework agreements. Subsequently these agreements can be fed into the national bargaining machinery for more substantive discussions. At the moment, this example is very much the exception. But the key issue is that the dialogue at the European level is integrated with the lower tiers of information sharing and negotiation inside the enterprise, thereby ensuring that the new Works Councils have a meaningful purpose. Creating additional vertical and horizontal information flows of this kind opens up the possibility of workers comparing conditions of employment across member-states with greater clarity. The result may be a more fertile discussion on the direction of employment and work change inside a company at the European level. In other words, if trade unions adopt creative strategies, they may be able to make more of the European Works Councils than first meets the eye.

As Chapter 5 highlighted, it is perhaps in the area of our third example, European employment policy, that learning by monitoring procedures has been most influential. Member-states have committed themselves to benchmarking specific public policies for the labour market in an effort to improve employment outcomes. Initial assessments suggest that this procedure itself will require a lot of 'learning by doing'. Yet, the member-states appear committed to this innovation. There is a general recognition that as no big plan exists for European unemployment, the only credible alternative is to learn from each other in this area. Thus, in forthcoming years the success or otherwise of particular employment programmes will be determined by a collaborative pan-European exercise as much as by nationally defined objectives. This is a significant departure, for benchmarking permits considerable national autonomy to persist while at the same time ensuring that tangible and meaningful connections are created between the member-states. The search for a symbiosis in EU social policy discussed in Chapter 7 nears fruition.

To some extent, these policy experiments may be foreshadowing the future political shape of the EU. Enacting learning by monitoring procedures across the policy spectrum might allow the supporters of a federal Europe to let go of their dream. At the same time, they would ensure that narrow intergovernmentalist bargaining was not at the centre of EU decision-making. The vision is of complementary institutional and social connections between the member-states in the context of blurred constitutional boundaries between the nation-state and the European centre. Learning by monitoring does not resolve the intergovernmental/supranational tension inside the EU. In fact, it is premised on the redundancy of this paradigm to European integration. It is founded on the notion that the relationship between national autonomy and European cooperation is inherently ambiguous, and that positive collaboration involving the two levels will be the outcome of deliberative and on-going efforts to seek political symbiosis. Learning by monitoring commits the member-states to a pattern of policy-making that facilitates such joint action.

The maintenance of national economic citizenship

The elements of a democratic agenda for the EU set out above do not amount to an EU rescue of the postwar social democratic settlement. However, they may help reduce some of the pressures that market integration is placing on national social and employment systems. Moreover, important institutional adaptations to the EU decision-making system may occur, should learning by monitoring procedures be introduced on a widespread basis. Overall, the most salient aspect of the proposed democratic agenda is that it is built around the assumption of a continuing close association between the nation-state and economic citizenship. There are too many political and social obstacles to the creation of a fully formed Europe-wide economic citizenship which stands above and takes precedence over national arrangements.

Arguing that the nation-state continues to be the most important arena for the holding together of employment and social systems cuts across much of the European debate about citizenship. With the growth of regional political movements as well as widespread administrative decentralisation, a popular argument is that the close ties between the nation and economic citizenship are weakening. Two rather different intellectual camps articulate this view. One is the 'new citizenship' group that argues that the growth of the EU alongside the demise of national political society has rescued citizenship from the grips of the nation-state. As a result, the rights and obligations through which people are incorporated into economic life are no longer contingent upon membership of a national polity. According to this view, citizenship underscores economic and social activity but not political identity. When citizenship rights are not reliant on national political institutions, they can be devised and maintained by the EU through the enactment of social laws. Indeed, the slow but steady growth of EU legal interventions in the labour market has been interpreted as the emergence of a new multiple citizenship in Europe. However, throughout this book the idea of multiple or dual citizenship has been treated with scepticism, partly because it overestimates the role of EU social policies in European economic life and partly because it considerably underestimates the continued importance of political sentiment to citizenship. These points are developed more fully later in this chapter.

The other intellectual group is camped around the notion of postnational political citizenship. This approach differs from the new citizenship argument in a number of important ways. First, postnationalists reject the abandonment of the political dimension of citizenship so that it is more or less based on social and economic activity. They see this as a recipe for a purely functional view of rights and obligations that could end up eroding the political bonds that underscore democratic practices. Thus, for example, Habermas (1990) argues for a new 'constitutional patriotism' that allows for the separation of the nation from the state. In this schema, the culture and ethnic bonds that heavily shape national identity constitute a different realm to that of the state, which is based on civic and political participation. As a result of this decoupling, the state becomes less of a cultural and historical unit and more grounded on the principle of the law. Bonds of ethnic identity still exist, but they become 'abstract processes and principles' which give people a link with the past. With political society perceived as civic practice, citizenship becomes post-national in the sense that it is not tied to any concrete historical or cultural community.

The notion of post-national citizenship facilitates the development of big models for European social development. For a start, it makes the concept of citizenship universal and all-inclusive. One of the negative effects of national economic and social rights is that boundaries to entitlements are created between residents and non-residents. Such social closure procedures end under post-nationalism. For example, since the state is centred on civic activity, foreigners entering the country are given full membership of the political community, which allows them to vote, participate in elections and so on. Thus the image of Europe is not only one of a single market, but also one that involves a new civic citizenship that is open and based on democratic practice.

This vision is supportive of a 'maximalist' Social Europe. Over the years, a persistent criticism of proposals such as that of a European Social Constitution is that the EU does not have the necessary political and cultural communities to sustain such arrangements. But since citizenship under post-nationalism becomes purely civic and is not connected to any particular historical or national sentiment, this criticism falls by the wayside. In other words, the EU can develop a model of economic citizenship based on the principles of 'universality, autonomy and responsibility' in the absence of an active political community (Ferry 1991). At the same time, post-nationalism also gives the Europe of the Regions project a shot in the arm. With the close association between the nation-state and economic citizenship weakened, lower tiers of government can develop new forms of social inclusion mechanisms. Thus post-national identity triggers a realignment of the institutional foundations of economic citizenship.

The idea of an open and civic economic citizenship is certainly attractive. But it is questionable whether the political and economic make-up of Europe can be described as post-nationalist. First of all, although the scope of governments to make regulatory interventions in the labour market has been constrained, economic citizenship and the nation-state still remain closely intertwined. Consider the furore when Hoover moved from France to Scotland in the search for attractive financial subsidies. This protest was nothing if not a spontaneous defence of *French* jobs and living standards. When a factory is uprooted from Berkshire to Scotland the outcry is nowhere near as intense precisely because the move has taken place within the territorial boundaries of one regime of economic citizenship. National frontiers still matter for social inclusion and political sentiment still matters for citizenship. Thus, the idea of filtering out the historical and cultural dimensions of citizenship until we arrive at purely civic practice is perhaps over-optimistic. With regard to the spheres of employment relations processes – the spheres of regulation, voice and cognition – it would be extremely difficult to perform such a filtering process, as labour market behaviour is as deeply rooted in the historical and cultural context as in prevailing productive structures.

Another way of making this point is that it took literally centuries in some instances to establish legitimate national spheres of economic and political action. To suggest that these traditions can be dissolved, even within a generation, seems wildly optimistic. At the same time, institutional procedures associated with economic citizenship are not immutable: they do evolve over time but the close association with the nation-state remains more or less constant. This observation opens up the bigger question about the desirability of ending the sibling-like relationship between the nation-state and economic citizenship. For Europe this is not a matter of theory or logic, but of history. Perhaps the most virtuous aspect of the nation-state in Europe is that it has contained ethnic and religious rivals in a manner that has allowed modernity to progress. As Schnapper aptly puts it,

> the singularity of the democratic nation compared to other forms of political organisation lies in the fact that in the final analysis, the civic ideal and the principle of citizenship must take precedence over ethnic or religious particularisms, over family or clan solidarities.
>
> (Schnapper 1997: 214)

Thus, while the intention of the post-national school in articulating open citizenship may be noble, the danger is that it may create a political environment in Europe which could open up old ethnic and religious divisions.

Macro-economic considerations also suggest limits to the post-nationalist model. In particular, destabilising the nation-state as a strategic site for economic citizenship may have negative implications for the macro-economic foundations to welfare and social protectionist systems. Important positive features of welfare states in Europe, such as continued cost effectiveness and universal coverage, are tied to national government decisions on taxation and public expenditure. In addition, national fiscal stabilisation and redistribution interventions ensure that the income gap between 'winning' and 'losing' regions does not get too wide. Furthermore, building a supply-side infrastructure for economic performance, including transport, science and communications, is bound up with macro-economic activity. Thus, macro-economics matters for economic citizenship. Severing the link between the nation-state and economic citizenship may actually be tantamount to dismantling some of the institutional structures that are important for the continuation of Social Europe. It would be ironic if the European left were to succeed in getting a monetary union established, with Europe's automatic stabilisers intact, only subsequently to diminish their importance by installing a variant of post-nationalist citizenship. This analysis does not mean that the EU will have no role in employment protection, but that its actions will simply supplement the main theatre for economic citizenship – national-level governance structures.

Recasting the spheres of economic citizenship

So far the argument has been that the EU cannot renew the postwar social-democratic settlement on a Europe-wide basis. Neither can it fully restore the economic functionality and social cohesion of existing welfare and employment regimes; all that can be done is to ease some of the problems that member-states are encountering. At the same time, the nation-state is still regarded as important for the operation of economic citizenship. In this situation, radical reform of each sphere of employment relations – regulation, voice and cognition – becomes even more central to renewing Social Europe. The discussion below will not focus on each sphere, but highlighs some of the themes that should be addressed in all three simultaneously. At the outset, it needs emphasising that no ready-made plan exists to solve the problems of Social Europe. Thus, renewing national employment relations institutions and processes is likely to be an open-ended affair. In this situation, European countries should commit themselves as far as possible to cross-country mutual learning, especially as they face similar strategic dilemmas with regard to the organisation of the labour market. Across Europe, governments are faced with three big dilemmas: the insider/outsider dilemma, the centralisation/decentralisation dilemma, and the public/private dilemma. Below, the nature of these dilemmas is briefly set out.

The insider/outsider dilemma

Extensive welfare provision has ensured that the 'outsider' problem in Europe is not as acute as in the USA, where a large under-class has emerged, etching out a living on the margins of the economy and through illegal activity. But the problem of exclusion is still pressing and likely to get more pronounced. The high levels of unemployment that exist across Europe are a major source of exclusion, particularly as individuals' self-esteem and health are bound up with the work they do. In addition, prospects for some groups in the labour market are distinctly worse than for others. Research shows that the future is fairly bleak for men without qualifications or who are low skilled. In the UK, for example, the proportion of unskilled prime-age males falling into economic inactivity has increased from one in twelve in 1976 to one in four in 1994 (Schmid and Wadsworth 1995). Furthermore, as several chapters have highlighted, women continue to get a raw deal in the labour market relative to their male counterparts. Thus, the problem of labour market outsiders has multiple dimensions.

There are many forces – economic, social and political – operating in the labour market to create an insider/outsider divide. It would be churlish to believe that collective labour market institutions are not implicated in some way. Indeed, the evidence is mounting that in an economic environment where unemployment is high and competitive pressures intense, key labour market institutions tend to pursue the interests of the more privileged workers. For example, Carlin and Soskice (1997) show that in the face of two macro-economic shocks, preparing for monetary union and dealing with the aftermath of reunification, German Works Councils have more or less focused on defending the interests of higher-skilled employees. In particular, many of the craft trade unions have acquiesced, as companies reorganise work systems to outsource semi-skilled productive activity and jobs to eastern Europe and elsewhere. A similar story can be told about other countries. Overall, this highlights the dominant role employers now enjoy in setting the industrial relations agenda across the region, and the increasing inability of trade unions to operate as guarantors of economic citizenship. Unsurprisingly, the outcome is that it is the most vulnerable and weak in the employment system who bear much of the cost of economic adjustment.

In this situation, many European countries have opted for more focused and selective interventions to promote the integration and protection of labour market outsiders, rather than for strengthening traditional collective bargaining institutions and practices. As shown in Chapter 5, a feature of employment policy almost everywhere in Europe is the design of active measures to connect the unemployed and other disadvantaged groups with the formal labour market. The policies actually pursued range from stricter rules for the claiming of benefits to offering people places on job creation and training programmes. Moves are afoot in some countries to introduce new labour laws to balance employer demands for flexibility and employee claims for security. For the most part, the focus is on creating a plinth of employment rights for atypical workers, the most rapidly growing section of the European labour force. Arrangements such as the minimum wage have found new favour in European capitals as they are seen as an effective way of placing a floor under earnings. Changes are being made to educational systems so that individuals have access to schooling at various points in their careers.

A wide range of initiatives is emerging to improve the lot of the most vulnerable in European societies. But all these initiatives share the same characteristic in that they are bypassing established collective employment institutions and aiming to upgrade the *status of individuals* as a way out of the social exclusion trap. To some extent, the new emphasis on individual rights is not in collision with the activities of collective institutions such as trade unions. For instance, in many situations trade unions have been the most effective enforcers of individual rights on the ground. But it is questionable whether this complementarity can be generalised across the entire spectrum of employment relations activity. For example, many governments are showing interest in promoting workplace innovations that emphasise individual rights and benefits, but which may at the same time weaken traditional forms of collective bargaining. Thus, the legitimacy and functionality of collective institutions in maintaining social integration, which have been vital aspects of each sphere of the postwar model of economic citizenship, may be destabilised by efforts to protect outsiders in the employment system. In other words, reconciling the collectivist and individualist dimensions to employment relationships is more pronounced than ever. Certainly, in present circumstances, it seems inappropriate to advocate traditional collective bargaining solutions to solving the problems of social exclusion.

The centralisation/decentralisation dilemma

A few years back a begrudging consensus emerged that decentralisation was an important dynamic in many European industrial relations institutions. Centralised bargaining looked increasingly moribund – defeated on the ground by the evolution of company-level employment systems. A debate opened up about the legal, social and political contexts of decentralised labour market activity. The notion of 'organised decentralisation' became more fashionable following the identification of Denmark as one country that had gone some way to resolve the tension between productive decentralisation and social cohesion (Due *et al.* 1995). Another example is Italy. In an extremely optimistic assessment, Regini (1995) argued that the Italian case showed that decentralised industrial relations activity can fully address the problem of macro-economic externalities. Despite these exaggerated claims, the notion of organised decentralisation was a promising formula, for it conceives of a downward shift as delegation: wherever possible, individual enterprises, local political and administrative units and civil associations are given responsibility to pursue economic modernisation and productive adaptation in a manner consistent with nationally defined social objectives. Central-level employment relations processes are not abandoned in this scenario, but they do perform a less constraining role. In particular, there is an increasing use of framework agreements that identify general objectives while leaving open the substantive means by which they are realised.

Yet as a renewal project for European industrial relations, organised decentralisation has been blurred by the recentralisation of collective bargaining in some countries. For the most part, this development can be explained as spillover from the moves toward monetary union. Governments are anxious to tie labour market behaviour, particularly wage bargaining, to the fiscal stabilisation programmes they are pursuing to meet the Maastricht criteria – they are trying to deepen the social legitimacy of the single currency project. In some instances, trade unions are eager participants in these arrangements, as they are considered an important institutional way of securing a role in economic governance in the new Euro-zone. Employers have acquiesced with these arrangements as they do not interfere with ongoing efforts at corporate reorganisation. Certainly, these new central agreements do not mark the return of social corporatism, which previously integrated the productive and distributive sides of the economy in some European economies. As argued in Chapter 2, the current wave of national pay determination falls short of such an organised model for the labour market.

If anything, the institutional configuration of many national systems appears distinctly dualistic. Tight regulation of the macro-economic aspects of the labour market is taking place alongside disorganised decentralisation that is giving employers a more or less free hand at productive reorganisation. It is not that these two developments are in collision: the idea that there is a new complementarity between the central and ground-level employment relations institutions cannot be fully dismissed. On this account, the competitive state is using centralised bargaining mechanisms to maintain macro-economic austerity, while employers pursue competitive restructuring inside the firm (Taylor 1993). However, this perspective probably makes too much of what is going on. For the most part, tight macro-regulation and spontaneous decentralisation sit check-by-jowl with each other but in a fairly disconnected way. The casualty in this process appears to be organised decentralisation. As a result, the horizontal and vertical connections between enterprises and public agencies that facilitate and guide economic modernisation remain paralysed. And of course with organised decentralisation held in check, the prospects for a positive realignment of economic citizenship also diminish.

The public/private dilemma

In a stark prediction, Marquand (1996) argues that European governments will soon have to choose between a free market and a free society. In making this assessment, he attempts to highlight the enormous social costs that go hand in hand with the relentless pursuit of neo-liberalism. Another worry, on top of this concern about social justice, is that placing the organisation of society secondary to business activity may not be a particularly efficient model of economic competition. For instance, Rubery (1997) shows how the growing wage differentials between workers may be producing unintelligible signals about the type and quality of investments required for training, thereby compounding the already complex problems associated with skill formation activity. While the social and economic costs arising from neo-liberalism may not justify Marquand's apocalyptic warning, they do raise the issue of reasserting the public interest over private sector activity as part of efforts to revitalise economic citizenship.

Crouch (1997) splendidly shows how this is the case with regard to training.

Over the past decade, and even before, government-funded bodies responsible for vocational education and training have lost their way somewhat. A number of factors in particular appear responsible for this situation. First of all, against the backdrop of major structural change and the diffusion of new technological and productive innovations, public institutions became uncertain about the form of training to promote and the best institutional mechanisms for its delivery. In these circumstances, the notion of private sector-led training became more prevalent. Meanwhile, as the casualties from economic reorganisation – the young, the long-term unemployed and the poorly educated – began to mount, an ever-increasing share of government-sponsored training was targeted on the hard-to-employ. As a result, the notion of a division between private sector 'proper' training and public-led residual training for employment 'failures' became engrained. The outcome almost everywhere was that the public agenda for vocational education and training was set by the private sector.

But, as Crouch stresses, this situation produces a paradox. Although the private sector may have acquired a decisive role in setting the public policy agenda for training, it is widely accepted that, left to their own devices, employers may not provide the quantity or quality of training considered socially acceptable. The fallout, of course, is that a key area of economic citizenship in the new complex economy may be under-provided. Solving this paradox will require ingenuity. Devising a monolithic vocational education and training programme that is imposed upon employers is certainly inappropriate. If the history of training teaches anything, it is that such a formula does not work. To reassert the public interest, government-sponsored institutions for the provision of training need to become more deliberative in character. They must be well-designed and resourced as well as maintained by highly qualified staff. They should have close associations with employers whether these take the form of neo-corporatist networks or looser partnerships. They need the capacity to make training as transparent as possible, both in terms of what is being done and with regard to identified outcomes. Not only does this allow for better monitoring and evaluation of performance, but it also lays the foundation for an internal process that seeks to interpret and understand the current direction of training practice, and to set guidelines for future policy. Underscoring this notion of mutual goal-setting and learning by the public and private sectors must be a commitment on the part of government to well-funded public education, and an acceptance by employers of socially devised frameworks for training. But securing either commitment in the present climate is far from certain. This echoes a point made in Chapter 5 that renewing economic citizenship in Europe cannot be done on the cheap.

The end of European exceptionalism?

European countries are experiencing the above employment relations dilemmas in varying degrees of intensity. But everywhere these dilemmas have their origins in the emergence of a new trajectory of economic and social development. The tentative, experimental and piecemeal way governments are addressing these dilemmas is a reflection of the deep-seated uncertainty that exists about how to manage the complexity of modern labour markets. At the same time, the reforms that are being pursued can be interpreted as attempts to modernise the institutional shape and content of economic citizenship in Europe. It is too early to say whether these reform strategies will succeed. But as they get further down the reform path, it is increasingly clear that few governments are attempting to move 'back to the future' by shoring up the organising principles of the postwar model of economic citizenship. Indeed, the evidence points to a departure from key elements of the regulatory, voice and cognitive spheres of the established model of Social Europe.

Consider the sphere of regulation. As Fredman (1997) rightly points out, labour law in the Fordist era was heavily influenced by the idea that employment legislation should create a 'space' for collective bargaining. Although there has been no widespread attempt to weaken this space, apart from in Britain, it is instructive that most governments are not attempting to strengthen it. None of the newly elected socialist governments in Europe, particularly in Britain and France, have adopted the legal extensions of collective bargaining rights as part of their programmes. Moreover, as Lord Wedderburn (1997) highlights in a passionate defence of the *ancien regime*, discussions of collective bargaining in policy circles across Europe, when they do occur, are now couched in a new, soft language that de-emphasises adversarialism and conflict, and promotes notions of partnership and consensus. Lord Wedderburn correctly interprets this as an effort to legitimise a new style of employment relations: the new warm words are part of an attempt to reinvent economic citizenship in a way in which traditional collective bargaining plays a less central role. Language as part of the cognitive structure of the labour market is being used to promote new conventions for employment relations.

Developments of this kind spell bad news for the Durkheim inspired view of organised labour markets as the institutional foundations of Social Europe. The most articulate advocate of this view is Wolfgang Streeck. As stressed on a number of occasions in this book, he sees organised labour markets bringing a number of benefits. They produce effective institutional constraints that oblige employers to follow employment policies consistent with high quality production. In addition, they promote the social integration of workers by conferring labour market status on particular occupational groups. One positive outcome is that workers are prepared to engage in organisational and technological change. Thus social integration and labour market adaptability go hand in hand. For some time this view has been a powerful convention in European employment relations. But it now seems to be in retreat, if not exhausted altogether. Nowhere does it seem to be working either smoothly or properly. Thus present developments in Europe can be interpreted as the fragmentation of Durkheimian labour markets.

Whether this amounts to the end of Social Europe is a matter of some controversy. Streeck (1997b) is certainly of the view that without collective rules European industrial relations will sooner or later be indistinguishable from an American-style employment system. But this assessment is perhaps too pessimistic. Social Europe continues to be an important political project, making it too early to say that neo-liberal employment relations have triumphed. At the same time, it is fair to conclude that Social Europe in the future will be without the big collective and encompassing rules that constrained employer behaviour in the past. Institutional influences outside the firm may continue to exist but they will be of a different kind.

For example, at the moment some countries seem to be building up a new framework of law that is designed to enhance the role of the individual as a labour market stakeholder, rather than to defend collective industrial relations institutions. So far much of the focus has been on increasing the employment protection of atypical workers. But any new legal framework must have a broader agenda if it is going to be an adequate substitute for collective bargaining arrangements in addressing asymmetric power between capital and labour. Consider the issue of employee communication and involvement. Across Europe there is evidence of employers opening up a third channel of communication, which in many instances is designed to undermine formalised employee representative bodies (Hyman 1997b). As Barenberg (1994) vividly shows, these new communication procedures alongside *unreciprocated* forms of teamwork could be the basis of a reconstituted form of labour domination inside the enterprise. Thus it seems appropriate that labour law should establish some ground rules for the new communication systems so that workers have a genuine influence over the internal organisation of the enterprise.

Apart from increasing the importance of the legal framework, a new role is opening up for institutions that stand between the macro-regulation of the labour market and enterprise-level employment policies. One positive feature of traditional corporatist structures was that they aggregated and articulated the particular preferences of workers. As a result, they ensured a connection between the macro- and micro-aspects of the labour market. But as already pointed out, these connections have weakened and looser relationships now prevail. The outcome is that while trade unions are incorporated into national pay systems – which should ensure their survival as formal labour market institutions – enterprises have a more or less free hand in restructuring workplace employment relations. Thus an important aspect of the governance gap in labour markets is a relatively underdeveloped 'public sphere' for any dialogue, or even conversation, about desired forms of employment relations processes. Bodies that promote equal opportunities, health and safety at the workplace, arbitration and conciliation, and economic development are ideally positioned to perform such a role.

Drawing on the principles of deliberative democracy, they should encourage exchanges about the direction of employment policy that is not overly tied either to the enterprise or to national wage bargaining systems. The idea is to develop shared solutions to labour market problems. The benefit of such a dialogue is that it draws employers into public debate about issues connected to social justice at the workplace, and gives trade unions the opportunity to make alliances with other social groups. Although the process is unlikely to produce big constraining rules for labour market action, it should none the less create a public agenda for employment relations reform, and promote norms of acceptable and non-acceptable work practices. Promoting deliberative labour market practices is a far cry from established models of labour management exchanges. Under the traditional model, employment relations processes are about reconciling fixed, opposing positions. Deliberative democracy presupposes more open-ended and less adversarial exchanges. It is an attempt to promote mutual understanding on employment topics and the political basis for common action between labour market actors.

Thus the message is that Europe will have to learn to live with less encompassing and restrictive labour market regulatory regimes. Employment protection has to be more selective, though not necessarily less meaningful. New, more discursive, forms of public action and agenda-setting have to be found to replace tightly integrated labour market collective goods. Maintaining Social Europe has become less a matter of putting the right type of 'binding' institution in place and more an on-going process of devising and revising methods of sustaining social inclusion. Not everybody will be happy with this scenario, for it means forsaking some of the cherished principles that have underscored

European industrial relations for decades. Neither can it be said in advance that reforms of this kind will rescue Social Europe from its sick bed. The political game between neo-liberal and Social Europe is still on. But the acid test for any reformed social dimension to the European economy is whether it can positively affect labour market outcomes. Lower unemployment, better labour market access, and more democratic and participatory workplaces are some of the key benchmarks which test whether egalitarian economic citizenship has been revived. If these targets are reached, then Europe can once again claim that it is exceptional in its capacity to marry economic efficiency with social justice.

Bibliography

Adonis, A. and Jones, S. (1991) *Subsidiarity and the Community's Constitutional Future*, Discussion Paper No. 2, Oxford: Nuffield College, Centre for European Studies.

Aglietta, M. (1988) *International Monetary and Financial Integration*, Boston: Kluwer.

Allsopp, C. and Vines, D. (1996) 'Fiscal policy and EMU', *National Institute Economic Review*, No. 158, October.

Anderson, T. (1997) 'Do institutions matter? Convergence and national diversity in the restructuring of employment in British and Danish banking', *European Journal of Industrial Relations*, Vol. 3, No. 1.

Arrowsmith, J. and Taylor, C. (1996) 'Moving toward EMU', *National Institute Economic Review*, No. 158, October.

Atkinson, A. (1995) *Income Distribution in OECD Countries*, Social Policy Studies, No. 18, Paris: OECD.

Baccaro, L. and Locke, R. (1998) 'The decline of egalitarian wage policies in Italy and Sweden', mimeograph, Dept of Political Science, MIT, Cambridge, MA.

Barenberg, M. (1994) 'Democracy and domination in the law of workplace cooperation: from bureaucratic to flexible production', *Columbia Law Review*, Vol. 94, No. 3.

Barro, R. J. and Sala-i-Martin, X. (1992) 'Convergence', *Journal of Political Economy*, Vol. 100, No. 2.

Bayoumi, T. and Eichengreen, B. (1996) 'The stability of the gold standard and the evolution of the International Monetary System', in T. Bayoumi and B. Eichengreen (eds) *Economic Perspectives on the Gold Standard*, Cambridge: Cambridge University Press.

Bean, C. (1993) 'European unemployment: a review of competing explanations', *Journal of Economic Literature*, Vol. 34, No. 2, 604–14.

Becker, G. (1964) *Human Capital: A Theoretical and Empirical Analysis with Special Reference to Education*, New York: NBER.

Begg, I. G. and Mayes, D. (1992) 'Cohesion as a precondition for monetary union in Europe', in R. Barrel (ed.) *Economic Convergence and Monetary Union in Europe*, London: Sage.

Bentolila, S. and Dolado, J. J. (1994) 'Labour flexibility and wages: lessons from Spain', *Economic Policy*, No. 18, April.

Bercusson, B. (1992) 'Maastricht: a fundamental change in European labour law', *Industrial Relations Journal*, Vol. 23, No. 1.
—— (1993) 'European labour law and sectoral bargaining', *Industrial Relations Journal*, Vol. 24, No. 2.
—— (1994) 'The dynamics of European labour law after Maastricht', *Industrial Law Journal*, Vol. 23, No. 1.
——(1995) 'The collective labour law of the European Union', *European Law Journal*, Vol. 1, No. 2.
Berggren, C. (1993) *The Volvo Experience: Alternatives to Lean Production in the Swedish Auto Industry*, London: Macmillan.
Bermann, G. (1994) 'Taking subsidiarity seriously: federalism in the European Community and the United States', *Columbia Law Review*, Vol. 94, No. 2.
Bishop, J. (1993) 'The French mandate to spend on training: a model for the United States?', *Industrial Relations Research Association*, Vol. 45, No. 2.
Blanchard, O. and Katz, L. (1992) *Regional Evolutions*, Brookings Papers on Economic Activity No. 1, Washington, DC: Brookings Institution.
Blanchard, O. and Summers, L. (1986), 'Hystersis and the European unemployment problem', *NBER Macroeconomics Annual*.
Blanchard, O., Dornbusch, R., Dreze, J., Giersch, H., Layard, R. and Monti, M. (1985) *Employment and Growth in Europe: A Two-handed Approach*, Brussels: Centre for European Policy Studies.
Blanchard, O. *et al.* (1995) *Spanish Unemployment: Is there a Solution?*, London: Centre for Economic Research.
Bovenberg, T. and De Jong, A. M. (1997) 'The road to monetary union in Europe', *Kyklos*, Vol. 49, No. 1.
Bowring, J. (1986) *Competition in a Dual Economy*, Princeton: Princeton University Press.
Boyer, R. (1993) 'The economics of job protection and the new emerging capital–labor relationship', in C. Buechtemann (ed.) *Employment Security and Labor Market Behaviour*, Ithaca, NY: ILR Press.
—— (1995) 'The future of unions: is the Anglo-Saxon model a fatality, or will contrasting national trajectories persist?', *British Journal of Industrial Relations*, Vol. 33, No. 4.
Boyer, R. and Freyssenet, M. (1993) 'L'Emergence de nouveaux modèles industrials: hypotheses, Premier Bilan et perspectives', paper presented to first international meeting of GERPISA, Paris.
Brewster, C. and Hegewisch, A. (ed.) (1994) *Policy and Practice in European Human Resource Management: Evidence and Analysis*, Routledge: London.
Buechtemann, C. and Soloff, D. (1994) 'Education, training and the economy', *Industrial Relations Journal*, Vol. 25, No. 3.
Buiges, P., Ilzkovitz, F. and Lebrun, F. J. (1990) 'The impact of the internal market by industrial sector: the challenge for the member states', *European Economy/Social Europe*, Special Edition.
Buiter, W., Corsetti, G. and Roubini, N. (1993) 'Excessive deficits: sense and nonsense in the Treaty of Maastricht', *Economic Policy*, No. 10, April.

Bunk, G. (1994) 'Teaching competence in initial and continuing vocational training in the Federal Republic of Germany', *Vocational Training*, Vol. 1, No. 2.

Burtless, G. (ed.) (1990) *A Future of Lousy Jobs?*, Washington, DC: Brookings Institution.

Calmfors, L. (1993) 'The economics of wage bargaining: a survey', *OECD Economic Studies*, Vol. 13, No. 3.

—— (1994) 'Active labour market policies and unemployment – a framework for the analysis of crucial design features', *OECD Economic Studies*, Vol. 14, No. 2.

Calmfors, L. and Driffell, J. (1988) 'Centralisation of wage bargaining', *Economic Policy*, No. 6.

Calmfors, L. and Skedinger, P. (1995) 'Does active labour market policy increase employment?', *Oxford Review of Economic Policy*, Vol. 10, No. 2.

Camuffo, A. and Volpato, G. (1995) 'The labour relations heritage and lean manufacturing at Fiat', *International Journal of Human Resource Management*, Vol. 6, No. 4.

Cappelli, P. and Rogovsky, L. (1994) 'New work systems and skill requirements', *International Labour Review*, Vol. 32, No. 2.

Carlin, W. and Soskice, D. (1997) 'Shocks to the system: German political economy under stress', *National Institute Economic Review*, No. 159.

Centre for Economic Policy Research (CEPR) (1993) *Making Sense of Subsidiarity: How Much Centralisation for Europe?*, London: CEPR.

Clarke, J. (1984) 'The juridification of industrial relations: a review article', *Industrial Law Journal*, Vol. 14, No. 2.

Cobham, D. (ed.) (1994) *European Monetary Upheavals*, Manchester: Manchester University Press.

Cremers, J. (1997) 'The modernisation debate viewed from a European angle', *Transfer*, Vol. 3, No. 2.

Crouch, C. (1993) *Industrial Relations and European State Traditions*, Oxford: Clarendon Press.

—— (1994) 'Beyond corporatism: the impact of company strategy', in R. Hyman and A. Ferner (eds) *New Frontiers in European Industrial Relations*, Oxford: Basil Blackwell.

—— (1995) 'Exit or voice, two paradigms for European industrial relations after the welfare state', *European Journal of Industrial Relations*, Vol. 1, No. 1.

—— (1997) 'Skill based full employment: the latest philosopher's stone', *British Journal of Industrial Relations*, Vol. 35, No. 3.

Crouch, C. and Traxler, F. (eds) (1995) *Organised Industrial Relations in Europe: What Future?*, Aldershot: Avebury.

Darbishire, O. and Katz, H. (1998) *Converging Divergences*, Ithaca, NY: Cornell University Press.

De Grauwe, P. (1996a) 'Reforming the transition to EMU', in P. Kenen (ed.) *Making EMU Happen: Problems and Prospects*, Princeton Essays in International Finance, No. 199, Princeton: Princeton University Press.

—— (1996b) 'The economics of convergence towards monetary union', in F. Torres (ed.) *Monetary Reform in Europe*, Lisbon: Universidade Catolica Editoria.

Dewatripoint, M. *et al.* (1995) *Flexible Integration – Towards a More Effective and Democratic Europe*, Monitoring European Integration, No. 6, London: CEPR.

Dibella, A., Edwin, N. and Gould, J. (1996) 'Understanding organisational learning capability', *Journal of Management Studies*, Vol. 33, No. 3.

Dore, R. (1994) 'Introduction', in R. Dore, R. Boyer and Z. Mars (1994) *The Return to Incomes Policy*, London: Pinter.

Dorf, M. and Sabel, C. (1997) 'A constitution for democratic experimentalism', mimeograph, Columbia Law School, New York.

Dreze, J. and Malvinaud, P. (1994) 'Growth and employment: the scope for a European initiative', *European Economy*, No. 1.

Dubious, P. (1996) 'Markets in organisations and organisations in markets', *Work, Employment and Society*, Vol. 10, No. 2.

Due, J., Madsen, J. S., Petersen, L. K. and Jensen, C. S. (1995) 'Adjusting the Danish model: towards centralised decentralisation', in Crouch, C. and Traxler, F. (eds) *Organised Industrial Relations in Europe: What Future?*, Aldershot: Avebury.

Dunford, M. (1995) 'Regional inequalities in the European Union', in A. Amin and J. Tomaney (eds) *Behind the Myth of the European Union*, London: Routledge.

Dunlop, J. (1958) *Industrial Relations Systems*, New York: Holt, Rinehart and Winston.

Edwards, R. (1993) *Rights at Work: Employment Relations in a Post Union Era*, Washington, DC: Brookings Institution.

Eichengreen, B. (1992) 'Should the Maastricht Treaty be saved?', *Princeton Studies in International Finance*, No. 74, December.

—— (1996) *A More Perfect Union?*, Princeton Essays in International Finance, No. 198, Princeton: Princeton University Press.

—— (1997) 'Saving Europe's automatic stabilisers', *National Institute Economic Review*, No. 159.

Eichengreen, B. and Frieden, J. (1993) 'The political economy of European Monetary Unification: an analytical introduction', *Economics and Politics*, Vol. 5, No. 3.

Emerson, M. (1988) *The Economics of 1992: The EC Commission's Assessment of the Economic Effects of Completing the Internal Market*, Oxford: Oxford University Press.

European Commission (1993) *Growth, Competitiveness, Employment: The Challenges and Ways Forward into the 21st Century*, Luxembourg: European Union.

—— (1996) *Employment Report 1996*, Luxembourg: European Union.

Falkner, G. (1995) 'Testing the Maastricht social agreement: the case of the European works council directive', mimeograph, University of Essex (Department of Government).

Fay, R. (1995) 'Enchancing the effectiveness of active labour market policies', mimeograph, OECD, Paris.

Ferry, J. (1991) *Les Puissances de l'experience*, Paris: Cerf.

Finegold, D. and Soskice, D. (1988) 'The failure of British training: analysis and prescription', *Oxford Review of Economic Policy*, Vol. 4, No. 3.

Franco, D. and Munzi, T. (1996) 'Public pension expenditure prospects in the European Union: a survey of national projections', *European Economy*, No. 3.

Fredman, S. (1997) 'Labour law in flux', *Industrial Law Journal*, Vol. 26, No. 4.

Freeman, R. (ed.) (1994) *Working Under Different Rules*, London: Sage.

Gill, C., Knudsen, H. and Lind, H. (1998) 'Are there cracks in the Danish model of industrial relations?', *Industrial Relations Journal*, Vol. 29, No. 1.

Glyn, A. and Rowthorn, B. (1992) 'The diversity of unemployment experience since 1973', *Structural Change and Economic Dynamics*, Vol. 1, No. 1.

Goodhart, C. (1996) 'The transition to EMU', *Scottish Journal of Political Economy*, Vol. 43, No. 3.

Gordon, R. (1990) 'What is New Keynesian economics?, *Journal of Economic Literature*,Vol. 28, No. 3.

Grahl, J. and Teague, P. (1994) 'Economic citizenship in Europe', *Political Quarterly*, Vol. 65, No. 4.

Greenwald, B. and Stiglitz, B. (1993) 'New and Old Keynesianism', *Journal of Economic Perspectives*, Vol. 7, No. 1.

Gregg, P. and Wadsworth, J. (1996) *More Work in Fewer Families*, London: Centre for Economic Performance.

Grimshaw, D. and Rubery, J. (1997) 'Workforce heterogeneity and unemployment benefits: the need for policy reassessment in the European Union', *Journal of European Social Policy*, Vol. 7, No. 4.

Habermas, J. (1990) *Ecrits Politiques*, Paris: Cerf.

Hanley, D. (ed.) (1994) *Christian Democracy in Europe: A Comparative Perspective*, London: Pinter.

Henley, A. and Tsaksolotos, E. (1994) *Corporatism and Labour Market Performance*, London: Edward Elgar.

Hepple, B. (1997) 'European rules on dismissals', *Comparative Labor Law Journal*, Vol. 18, No. 2.

Herrigel, G. (1995) *Industrial Constructions: The Sources of German Industrial Power*, Cambridge: Cambridge University Press.

—— (1996) 'Crisis in German decentralised production', *European Urban and Regional Studies*, Vol. 3, No. 1.

Herrigel, G. and Sabel, C. (1994) 'Craft production in crisis: industrial restructuring in Germany during the 1990s', mimeograph, Department of Political Science, MIT, Cambridge, MA.

Hobsbawn, E. (1994) *The Age of Extremes: A History of the World 1914–1991*, New York: Patheon Books.

Hollingsworth, J., Schmitter, P. and Streeck, W. (eds) (1994) *Governing Capitalist Economies*, Oxford: Oxford University Press.

Hyman, R. (1994) 'Industrial relations in Europe: an era of ambiguity?', *Industrial Relations*, Vol. 35, No. 1.

—— (1997a) 'Trade unions and interest mediation in the context of globalisation', *Transfer*, Vol. 4, No. 3.

—— (1997b) 'The future of employee representation', *British Journal of Industrial Relations*, Vol. 26, No. 4.

International Labour Organisation (ILO) (1996) *Employment Policies in a Global Context*, Geneva: ILO.

Jackman, R., Layard, R. and Nickell, S. (1994) *Unemployment: Macroeconomic Performance and the Labour Market*, Oxford: Oxford University Press.

Jacquemin, A. and Sapir, A. (1996) 'Is a European hard core credible?', *Kyklos*, Vol. 49, No. 2.

Jacobi, O. (1997) 'Contours of a European collective bargaining system', in P. Flood *et al.* (eds) *The European Union and the Employment Relationship*, Dublin: Oak Tree Press.

Jacobi, O. and Hassel, A. (1996) 'Does direct participation threaten the German model?', in I. Regalia and C. Gill (eds) *The Position of the Social Partners in Europe on Direct Democracy*, Vol. 11, Working Paper 95/35/EN, Dublin: European Foundation for the Improvement of Living and Working Conditions.

Jurgens, U. (1994) *Lean Production and Codetermination: The German Experience*, Detroit: Labor Studies Center, Wayne State University.

Kahn, L. (1998) 'Against the wind. Bargaining recentralisation and wage inequality: Norway 1987–1991', *Economic Journal*, Vol. 108, No. 448.

Keating, M. (1993) 'The political economy of regionalism', mimeograph, Department of Politics, University of Western Ontario, London, Ontario.

Kenner, J. (1995) 'Introduction', in J. Kenner (ed.) *Essays on European Social Policy, Essays in Memory of Malcolm Mead*, Aldershot: Darmouth.

Kerr, C. (1960) *Industrialism, Industrial Man: The Problems of Labour and Management in Economic Growth*, Cambridge, MA: Havard University Press

Kiel, M. and Newell, A. (1993) 'Lessons from the OECD experience of unemployment', mimeograph, Department of Economics, University of Sussex, Brighton.

Klodt, H. *et al.* (1994) *Standort Deutschland: strukturelle Herausforderungen im neuen Europa*, Tübingen: J. C. B. Mohr.

Krugman, P. (1991) 'Increasing returns and economic geography', *Journal of Political Economy*, Vol. 99, No. 3.

Lane, C. (1995) *Industry and Society in Europe: Stability and Change in Britain, Germany and France*, Aldershot: Edward Elgar.

Layard, R. (1990) 'Getting agreement that inflation is like litter', in P. Philpott (ed.) *Trade Unions and the Economy: Into the 1990s*, London: Employment Institute.

—— (1995) 'Preventing long-term unemployment in Europe', Working Paper No. 565, London: Centre for Economic Performance, London School of Economics.

—— (1997) 'Sweden's road back to full employment', *Economic and Industrial Democracy*, Vol. 18, No. 1.

Layard, R. and Nickell, S. (1992) 'Unemployment in the OECD countries', Discussion Paper No. 81, London: Centre for Economic Performance, London School of Economics.

Lenoir, D. (1994) *L'Europe sociale*, Paris: La Decouverte.

Lipietz, A. (1996) 'Social Europe, the post Maastricht challenge', *Review of International Political Economy*, Vol. 3, No. 3.

—— (1997) 'The post-Fordist world: labour relations, international hierarchy and global ecology', *Review of International Political Economy*, Vol. 4, No. 1.

Locke, R. (1990) 'The resurgence of the local union: industrial restructuring and industrial relations in Italy, *Politics and Society*, Vol. 18, No. 3.

Locke, R., Kochan, T. and Piore, M. (1995) 'Reconceptualising comparative industrial relations: lessons from international research', *International Labour Review*, Vol. 134, No. 2.

Lorenz, E. (1993) 'Flexible production systems and the social construction of trust', *Politics and Society*, Vol. 21, No. 3.

Lynch, L. (1994) 'Payoffs to alternative training strategies at work', in R. Freeman (ed.) *Working Under Different Rules*, London: Sage.

Machin, S. (1996) 'Wage inequality in the UK', *Oxford Review of Economic Policy*, Vol. 12, No. 2.

Marginson, P. and Sissons, K. (1998) 'European collective bargaining: a virtual project', mimeograph, University of Warwick.

Marquand, D. (1996) 'The stakeholder society', mimeograph, Centre for Political Economy, University of Sheffield.

Marsden, D. (1994) 'Industrial change, "competencies" and labour markets', *Vocational Training*, Vol. 1, No. 1.

—— (1997) 'Public service pay reforms in European countries', *Transfer*, Vol. 3, No. 1.

Maurice, M., Sellier, F. and Silvestre, J.-J. (1986) *The Social Foundations of Industrial Power: A Comparison Between France and Germany*, Cambridge, MA: MIT Press.

Mayhew, D. and Kweep, E. (1994) *Skilling The Jobless – Time for a New Deal?*, London: Employment Policy Institute.

Mitchell, D. (1993) 'Keynesianism, Old Keynesianism and New Keynesianism and wage nominalism', *Industrial Relations*, Vol. 26, No. 2.

Mosley, H. (1997) 'Market share and market segment of employment services in the EU', *MISEP Policies*, No. 57, Spring.

Mueckenberger, U. (1984) 'Labour Law and Industrial Relations', in O. Jacobi *et al.* (eds) *Economic Crisis, Trade Unions and the State*, London: Croom Helm.

—— (1996) 'Towards a new definition of the employment relationship', *International Labour Review*, Vol. 135, No. 6.

Mueckenberger, U., Stroh, C. and Zoll, R. (1995) 'The challenge of modernisation: toward a new paradigm of trade unions in Europe', *Transfer*, Vol. 1, No. 1.

Muller-Jentsch, W., Rehermann, K. and Speeling, W. (1992) 'Social–technical rationalisation and negotiated work organisation: recent trends in West Germany', in OECD (ed.) *New Directions in Work Organisation: The Industrial Relations Response*, Paris: OECD.

Oliver, N., Delbridge, R. and Lowe, J. (1996) 'Lean production practices: international comparisons in the auto components industry', *British Journal of Management*, Vol. 7, No. 1.

Organization for Economic Cooperation and Development (OECD) (1997) *Employment Outlook*, Paris: OECD.

Orlean, A. (ed.) (1994) *Analyse – Economique des conventions*, Paris: PUF.

Orr, J. (1996) *Talking About Machines*, Ithaca, NY: ILR Press.

Padoa-Schioppa, T. (1994) *The Road to Monetary Union in Europe*, Oxford: Oxford University Press.

Piore, M. (1994) 'Trade unions: a reorientation to survive', in C. Kerr and D. Strudohar (eds) *Labor Economics and Industrial Relations*, Cambridge MA: Harvard University Press.

—— (1996) 'Review of the *Handbook of Economic Sociology*', *Journal of Economic Literature*, Vol. 34, No. 2.

Piore, M. and Sabel, C. (1984) *The Second Industrial Divide*, New York: Basic Books.

Pizzorno, A. (1978) 'Political exchange and collective identity in industrial conflict', in C. Crouch and A. Pizzorno (eds) *The Resurgence of Class Conflict in Western Europe since 1968*, London: Macmillan.

Redher, R. (1994) 'Saturn, Uddevalla, and the Japanese lean systems: paradoxical prototypes for the twenty-first century', *International Journal of Human Resource Management*, Vol. 5, No. 1.

Regini, M. (1995) *Uncertain Boundaries: The Social and Political Reconstruction of European Economies*, Cambridge: Cambridge University Press.

—— (1997) 'Still engaging in corporatism? Recent Italian experience in comparative perspective', *European Journal of Industrial Relations*, Vol. 3, No. 3.

Rhodes, M. (1997) 'Competitive corporatism', mimeograph, European University Institute, Schumann Centre, Florence.

Robinson, P. (1995) *The Limits to Active Labour Market Policies*, Employment Institute Report, London: Employment Institute.

Rodgers, J. and Streeck, W. (1994) 'Productive solidarities: economic strategies and the left', in D. Miliband (ed.) *Reinventing the Left*, Oxford: Polity.

Romer, P. (1993) 'The New Keynesian synthesis', *Journal of Economic Perspectives*, Vol. 7, No. 1.

—— (1994) 'The origins of endogenous growth', *Journal of Economic Perspectives*, Vol. 8, No. 1.

Rowthorn, R. (1992) 'Centralisation, employment and wage dispersion', *The Economic Journal*, Vol. 102, May.

Rowthorn, R. and Ramaswamy, R. (1997) 'Deindustrialisation: causes and implications', IMF Working Paper, No. 42, Washington, DC: IMF.

Rubery, J. (1997) 'Wages and the labour market', *British Journal of Industrial Relations*, Vol. 35, No. 3.

Sabel, C. (1991) 'Decentralised production systems and trust relations', mimeograph, Department of Politics, MIT, Cambridge, MA.

—— (1992) 'Studied trust: building new forms of co-operation in a volatile economy', in F. Pyke and W. Sengenberger (eds) *Industrial Districts and Local Economic Regeneration*, Geneva: ILO.

—— (1994) 'Learning by monitoring: the institutions of economic development', in N. Smelser and R. Swedberg (eds) *Handbook of Economic Sociology*, Princeton: Princeton-Sage.

—— (1995) 'Bootstrapping reform: rebuilding firms, the welfare state and the unions', *Politics and Society*, Vol. 23, No. 1.

Sabel, C. and Zeitlin, J. (1997) *World of Possibilities: Flexibility and Mass Production in Western Industrialisation*, Cambridge: Cambridge University Press.

Saglio, J. (1993) 'Localised industrial systems in France: a particular type of industrial system', in A. Scott and M. Storper (eds) *Pathways to Industrialisation*, Routledge: London.

Sako, M. (1993) 'Training practices in Japanese, British and German firms', *Rivista Internazionale di Scienze Economiche e Commerciali*, Vol. 50, No. 12.

Salais, R. and Storper, M. (1997) *Worlds of Production: Action Frameworks of the Economy*, Cambridge, MA: Harvard University Press.

Scharpf, F. (1997) 'European integration and welfare states', *Journal of European Public Policy*, Vol. 3, No. 2.

Scheltex, K. (1991) 'La subsidiarité – principle directeur de la future Europe', *Revue du Marché Commun*, Vol. 34, No. 4.

Schmid, J. and Wadsworth, J. (1995) 'Why are two million men inactive: the decline of male labour force participation', Working Paper No. 338, London: Centre for Economic Performance.

Schmid, G. (1997) 'The Dutch employment miracle? A comparison of the employment systems in the Netherlands and Germany', *Infor Misep*, No. 59.

Schmittter, P. (1996) 'Some alternatives for the European polity and their implications for European public policy', in Y. Mény, P. Muller and J.-L. Quermonne (eds) *Adjusting to Europe*, London: Routledge.

Schnapper, D. (1997) 'The European debate on citizenship', *Daedalus*, Vol. 126, No. 3.

Sciarra, S. (1995) 'Social values and multiple sources of European social law', *European Law Journal*, Vol. 1, No. 1.

Scott, A., Peterson, J. and Millar, D. (1994) 'Subsidiarity: a Europe of the regions v. the British Constitution?', *Journal of Common Market Studies*, Vol. 32, No. 1.

Sengenberger, W. (1992) 'Intensified competition, industrial restructuring and industrial relations', *International Labour Review*, Vol. 34, No. 2, 131.

Shackleton, J. R. (1995) *Training and Unemployment*, Employment Institute Report, London: Employment Institute.

Silver, H. (1994) 'Social exclusion and social solidarity: three paradigms', *International Labour Review*, Vol. 133, No. 5–6.

Snower, D. (1995) 'Unemployment reforms: an assessment of proposals for reform', *International Labour Review*, Vol. 134, Nos 5–6.

Snyder, F. (1994) 'Soft law and institutional practice in the European Community', European University Institute (EUI) Working Paper, Law 93/5, Florence: EUI.

Solow, R. (1990) *The Labour Market as a Social Institution*, Oxford: Oxford University Press.

Soskice, D. (1990) 'Wage determination: the changing role of institutions in advanced industrialised economies', *Oxford Review of Economic Policy*, Vol. 6, No. 2.

—— (1994) 'Reconciling markets and institutions: the German apprenticeship system', in L. Lynch, (ed.) *Training and the Private Sector*, Chicago and Paris: University of Chicago Press.

Spencer, J. (1992) 'European Monetary Union and the regions', mimeograph, Queens University, Belfast.

Steedman, H. (1994) 'Assessment, certification and recognition of occupational skills and competencies', *Vocational Training*, Vol. 1, No. 1.

Streeck, W. (1992a) 'National diversity, regime competition and institutional deadlock: problems in forming a European industrial relations system', *Journal of Public Policy*, Vol. 12, No. 2.

—— (1992b) *Social Institutions and Economic Performance*, London: Sage.

—— (1993) 'The rise and decline of neocorporatism', in L. Ulman, B. Eichengreen and W. Dickens (eds) *Labour and an Integrated Europe*, Washington, DC: Brookings Institution.

—— (1994) 'Pay restraint without incomes policy: institutionalised monetarism and industrial unionism in Germany', in R. Dore, R. Boyer and Z. Mars (eds) *The Return to Incomes Policy*, London: Pinter.

—— (1995) 'Neo-voluntarism: a new European social policy regime', *European Law Journal*, Vol. 1, No. 1.

—— (1996) 'Lean production in the German automobile industry: a test-case for convergence theory', in S. Berger and R. Dore (eds) *National Diversity and Globalisation*, Ithaca, NY: Cornell University Press.

—— (1997a) 'Neither European nor works councils: a reply to Paul Knutsen', *Economic and Industrial Democracy*, Vol. 18, No. 2.

—— (1997b) 'German capitalism: does it exist? can it survive?', in C. Crouch and W. Streeck (eds) *Modern Capitalism or Modern Capitalisms*, London: Sage.

—— (1998) *The Industrialization of Industrial Relations in Europe: Prospects and Problems*, Working Paper No. 1, Madison: International Institute of the University of Wisconsin.

Streeck, W. and Schmitter, P. (1985) *Private Interest Government: Beyond Market and State*, London: Sage.

—— (1991) 'From national corporatism to transnational pluralism: organised interests in the single market', *Politics and Society*, Vol. 19, No. 2.

Streeck, W and Visser, J. (1997) 'The rise of the conglomerate union', *Journal of European Industrial Relations*, Vol. 3, No. 1.

Suriot, A. (1995) *Critique du droit de travail*, Paris: POF.

Taylor, G. (1996) 'Labour market rigidities, institutional impediments and managerial constraints: some reflections on the recent experience of macro-political bargaining in Ireland', *Economic and Social Review*, Vol. 27, No. 3.

Taylor, P. (1993) *International Organisations in the Modern World*, London: Pinter.

Teague, P. (1989) *The European Community: The social dimension*, London: Kogan Page.

—— (1994) 'Employment policy in the European Union: between New Keynesianism and deregulation', *Journal of European Public Policy*, Vol. 1, No. 3.

Teague, P. and Grahl, J. (1992) *Industrial Relations and European Integration*, London: Lawrence & Wishart.

Thornley, C., Contrepois, S. and Jeffreys, S. (1997) 'Trade unions, restructuring and individualisation in French and British banks', *Journal of European Industrial Relations*, Vol. 3, No. 1.

Traxler, F. (1994) 'Collective bargaining: levels and coverage', *OECD Employment Outlook*, Paris: OECD.

—— (1995) 'Farewell to labour market associations? Organised versus disorganised decentralisation as a map for industrial relations', in Crouch, C. and Traxler, F. (eds) *Organised Industrial Relations in Europe: What Future?*, Aldershot: Avebury.

—— (1996) 'Collective bargaining and industrial change: a case of disorganisation?', *European Sociological Review*, Vol. 12, No. 3.

Traxler, F. and Schmitter, P. (1995) 'The emerging Euro-polity and organised interests', *European Journal of International Relations*, Vol. 2, No. 1.

Van Kersbergen, K. and Kerbeck, B. (1994) 'The politics of subsidiarity in the European Union', *Journal of Common Market Studies*, Vol. 32, No. 2.

Wallace, W. (1990) *The Transformation of Western Europe*, New York: Council on Foreign Relations Press.

Wallerstein, M. and Golden, M. (1997) 'The fragmentation of the bargaining society: wage setting in the Nordic countries, 1950–1992', *Comparative Political Studies*, Vol. 50, No. 5.

Wedderburn, Lord W. (1990) *The Social Charter, European Company and Employment Rights*, London: Institute of Employment Rights.

—— (1997) 'Consultation and collective bargaining in Europe: success or ideology?', *Industrial Law Journal*, Vol. 26, No. 1.

Weiler, J. H. H. (1994) 'A quiet revolution: the European Court of Justice and its interlocutors', *Comparative Political Studies*, Vol. 26, No. 3.

—— (1995) 'Does Europe need a constitution? Reflections on demos, telos and the German Maastricht decision', *European Law Journal*, Vol. 1, No. 3.

Womack, J., Jones, D. and Ross, D. (1990) *The Machine that Changed the World*, New York: Rawson.

Wright, M. (1989) 'Comparative industrial policies: the role of the policy communities', *Politicial Studies*, December.

Index